Computers and Computing in Education
An Introduction

Computers and Computing in Education
An Introduction

William C. Bozeman

University of Iowa

Gorsuch Scarisbrick Publishers
Scottsdale, Arizona

Photo Credits

The photos contained in this book are courtesy of the following people and organizations. We are most appreciative of their cooperation.

Apple Computer, Inc. Figures 1.1, 1.2, 7.1, 7.2, 7.3

AT&T, Bell Laboratories Figures 2.10, 2.12

Cincinnati Milacron, Inc. Figure 5.15

Corvus Systems, Inc. Figure 3.36

Digital Equipment Corporation Figures 2.14, 3.2, 3.8

Hayes Microcomputer Products, Inc. Figure 3.39

Heath Company Figure 5.16

Hewlett Packard, Data Systems Division Figures 2.16, 2.17

Intel Corporation Figure 3.25

International Business Machines (IBM) Figures 2.2, 2.3, 2.4, 2.5, 2.9, 2.11, 2.13, 7.4

Iowa State University Figures 2.6, 2.6a

Microsoft Corporation Figure 3.16

Milliken Publishing Company Figure 5.2

Popular Electronics Figure 2.15

Qume, A Subsidiary of ITT Figures 3.17, 3.21, 3.22

Recognition Equipment Inc. Figures 3.11, 5.14

Richardson, Robert and Janet Gilchrist Figures 3.19, 3.20

Sperry Corporation Figures 2.7, 2.8

Tandy Corporation Figure 1.3

University of Iowa, Weeg Computing Center Figures 3.13, 3.14, 3.18, 3.26, 3.27, 3.28, 3.29, 3.31, 3.33, 3.37, 5.4, 5.5, 5.9

U.S. Robotics, Inc. Figure 3.38

Wei, Yin-min and Richard Post Figure 2.1

Gorsuch Scarisbrick Publishers
8233 Via Paseo del Norte, Suite E-400
Scottsdale, AZ 85258

10 9 8 7 6 5 4 3 2 1

ISBN 0–89787–407–2

Contents

Acknowledgements

Acknowledgements are a pleasure to write because they represent one of those all too few occasions which one can formally express appreciation for contributions and assistance. Acknowledgements are also difficult to write because there are so many persons who contributed in some way. Among those persons who generously offered their time were my graduate students—especially Bill Hall, Rob Molek, Sandi Moradi, and Chris Olsen. A special debt of graditude is owed Donald McClain, Director of The University of Iowa CAI Laboratory. Don not only served as a technical editor, but also provided many valuable suggestions. Production of the text was greatly facilitated by Richard Clark, my manuscript editor and Greta Gorsuch who worked diligently at finding the needed photographs and figures. I also wish to thank John Gorsuch for his patience and encouragement throughout the development of the text. Finally, I must add a special note of thanks to Jean Gilmer. She must be the ideal secretary.

Preface

If you have not asked already, the question most readers should be asking is "Why another book about computers?" It is certainly a fair question given the increasing number of computer-related texts over the past few years. Even a quick perusal of the bookstore shelves reveals dozens of texts on microcomputers, programming, data base management systems, spreadsheet applications, operating systems, graphics, and many other important topics. Within the field of education, a number of good texts have emerged on subjects such as computer literacy, Logo, applications in specific subject areas, programming, and computer-assisted instruction/computer-managed instruction (CAI/CMI). While the book lists are replete with good texts related to computer-based education, there appears to be a void in one critical area. This area is the introduction of students of teacher education to the use of computers in education.

The motivation for preparing this text grew out of two basic beliefs. First, the computer will be the most powerful tool for the improvement of education in this century. The true potential for the applications of computing has hardly been realized. Secondly, until students in teacher education programs (both at the pre-service and in-service level) receive adequate preparation in this area, this tool will continue to be neglected. Hopefully, this text will contribute to the improvement of teacher education programs as well as the technical and conceptual competencies of the educator.

The assumption throughout the text is that the reader has little or no background in computing. Given this assumption, we begin our study with an introduction to computing and an overview of the historical evolution of the technology, in chapters 1 and 2. This is followed by a presentation of the functional components of a computer in chapter 3. In this section, particularly, the view is taken that educators require some familiarity with computers beyond the personal or microcomputer level. Therefore, such topics as operating systems, time-sharing, and communications are included.

An introduction to computer programming in BASIC is offered in chapter 4. While this chapter is not intended to be a comprehensive treatment of the subject, it does provide fundamentals of algorithms, program development, flow charts, and structured programming. Chapter 5 examines several important areas in computer-based education. Topics addressed are computer literacy, computer-assisted instruction, computer-managed instruction, computer science, administrative data processing, information retrieval, and vocational education. Current literature and research are cited extensively in these areas in an attempt to provide a state-of-the-art discussion. A number of societal issues related to the use of computers are raised in chapter 6—personal privacy, computer ethics, computer fraud, software piracy, economic implications of computing, and computer security.

The final chapter concerns the successful implementation and integration of computer-based technology into our schools. This chapter is a departure from the usual content of a text on computer science. Essentially, it seeks to address a question which pervades our nation's schools: "Now that we have computers, how can we utilize this technology in the classroom?" Two important dimensions of this question are discussed: (a) concepts, theory, and research related to organizational change, and (b) a strategy for planning, design, and implementation of computer-based technology.

This is text written by an educator for educators. It reflects the needs of the classroom teacher. Furthermore, the text is based on a perspective gained from over seventeen years in the profession as a teacher, administrator, and professor. Content is drawn from research, theory, and, perhaps most important, experience. Computers can be one of the most exciting experiences of one's education. If this text can facilitate the sharing of that excitement, it will be a successful effort.

1

Computers In Education

The advent of low-cost, state-of-the-art computers has opened a door for education that could not have been imagined only a decade ago. For many years, computing was the province of the engineer, the scientist, or the guru of data processing. So quickly has the scene changed! In the last few years accessibility to computers, especially through personal computers, has served to remove the cloak of mystique that once veiled the technology. Educational computing that was once available to only a few students in a few schools and districts has now become almost commonplace—even in the smallest of schools.

Consider, if you will, three scenarios to illustrate this point. The first is a 1972 scenario. A high school wishes to offer a few courses in computer science complete with an introduction to computer programming. There are two options available to the school: (a) purchase or lease a small computer system (such as IBM 1401, System/3, HP 2000, or PDP minicomputer); or (b) purchase computer access time from a business, bank, or service bureau computer department. The costs associated with the first option are prohibitive for most school districts, especially the smaller ones. Purchase price of even a small system will probably range from $40,000 to $80,000 not including peripheral equipment, terminals, and keypunch machines. Lease of a system would also be expensive with costs probably ranging from $1200 to $2000 per month. The logistics associated with the second option would present many problems for teachers and students. The input media would probably be punched cards. The card decks and printouts would have to be delivered by courier from the school to the computer center. Turnaround (i.e., the time required to receive the computer output) on the programs would be slow and greatly impede the teaching/learning process. Time-sharing via remote terminals was not particularly attractive at this time because of systems availabilty and communication requirements. Needless to say, the 1972 scenario for computers in the schools was a bleak one.

Advance the calendar, if you will, ahead a decade to a 1982 scenario. The same high school can now purchase a stand-alone microcomputer for less

Figure 1.1
Portable microcomputers are becoming an important part of college
studies. (Courtesy of Apple Computer, Inc.)

than $2000. This price includes sufficient memory for significant program-
ming applications, and disk storage and a monitor. The system is programmable "off-the-shelf" in BASIC and can be expanded to support other languages. Additionally, a considerable amount of software is already available
with more on the way. Perhaps most importantly, the computer is beginning
to appear user friendly.

Now advance the calendar just a bit into the future for a glimpse into our
cloudy crystal ball at a 1987 scenario. Computing has become quite commonplace, not only at the high school, but also at the elementary and middle
schools. Computer applications are found in most academic areas with uses
ranging from total instructional tutorials, remediation, practice, and management of learning to entertainment. Clusters of microcomputers together
with intelligent, interactive videodisks are found everywhere in the schools—
not just the areas associated with computer science. Many students own their
own personal computers. They are brought to school with the same ease as
books or a calculator. The power of the computers meets all of their present
requirements. Many of these same computers may even accompany the students to college. In some districts, computers will be supplied to students just
as textbooks are supplied today. Is this 1987 scenario unrealistic? Not at all!
In fact, there are schools today which closely resemble this description.

There is little doubt or argument today that the computer is the pervasive
technology of our age and our society. Both the cost and size of computer
hardware are decreasing exponentially while power and capacity are increasing exponentially. This phenomenon has been contrasted with the automotive
industry. If automobiles had experienced a similar change over the past thirty
years, we would be able to buy for a few dollars a Rolls Royce which would
get a couple of million miles per gallon. As Nobel Laureate Herbert Simon

Figure 1.2
Macintosh can be mastered in just a few hours and takes up only a small amount of desk space. It allows business people, professionals, and students to work in familiar ways, but more quickly and efficiently. (Courtesy of Apple Computer, Inc.)

observed, "The computer is an innovation of more than ordinary magnitude, a one-in-several-centuries innovation and not a one-in-a-century innovation or one of these instant revolutions that are announced every day in the papers or on television."

Just as there is little argument that the computer is the pervasive tool of our age and society, there is little argument that the computer and associated information technology can be and should be an integral part of our institutions for learning. A number of powerful forces which educators cannot ignore are converging at this very time.

For one, popular interest in computing and our free enterprise system, aided by phenomenal improvements in computer cost, size, and power, have caused a veritable flood of small computers into homes, businesses, and schools. This flood of computers into our nation's schools, sometimes dubbed *micromania,* has not been a completely positive occurrence. For the greater part, educators have not been prepared to integrate this technology into the schools intelligently. It has become in vogue for schools to possess computers. Unfortunately, teachers and administrators often ask the question, "Now that we have the computers, what do we do with them?"

In all fairness to the faculties of schools moving toward computer applications, our colleges of education have not been responsive to the needs of teachers in professional pre-service programs. This has been cited time and again as a significant problem—the proper training of teachers. Teachers who are specialists and possess expertise in computing are drastically needed in our schools, for there is no question that the successful implementation of computer technology in a school ultimately resides with the faculty.

A second force impacting upon education is the renewed interest in the quality of education, not just the quality of courses being offered our students. This concern was clearly expressed in the National Commission on Excellence in Education Report, *A Nation At Risk* (1983). A conclusion of that report was that too many schools offer a smorgasbord of courses while neglecting important core courses. The Commission concluded that, "Secondary school curricula have been homogenized, diluted, and diffused." Computing in our schools is also mentioned in the Commission's report. Note was taken that "computers and computer-controlled equipment are penetrating

Figure 1.3
Personal computers in the home may provide exciting education and recreation.

every aspect of our lives—homes, factories, and offices." One of the recommendations of the Commission was that all students seeking a high school diploma be required to take one-half year of computer science. The position of the Commission reflects a growing belief that the role and purpose of schools is to provide a place of learning—not simply a place of academic content presentation.

Because of the availability of computing power, teachers and future teachers throughout the nation are seeking skills and knowledge which will permit them to utilize the vast and rich array of potential applications. It is for these persons that this text is written.

How much about computing and computer-based education do teachers need to know? What competencies should be considered necessary and sufficient? Of course, there are many answers to these questions and these answers probably depend upon whom one asks. The position of this text is that teachers should have some fundamental knowledge about computing in five areas: (1) the development and evolution of computing, especially the technological advances that have occurred in recent years; (2) concepts and components resident in computer systems; (3) software and programming, at least to the extent that the teacher appreciates the "language of the computer;" (4) educational computing including concepts of computer literacy, computer-assisted instruction, computer-managed instruction, computer science, administration applications, data analysis, and information retrieval; and (5) general topics such as software evaluation, societal considerations, privacy and security of information, career opportunities in data processing, and acquisition of equipment.

This text is offered to assist the person seeking entry into the realm of computer applications in education. Exhaustive discussions of the topics herein are clearly beyond the scope or purpose of the work. The text should be viewed, therefore, as a means of gaining one's first glimpse of the world of computing. It is hoped that this will provide the foundation and encouragement for future study.

2
Historical Evolution of Computing

Early Roots of Computational Devices

One of the many marvelous attributes exhibited by humans throughout history has been their never-ending search for devices which would expand their physical capacities and make their life and work easier. Simple machines provided early man with capabilities to perform tasks that would have otherwise been impossible. Such was the case with counting. Since the time people perceived a need for calculating and counting beyond the most primitive level, tools or machines have been required to relieve most of this burdensome and time-consuming task.

At first, fingers were sufficient for counting. Gradually, as societies developed and especially as trade increased, an improvement on simple finger-counting became necessary. Some type of machine was required to overcome man's physical limitations. Herein, we have the beginnings of a story that is ever-present in modern times and still continues to evolve. As our environment becomes more complex, different and more sophisticated devices will be required and will be developed to cope with the associated problems. The computer is one such device.

While the roots of modern computing devices can be traced far back in history, it is important to note a few of the milestones along the way. One of the earliest counting machines was the abacus, a powerful instrument when used by a skilled person. The abacus dates back many hundreds of years B.C. and is generally considered the oldest known computational aid. Basically, the abacus works on the principal that a number can be represented (in units, tens, and so forth) by the position of counters—a series of beads strung on parallel wires within a frame. As we shall see later, the concept of representing numbers physically, mechanically, or electrically is still a most important element in our modern computing devices. The abacus was used in many ancient countries. While the design varied somewhat (e.g., the Chinese "suan-pan," the Japanese "soroban," or the Russian "s'choty"), the basic principles were quite similar. Figure 2.1 shows a typical abacus.

Figure 2.1
Abacus. (Reprinted from Yin-Min Wei and Richard Post, *Elements of Computers and Programming with WATFIV,* 1985 by Gorsuch Scarisbrick, Publishers, Scottsdale, Arizona.)

Some other early civilizations developed different means of counting. Before the arrival of the European discoverers, the Indians of South America used a method of computing with counters (often pebbles or kernels) on a board. The natives of Peru used knotted cords for keeping accounts. These cords (or "quipus") were used to record the results from the counting table (Smith & Ginsburg, 1956, 442–64).

An important device of the early seventeenth century was *Napier's bones,* a system of numbering rods based on logarithms and invented by John Napier, an eminent Scottish mathematician. This concept led a few years later to the slide rule. The slide rule, of course, was an essential tool for calculation until the advent of electronic calculators. Napier was also intrigued by the binary or base 2 number system. Little did he realize how important his discovery of logarithms and the concept of binary arithmetic would be in the development of electronic digital computers.

In the 1640s, Blaise Pascal, a French mathematician, built the first adding machine—a forerunner to the mechanical desk calculator. Three decades later, the German mathematician, Leibnitz, devised a similar machine which could also multiply and divide. Much of the work throughout the eighteenth century was an extension and refinement of these calculating machine concepts. Figure 2.2 is a picture of Pascal's calculator and figure 2.3 shows Leibnitz's machine.

During that time, however, considerable interest was shown in the area of automation. One example was the Jacquard loom which provided for the weaving of intricate patterns under the control of machine-internal instructions coded on punched cards. The importance of this invention cannot be understated. Herein was one of the first examples of a machine which performed a task without continuous human intervention.

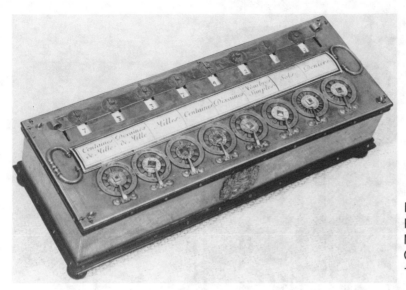

Figure 2.2
Pascal calculator. (I.B.M. Archives, Management Development Center, Old Orchard Road, Armonk, NY 10504.)

Figure 2.3
Leibnitz's machine. (I.B.M. Archives, Management Development Center, Old Orchard Road, Armonk, NY 10504.)

One of the first automatic devices for computing was Charles Babbage's *difference engine.* Babbage, an English mathematician, wanted a machine which could perform various computations (such as are required in the calculation of mathematical tables) without direct human intervention. He began developmental work in 1812 but never completed the engine because of technical obstacles and constraints. Another Babbage concept never carried to completion was the *analytical engine* designed in 1823. If the construction of the analytical engine had been finished, it would have been the first general-purpose digital computer. An excellent scientist, mathematician, and inventor, Babbage's contributions to the annals of computing must be considered among the most noteworthy.

Working with Babbage on his analytical engine was Lady Ada Augusta Lovelace, daughter of Lord Byron, the English poet. Lady Lovelace became quite interested in his inventions and contributed a number of significant ideas of her own. One of her more notable inventions was the concept of the *loop* which permitted the repetition of a set of instructions. Historians consider Lady Lovelace the first computer programmer. Recently, the programming language "Ada" was named in her honor. Figure 2.4 shows the general appearance of one of Babbage's "engines."

Figure 2.4
Charles Babbage difference engine. (I.B.M. Archives,
Management Development Center, Old Orchard Road,
Armonk, NY 10504.)

Another milestone in the history of computational devices was Herman
Hollerith's late nineteenth century employment of punched cards in data processing. Punched cards similar to ones in use today were used to sort and analyze data. A major event was the application of this system to facilitate data
handling in the 1890 U.S. census. Machines using Hollerith's punched cards
completed the work in one-third the time that had been required to calculate
the 1880 census. In 1896, he formed the Tabulating Machine Company which
was absorbed in 1911 by IBM. Figure 2.5 shows a picture of Hollerith's census engine.

Throughout this period and into the early twentieth century, work pro-
gressed in the advancement of mechanical calculators, and in 1911 the widely
used Monroe Calculator was produced. This machine was capable of relatively
fast multiplication and division. Important as all these devices and machines
may have been, the electronic and electromechanical computer industry's
birth did not occur until the 1930s and 1940s.

Figure 2.5
Hollerith's census machine. (I.B.M. Archives,
Management Development Center, Old Orchard
Road, Armonk, NY 10504.)

Three Generations of Computers

In the late 1930s, John Atanasoff, a mathematics professor at Iowa State
University, and his assistant, Clifford Berry, designed the Atanasoff-Berry
Computer (or ABC). Their 1939 prototype, built in the basement of the old
Physics Building, represented the first electronic digital computer, bringing
Atanasoff eventual recognition as the true father of the computer industry.
See figure 2.6.

As often happens in the process of technological advance, Atanasoff was
not alone in his pursuits of such a computing machine. In 1944 the automatic
sequence-controlled calculator, Mark I, was completed by IBM and Harvard
University scientists. It was an electromechanical system designed to solve
mathematical problems and prepare tables; it used punched cards for data input and output. The instructions for the system were encoded on a paper
tape.

The first large-scale electronic computer was ENIAC (Electronic Numerical Integrator and Calculator) built by John W. Mauchly and J. Presper Eckert at the University of Pennsylvania. This computer was intended to produce
ballistics tables for the war effort, but in fact was not completed until 1946.
ENIAC was an engineering feat; it contained about 20,000 vacuum tubes,
weighed over 30 tons and occupied as much floor space as an average family

Figure 2.6
Atanasoff-Berry Computer (The ABC).
(Information Service, Iowa State
University of Science and
Technology, Ames, Iowa 50010.)

Figure 2.6a
John Vincent Atanasoff. (Information
Service, Iowa State University of
Science and Technology, Ames,
Iowa 50010.)

dwelling. ENIAC was used until 1955 for construction of tables, calculations related to weather forecasting, solution of atomic energy equations, and for many other purposes. See figure 2.7.

Another central figure in the history of computing is Konrad Zuse, a German engineer. Though Zuse made a number of important discoveries during the 1930s and 1940s in computing, his work has gone largely unmentioned in many historical accounts. His Z3 computer, completed in 1941, was the first fully functional, program-controlled computer. Designed for use in material stress analysis and aircraft wing structure, it was, in fact, a functional general-purpose computer. Many factors, including the war, have resulted in the work of Zuse being ignored by many writers and historians.

During the 1940s, one of the United States' preeminent scientists and mathematicians was John von Neumann. In 1944 he began work with the staff at the University of Pennsylvania on the EDVAC (Electronic Discrete Variable Automatic Calculator). Von Neumann is largely credited with the development of the stored-program concept—that is, storing instructions in the computer's memory in a manner similar to storing numerical data. Heretofore, programming the computer (i.e., providing the system with instruc-

Figure 2.7
ENIAC. (Public Relations, Sperry Corporation, Computer Systems, P.O. Box 500, Blue Bell, PA 19424.)

tions) required the manipulation of many wires and switches. The first computer to use the stored-program concept was EDSAC (Electronic Delay Storage Automatic Calculator) at Cambridge University in England.

Computing, to this date, had been primarily associated with scientific, engineering, or war-related efforts. The year 1951 marked the end of the one-of-a-kind computer with the delivery of the UNIVAC I to the U.S. Bureau of the Census. The UNIVAC I (Universal Automatic Computer), designed by Mauchly and Eckert and sold by Remington Rand, was the first commercially available computer. See figure 2.8.

The computers built in the period from the late 1930s to the late 1950s are typically characterized as first-generation computers. They used vacuum tubes; they were quite large and slow by modern standards; they were expensive, relative to capability and somewhat unreliable due to the electronic technology of the day (vacuum tubes and the associated heat produced a troublesome failure rate). Programming the first-generation computers was also

Figure 2.8
UNIVAC I. (Public Relations, Sperry Corporation, Computer Systems, P.O. Box 500, Blue Bell, PA 19424.)

cumbersome as only machine languages or symbolic notation could be used in programming until the late 1950s. Other first-generation computers included the IBM 701, 650, and 705, UNIVAC II, RCA 501, and the NCR 304. During the 1950s, IBM gained the dominant position in the computer industry, a position which it maintains today. See figure 2.9.

A major event occurred in the electronics industry in 1947 with Bell Laboratories' development of the transistor. The advent of solid-state devices, or transistors, was to have ripple effects in the communications, electronics, and computer industries. Development of solid-state devices occurred almost simultaneously with the development of stored-program digital computers. The resultant synergetic effect had profound influences on all three industries. See figure 2.10.

The use of transistors in place of vacuum tubes marked the beginning of second-generation computers. These systems, built from the late 1950s until about 1964, were considerably smaller and more powerful than their predecessors. Second-generation machines were also less expensive, more reliable, faster, and more efficient. Representative computers of this period were the IBM 1401 business-oriented computer, and the 7090–7094. Figure 2.11 shows the IBM 1401.

Third-generation computers appeared about 1965. The principal characteristic of these machines was the use of integrated circuits. Integrated circuits (IC's or "chips") made it possible to put thousands of electronic components such as transistors, resistors, and capacitors on a single small silicon chip about one-quarter–inch square. This construction, known as large scale integration (LSI), provided for an enormous decrease in physical size with an inversely proportional increase in computing power. In addition to the use of integrated circuits, third-generation computers possessed increased program-

Figure 2.9
IBM 650. (I.B.M. Archives,
Management Development
Center, Old Orchard Road,
Armonk, NY 10504.)

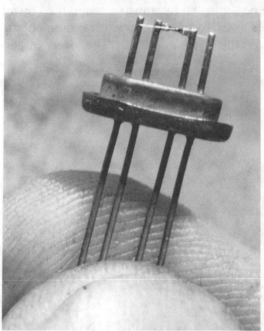

Figure 2.10
Junction transistor. (AT&T,
Bell Laboratories, 150 John F.
Kennedy Parkway, Short Hills,
NJ 07078.)

Figure 2.11
IBM 1401. (I.B.M.
Archives,
Management
Development
Center, Old
Orchard Road,
Armonk, NY
10504.)

ming and peripheral device sophistication and overall miniaturization of hardware. Computers of this generation included the IBM System/360 and System/3, CDC 6400, DEC PDP-8, and the Univac 1108. Figures 2.12 and 2.13 will give you an idea of the physical appearance of silicon chips.

Smaller Is Better

Beyond the third generation, it is difficult to determine what exactly constitutes a generation. Computers continued and still continue to be improved with regard to speed, reliability, and efficiency. Costs and physical size are continually shrinking as a result of technological innovations, marketing, production, and, most important, development of microelectronics. Figure 2.14 shows a modern data-processing facility.

To illustrate the changes made possible first by transistors and then by microelectronics, turn your thoughts away from computers for a moment and think about the portable radios of the 1940s and 1950s. They were large—

Figure 2.12
Vacuum tube, transistor, and integrated circuit. (AT&T, Bell Laboratories, 150 John F. Kennedy Parkway, Short Hills, NJ 07078.)

Figure 2.13
Vacuum tubes, transistors, integrated circuits, and large-scale integrated circuits: components of four generations of computers. (I.B.M. Archives, Management Development Center, Old Orchard Road, Armonk, NY 10504.)

Figure 2.14
Modern data processing facilities. (Photo courtesy of Digital Equipment Corporation. Digital Equipment Corporation, 200 Baker Avenue, Concord, MA 01742.)

about the size of a small briefcase. They were heavy and required huge, expensive batteries to supply the necessary current for their vacuum tube circuitry. They were expensive (probably over $100 in constant dollars) and battery life was fairly short. Then in the late fifties, transistor radios became commercially available. They were still expensive compared to their present prices, but were only a fraction of the size of their predecessors. Also they used low-voltage batteries which lasted much longer. With the further development of integrated circuits, radios can now be made almost as small as desired. They are also inexpensive and reliable.

Of course, radios are only part of the microelectronics revolution. Microelectronic components are the heart of products ranging from watches, calculators, telephones, automobile emission control systems and vending machines to intelligent weaponry. The progress associated with this technology has been and continues to be astounding. Equally impressive is the degree of cost reduction. A small computer today costing only a few hundred dollars has more computing power than ENIAC. It is many times faster, has more memory, thousands of times more reliability, and occupies only a small table top rather than a building.

Another milestone as impressive as the previous advances in computer technology occurred in 1975. In that year MITS, a small business venture in New Mexico, marketed a computer kit—the Altair 8800, for about $500. Based on the Intel 8080 chip, the Altair was a desktop computer which could support high-level programming languages and sufficient memory for important applications. The response to this computer was overwhelming and, in a sense, a new market was formed. See figure 2.15 for a picture of this historic computer.

The rest of the microcomputer or personal computer story is familiar history to most of us. Other small companies rapidly appeared (and a few rapidly disappeared). Apple, IBM, Radio Shack, Hewlett Packard, Atari, Texas Instruments, and many other manufacturers have produced personal comput-

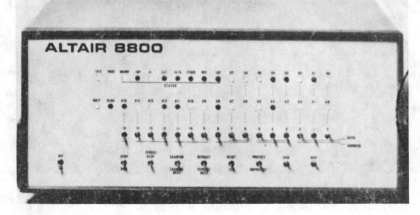

Figure 2.15
Altair. (*Popular Electronics,* January, 1975.)

Figure 2.16
Personal computer. (Hewlett Packard, Data Systems Division, 11000 Wolfe
Road, Cupertino, CA 95014–9974.)

Figure 2.17
Personal computer. (Hewlett Packard, Data Systems Division, 11000 Wolfe
Road, Cupertino, CA 95014–9974.)

ers which have become popular and prevalent in homes, offices, and schools, as in figure 2.15.

Summary

As we have seen in this chapter, the machine we call the electronic digital computer is a relatively new device even though the history of computation dates back to prehistoric times. In less than three decades computers evolved from UNIVAC I, the first commercially available, assembly-line produced computer to the sophisticated systems of today. Several forces in different areas of both the public and private sectors fueled the 1940–1980 computer revolution. Central to the amazing progress in computing was the invention of the monolithic integrated circuit which contained thousands of transistors on a single tiny chip. Economic and technical developments in many diverse industries produced unforeseeable growth and evolution. In the past twenty years, the cost of computer hardware has decreased at a rate of about 25 percent per year. The shrinking cost of computing and the availability of small computers have removed information technology from its early status as the exclusive domain of government, big business, and higher education. And we have not even mentioned the related information technologies such as videodisk, two-way cable TV communication, satellite systems, and data networks. Interestingly, while the cost of human services and the work force continued to rise, the cost of electronic computer technology was decreasing dramatically.

During the 1970s this technology continued to evolve, permitting thousands of integrated circuits to be placed on a single chip. This production, using very large scale integration (VLSI), continues to advance to areas and capabilities unimaginable only a few years ago. With this knowledge of microelectronics, scientists and engineers can incorporate data-processing capabilities into everything from radios to missile guidance systems. Truly, electronic miracles have changed and will continue to change the course and destiny of mankind.

References

Smith, D.E., & Ginsburg, J. (1956). From numbers to numerals and from numerals to computation. In J.R. Newman (Ed.), *The World of Mathematics* (pp. 442–464). New York: Simon and Schuster.

Suggested Readings

Adams, J.M., & Haden, D.H. (1976). *Social effects of computer use and misuse.* New York: John Wiley and Sons.

Annals of the History of Computing. Reston, VA: AFIPS Press, 1899 Preston White Boulevard.

Bohl, M. (1984). *Information processing.* Chicago: SRA.

Graham, N. (1980). *The mind tool.* St. Paul: West Publishing Company.

Laurie, E.J. (1979). *Computers, automation, and society.* Homewood, IL: Richard D. Irwin, Inc.

London, K. (1976). *The people side of systems.* London: McGraw-Hill Co.

Spencer, D.D. (1974). *Computers in society.* Rochelle Park, NJ: Hayden Book Co.

Wu, M.S. (1979). *Introduction to computer data processing.* New York: Harcourt Brace Jovanovich, Inc.

3
Computers: An Introduction

"What is a computer?" "How does it work?" "Where do I begin?" These are familiar and legitimate questions that newcomers to computing always ask. These questions can and will be answered in time. Like most everything new and worthwhile, it is best to proceed slowly at first.

Explaining the functions and operations of a computer is much like explaining how an automobile works to someone who isn't a mechanic. Words and terminology immediately get in the way. If we start talking about carburetors, manifolds, ignition systems, transmissions, differentials, and so on, we probably lose our audience right away. So it is with computers. But we can explain in a relatively nontechnical way the basics of an automobile and gradually introduce a new term here and there. That's the way we shall approach computing. Then, just as the newcomer to automotive mechanics would soon learn how to check the oil and other fluids, we will learn something about the operations of a computer.

Since this book is not intended to be a computer science text, we shall not attempt to go into too much detail. There are many reference sources better suited for this. Also, there are system-specific details which may vary among the many different computers. A statement which is accurate for an Apple II may not be exactly true for an IBM PC. That's what makes this business interesting. To maintain our analogy to automobiles, Fords and Chevys both have electrical systems which operate in basically the same way. A tune-up procedure, however, on the Chevy will be a little different from the Ford. Parts are not in quite the same place or they may look somewhat different. Specifications will vary between the two and the tools required may differ also.

A computer is somewhat like a jigsaw puzzle. It's much easier to understand how the pieces fit together once you have seen the complete picture. That's the approach this chapter will take. First, a computer system will be reviewed without too much regard for details. We will then examine how data are represented in a computer. This will be followed by a look at several input/output devices and their operation. Given this foundation, we can then examine the operation of the central processing unit, main memory, and secondary storage in order to gain some insight into storage and processing.

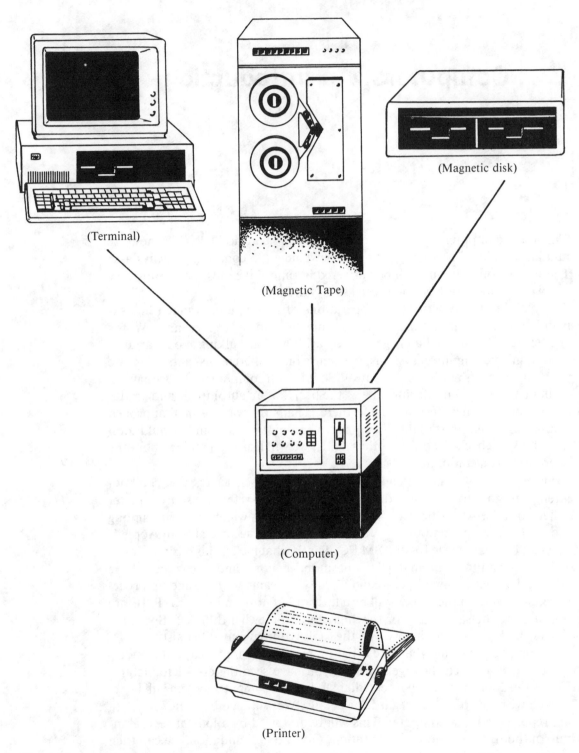

(Terminal)

(Magnetic Tape)

(Magnetic disk)

(Computer)

(Printer)

Figure 3.1
Data Processing Components

A Typical Computer System

Fortunately, just as we are able to make some general statements about the mechanics and principles of automobiles, we are also able to discuss computers at a certain general level. The purpose of a computer is to process data—data being a formal representation of facts, ideas, or instructions. A data-processing (DP) system has four necessary, fundamental functions: input, storage, processing, and output. Essentially, data and instructions enter the system through input devices. Common input devices are the computer terminal and storage facilities such as magnetic tape or disk. Other input devices are graphics tablets, game paddles, voice/music synthesizers, and the mouse which is especially gaining in popularity. Once *input*, the data reside in the main memory of the computer and are *processed* by the electronic circuitry of the system. The results are then *output* to some output device such as a printer. This process is illustrated in figure 3.1.

For example, a teacher collects data on each student in a class during the semester. Data will include grades on assignments, quizzes, projects, exams, etc. At the end of the term, the grades (data) will be "processed," which generally includes weighting and averaging. Then a numeric or letter grade will be determined by the teacher.

Here is the sequence of events that might occur if the semester grades were determined using a computer. First, the teacher might sit down at a micro-computer and *load* a program (a set of instructions for the computer) which tells the computer how to calculate the semester grades given the raw data. This program could be stored on a tape (probably an audio cassette) or a magnetic diskette (sometimes called a floppy disk). If the program was stored on a tape, the tape would be "played" or loaded to the computer on an ordinary cassette tape recorder connected to the computer. If it were stored on a disk, the program would be loaded using a disk drive. In either case, once the program is loaded, it then resides in the computer's memory. See figure 3.2.

Figure 3.2
Data/Programming Storage Using Floppy Disk. (Photo courtesy of Digital Equipment Corporation.
Digital Equipment Corporation, 200 Baker Avenue, Concord, MA 01742)

Now the teacher may enter (input) the grade data for each student. Once this step is completed, the data (grades for a student) AND the program (instructions as to what to do with the data) are in the computer's main memory. Processing can now begin. The computer central processing unit (CPU), the "brains" of the computer, can go to work and calculate the student's semester grade. When this processing is complete (and it would require only a fraction of a second), the computer would then display the results.

To summarize, three important events occurred in this data processing cycle:

1. INPUT (of both the program and data)
2. PROCESSING (according to the instructions in the program)
3. OUTPUT (display or printing of the completed results)

Figure 3.3 depicts this procedure schematically.

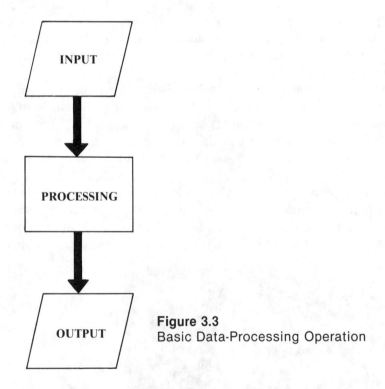

Figure 3.3
Basic Data-Processing Operation

In most applications, this data-processing cycle includes devices and operations related to mass storage of data. Secondary storage devices such as magnetic tape or disk allow the user to save and retrieve data or programs. This would be important in the above application since the teacher would not wish to reenter grades and the instructions each time the system were used. Figure 3.4 illustrates this addition of the secondary storage component in the data-processing cycle.

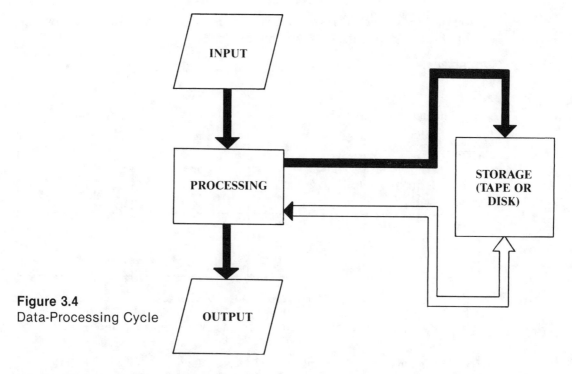

Figure 3.4
Data-Processing Cycle

Data Representation

In the preceding pages we saw an illustration of the basic data-processing cycle—input, processing, and output. We also gained a glimpse of some of the more common input, output, and storage devices. We conveniently omitted any discussion of how all this "magic" occurs. In order to gain some understanding of exactly what goes on from the time data are entered until the final report is printed, we must first examine the concepts of computer data representation.

Computers use data that have been converted into some electronic form, whether the data are being transmitted, stored, or processed. In the final analysis, this electronic form of data relies upon the binary number system or base 2 system. Various computer systems may use extensions of binary numbers, binary arithmetic, and other number systems but we shall begin with a discussion of base two and then gradually move forward.

Binary Numbers

As you well know, our everyday system of counting is the base 10 or *decimal system* (which literally means proceeding by tens). This should not be surprising since the first method of calculation was counting on the ten fingers. Hence we have ten symbols (0, 1, 2, . . . 9) or digits (from the Latin word meaning finger) in our system of counting. In order to represent amounts greater than nine, we place the digits side by side forming the units, tens, hundreds places and so on. Therefore, if we wish to represent the amount, three thousand two hundred forty-five, we write 3245. Table 3.1 shows how this looks broken into units, tens, and hundreds.

Table 3.1

Thousands	Hundreds	Tens	Units
3 × 1000	2 × 100	4 × 10	5 × 1
3000	200	40	5

3000 + 200 + 40 + 5 = 3245

This example can be presented also using exponents:

Thousands	Hundreds	Tens	Units
3×10^3	2×10^2	4×10^1	$5 \times 10^{0*}$
3000	200	40	5

Again, the sum of the places equals 3245
(*any base to the zero power equals 1)

The base of all our exponents is 10, hence the name "base 10" number system. There is nothing to prevent the use of number systems using bases other than 10. In fact, in order to handle data electronically, it is necessary to use a base of 2 rather than 10. This is because binary, or two-state (either on or off) devices are the simplest and most efficient form of electrical, electronic, or even mechanical switches. For example, a light switch in your home is a binary device; it's either open or closed (on or off). A light bulb is also a binary device; it too is either turned on or turned off. There are many such binary devices in computing machinery that can be switched on or off, or more technically, can exist in two states. In the case of computers, these states may be open/closed, on/off, charged/not charged, magnetized/not magnetized, and so on.

In the base 2 number system, there are two symbols—0 and 1. The system is called the *binary number system* (the prefix "bi" meaning two). Everything works the same as in base 10 representation except that: (a) now we have only the two symbols (0 and 1) whereas in the decimal system there are ten symbols; and (b) the base for exponents is 2 instead of 10. Consider, for example, the number 10 (base 2). What does this quantity equal in base 10?

$$
\begin{array}{ll}
\text{BINARY} & \text{DECIMAL} \\
10 = \quad 0 \times 2^0 = & 0 \\
\quad\quad + 1 \times 2^1 = & \underline{2} \\
\quad\quad \text{TOTAL} = & 2
\end{array}
$$

Therefore, 10 (base 2) is equal to 2 (base 10). What about 101 (base 2)? Converting this to decimal we have:

$$
\begin{array}{ll}
\text{BINARY} & \text{DECIMAL} \\
101 = \quad 1 \times 2^0 = & 1 \\
\quad\quad + 0 \times 2^1 = & 0 \\
\quad\quad + 1 \times 2^2 = & \underline{4} \\
\quad\quad \text{TOTAL} = & 5
\end{array}
$$

Therefore, 101 (base 2) is equal to 5 (base 10). Table 3.2 shows the first twenty base 10 numbers and their binary equivalents. The reader should convert a few of these as exercises to establish that the process works as described.

Table 3.2
Decimal/Binary Number Equivalents

DECIMAL	BINARY	DECIMAL	BINARY
1	1	11	1011
2	10	12	1100
3	11	13	1101
4	100	14	1110
5	101	15	1111
6	110	16	10000
7	111	17	10001
8	1000	18	10010
9	1001	19	10011
10	1010	20	10100

Using just what we have studied so far, electrical representation of numbers (and other symbols) is really quite easy. The common light bulb will allow us to illustrate this concept. Suppose we have a row of seven light bulbs as in figure 3.5. These light bulbs in their respective positions will represent binary place positions. Let's define a light being "on" to mean a one and "off" to mean a zero. In order to represent the decimal number 10, we simply turn on the fourth and sixth lights. This gives us the binary number 0001010 which is equivalent to the quantity 10 (base 10). What if we turn on lights two, three, and seven? We have binary number 0110001 which equals 49 (base 10). See figure 3.5. By using enough lights, we could represent any decimal number (and as we shall see later, any alphabetic or special character). Obviously, the computer does not use light bulbs. It uses integrated circuits and electronic components which can exist in a binary state. These devices can electrically represent numbers and characters in a binary form.

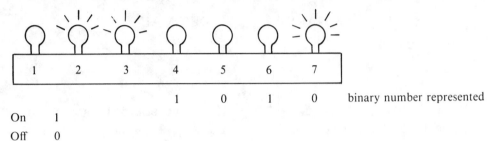

On   1
Off   0

Converting 1010 (base 2) to its decimal equivalent we have:

$$
\begin{array}{rcl}
0 \times 2^0 & = & 0 \\
+ 1 \times 2^1 & = & 2 \\
+ 0 \times 2^2 & = & 0 \\
+ 1 \times 2^3 & = & 8 \\
\hline
\text{TOTAL} & = & 10
\end{array}
$$

The 1010 (base 2) is equivalent to 10 (decimal)

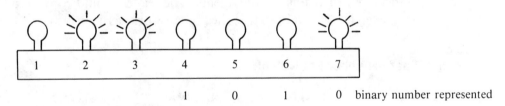

Converting 110001 (base 2) to the decimal equivalent:

$$
\begin{array}{rcl}
1 \times 2^0 & = & 1 \\
+ 0 \times 2^1 & = & 0 \\
+ 0 \times 2^2 & = & 0 \\
+ 0 \times 2^3 & = & 0 \\
+ 1 \times 2^4 & = & 16 \\
+ 1 \times 2^5 & = & 32 \\
\hline
\text{TOTAL} & = & 49
\end{array}
$$

Therefore 110001 (base 2) do represented by the lights is equivalent to 49 (decimal)

Figure 3.5
Electrical Representation of Numbers

Bits and Bytes

The computer contains an enormous collection of devices which represent zeros and ones. Each of these zeros and ones is called a bit, which is short for Binary digIT. By stringing together a group of bits we have a byte. In many computer systems, a byte contains eight bits so we say that such a byte is eight bits long.

The code used for data representation in many computers, both large and small, is ASCII (American Standard Code for Information Interchange). ASCII is a seven-bit code developed years ago in an effort to standardize systems communication. Because there are seven bit positions in the code, each being either zero or one, there can be $2 \times 2 \times 2 \times 2 \times 2 \times 2 \times 2$ or $2^7 = 128$ possible ASCII codes. This provides enough possible binary codes for the ten numeric symbols, the alphabet (upper and lower case), special symbols (!,",#,$, %, etc.), and other necessary codes such as form feeds, back spaces, etc. The codes from 32 to 127 (decimal) are the *printable codes*, which means they will produce a printed, visible character. The two exceptions are ASCII 127 which deletes characters and ASCII 32 which is a space or separator. The remaining 32 ASCII (0 through 31 decimal) codes are so-called control codes which do not represent a printable character but serve special functions such as causing a bell or beep to sound, effecting a carriage return or form feed, and so on.

Let us examine closer how the ASCII code provides a method of data representation. Imagine a row of seven pidgeonholes or boxes, each capable of containing a zero or a one, with a light above each pigeonhole. Consistent with our earlier definition, a light turned on means the box contains a one and a light not turned on represents a zero. Figure 3.6 shows how we represent an "A," "B," and "C" and table 3.3 provides a listing of the 96 printable ASCII codes.

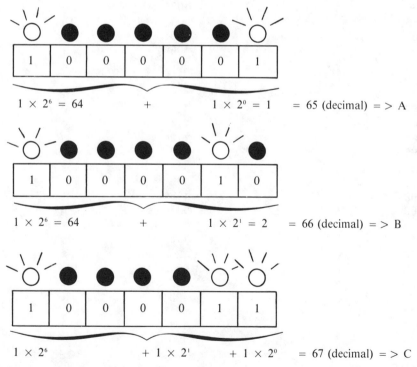

Figure 3.6
ASCII Representation of A, B, and C

Table 3.3
ASCII Character Codes

32	space	80	P
33	!	81	Q
34	"	82	R
35	#	83	S
36	$	84	T
37	%	85	U
38	&	86	V
39	'	87	W
40	(	88	X
41	)	89	Y
42	*	90	Z
43	+	91	[
44	'	92	\
45	-	93	]
46	.	94	^
47	/	95	__
48	0	96	'
49	1	97	a
50	2	98	b
51	3	99	c
52	4	100	d
53	5	101	e
54	6	102	f
55	7	103	g
56	8	104	h
57	9	105	i
58	:	106	j
59	;	107	k
60	<	108	l
61	=	109	m
62	>	110	n
63	?	111	o
64	@	112	p
65	A	113	q
66	B	114	r
67	C	115	s
68	D	116	t
69	E	117	u
70	F	118	v
71	G	119	w
72	H	120	x
73	I	121	y
74	J	122	z
75	K	123	{
76	L	124		
77	M	125	}
78	N	126	~
79	O	127	DEL

Earlier we mentioned that many computers use an eight-bit byte. Since ASCII code only requires seven of these bits, the eighth bit can either be ignored or can be used for other purposes. Some systems use the eighth bit (sometimes called the high-order bit) for parity checks or error detection. The eighth bit in an Apple II computer, for example, tells the system that a key on the keyboard has been pressed. For example, when you press an "A" on an Apple keyboard the following "lights" turn on and corresponding numbers appear in the boxes (see figure 3.7):

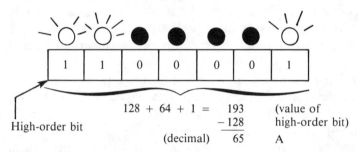

Figure 3.7
Use of Eighth Bit in ASCII Code

Converting these eight bits to decimal, we have 193. The high-order bit (or the extreme left bit) is "on" and represents one. This is a signal called a keyboard strobe that tells the computer that some key on the keyboard has been pressed. The next seven bits total 65 (or 193–128). 128 is the decimal value of the high-order bit. Therefore 65 represents the ASCII code for "A," signifying that the "A" key was pressed. Fortunately, all these codes and operations are "transparent" to the computer operator or user.

So we see that all data representation in the computer involves numbers. The "brains" of the computer, the central processing unit (CPU), deals with these numbers a byte at a time.

To review what's been said already, a bit is a binary digit (i.e., a zero or a one). A fixed sequence of bits is a byte (on the Apple, TRS-80, Atari, and many other microcomputers a byte contains eight sequential bits). The CPU of the computer works with the data one byte at a time. Stated another way, the byte is the smallest unit that can be handled or accessed. Many computers, especially micros, use an eight-bit byte. Now if you have already done some arithmetic you discovered that given eight bits in a row, the largest number which can be represented is 256 or 11111111 (base 2). Since we shall need to work with larger numbers than this, the computer combines or links two or more consecutive bytes. These bytes taken together form a *word*. Therefore, a two-byte word would be sixteen bits long and could represent a maximum decimal number of 65,635. Larger numbers can be handled using additional bytes and exponential notation (numbers times 10 to a power). Likewise, very small numbers can be handled using negative exponents. For most general-purpose applications, word lengths are not a critical concern of the user. It does, however, become very important to the user who requires high levels of precision or a large number of significant figures.

Components of a Computer

The components of a computer are generally classified into two categories: hardware and software. *Hardware* refers to the physical equipment and me-chanical/electronic devices used in a system. Examples of hardware include input and output devices, processing units, and storage devices. *Software* typically refers to computer programs, instructions and documentation, and systems procedures.

In the earlier example of the teacher's use of the computer for averaging grades, it was clear that even the simplest data-processing activity requires in-put and output. All dialogues or transactions with a computer require an in-put and output device of some type. Data in a form people generally use (e.g., the numbers in a gradebook) are converted by the input device into a form which can be processed by the computer. In that previous example, the teacher had recorded scores for each student in a gradebook. These data were sup-plied to the system via a data entry terminal, or *keyboard*. The processed data (semester grades) were, in turn, printed. Data entry terminals or keyboards and printers are examples of input and output devices. There are many others as we shall see.

Input Devices

Input devices provide a means of communication of data between the user and the CPU. Types of input devices will vary from system to system accord-ing to application requirements and the type of computer—especially the size of the computer. Common input devices include:

- Data entry terminal/keyboard
- Magnetic-ink character readers
- Optical character recognition systems
- Punched cards/reader
- Magnetic tape
- Magnetic disk

With the exceptions of magnetic tape and magnetic disk, each of these meth-ods will be discussed one by one. Tape and disk storage will be covered in the section on secondary storage devices.

Data entry terminal.   The most popular mode of computer input is the data entry terminal or, as it is usually called, a computer terminal. These input de-vices typically use a typewriter-style keyboard (with a few additional keys) and a television-like screen (cathode ray tube or CRT) or a printer. (Please refer to the next section on output devices for a discussion of CRTs). The user enters data in a manner similar to typing. Once the data have been entered by the operator, the data are transmitted to the computer over some communication facility. The data can then be saved electronically in the computer's main memory or in a secondary storage device. Figure 3.8 shows a typical data entry terminal and CRT.

Figure 3.8
Use of a Terminal and CRT for Data Input. (Photo courtesy of Digital Equipment Corporation. Digital Equipment Corporation, 200 Baker Avenue, Concord, MA 01742)

Terminals which simply communicate with the computer and pass data to and from the computer system are often called *dumb terminals*—not to be derogative, but to simply indicate that no processing of data occurs in the terminal itself. The sole function of the terminal is data input and output.

When data entered at the terminal can be processed, at least to some degree, before transmission to the computer, the device is called an *intelligent terminal* or *smart terminal*. Intelligent terminals can be quite valuable in organizations using remote-site data entry. In effect, the intelligent terminal is a small computer performing certain data-processing activities without communicating with the main computer. This off-line processing frees the main computer to do other things. It also reduces communication time and expense.

Once a data set is entered and saved in the computer system, it can be processed. The data set can also be easily stored, retrieved, edited, and manipulated. Magnetic media are rapidly becoming the most familiar method of data input and storage. These methods will be discussed in more detail in a later section.

Magnetic-ink-character recognition. All of us are quite familiar with magnetic-ink-character-recognition (MICR). MICR was introduced in the 1950s for the automated processing of bank checks. Without such a system, banks would fall hopelessly behind in the handling of check transactions. In this type of input device high-speed sensors read specially shaped characters printed in magnetic ink and transmit the scanned data to the computer; this permits extremely rapid recording, identification, and routing of checks. See figure 3.9.

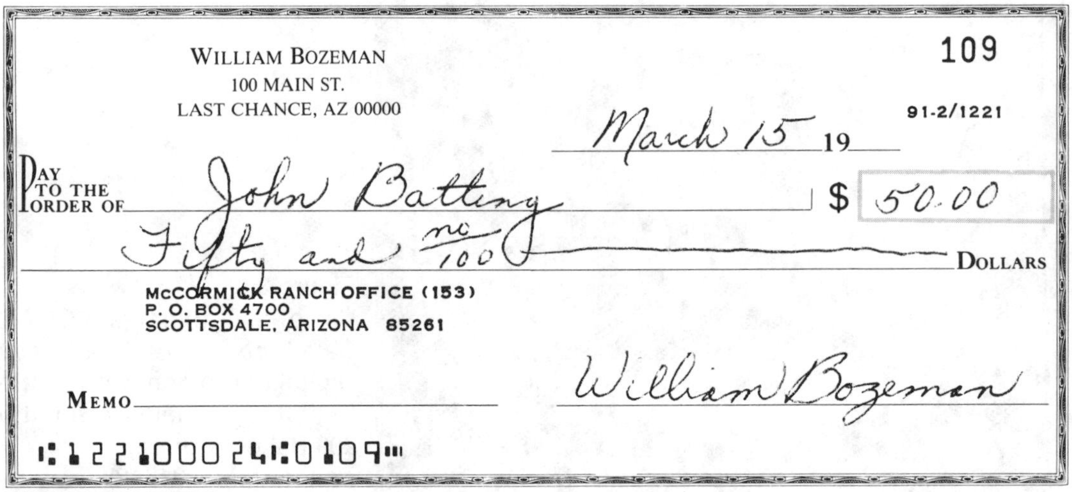

Figure 3.9
Use of Magnetic-Ink Characters on a Personal Check for Computer Data Input

Optical character recognition. A data input system that has gained popularity in education as well as in business and industry employs *optical character recognition* (OCR). OCR systems read data recorded as marks, bar codes, or characters. Optically readable marks are probably the most familiar method among educators since this has been a popular test-scoring medium for many years. Optical bar codes, however, are rapidly gaining in use in supermarkets and department stores. Basically the system uses printed bars of varying width separated by nonprint areas of varying width (see figure 3.10). These bars and blanks are read by a *scanner.* The scanner may be a hand-held wand or the stationary laser often used in checkouts of stores or libraries.

Optical character scanning is useful when the character must be readable by humans as well as machines. While most OCR characters are typed/printed using a standard font (see figure 3.11), handwritten document scanning is becoming available also.

Figure 3.10
Bar Code Illustration

IBM

Figure 3.11
Optical Character
Recognition.
(Recognition Equipment
Inc.,
P.O. Box 660204,
Dallas, Texas 75266-0204)

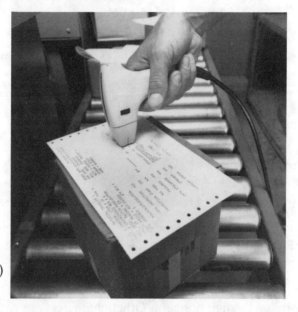

Punched cards.　　The punched card was the first important medium for entering data into a computer and is still used in many computer centers. Even though the use of cards as an input medium is diminishing, it does deserve attention and discussion. As mentioned in chapter 2, the punched card was developed in the 1880s by Herman Hollerith for use in tabulating and completing the 1890 U.S. Census. Dr. Hollerith applied a concept used earlier in the Jacquard loom, a loom which could weave intricate patterns under the production control of a punched card. By changing the code, or holes in the card, a different design could be created. Using Hollerith's punched cards, the Bureau of the Census was able to complete its task in only a fraction of the usual time.

The Hollerith card (sometimes called the IBM card) contains twelve horizontal rows and eighty vertical columns. Data are represented by the presence (or absence) of holes in the cards according to Hollerith code. An example of a punched card is shown in Figure 3.12. As the figure illustrates, the alphabet, A-Z, is represented by two holes—a *zone punch* (row) and a *digit punch* (column). For example, "Z" is a zero row punch plus a nine punch; "J" is a zone punch (specifically, a zone eleven punch) and a one punch; "A" is a combination of a zone twelve punch and a one punch. The numbers zero through nine

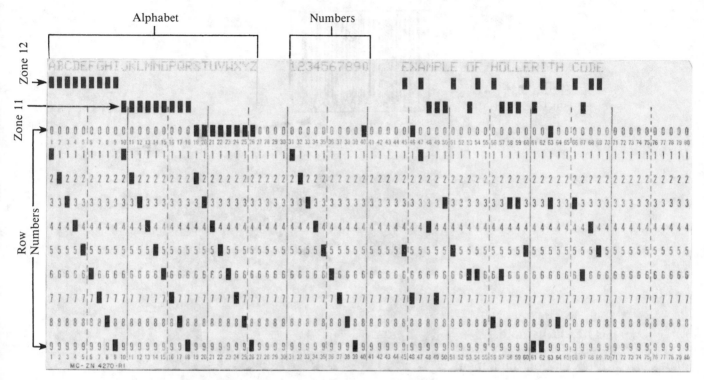

Figure 3.12
Hollerith or IBM Punched Card

are single digit punches. Other characters are various combinations of two or three punches. In any case, there can only be one character per column and a maximum of eighty characters per card.

Data are recorded on punched cards using a keypunch machine (see figure 3.13). The machine uses a keyboard similar to a typewriter and can punch cards with or without printing the characters at the top of the card.

Once the data have been entered on the punched cards, the deck of punched cards is fed to a punched card reader. This device senses where the holes are located in the cards and converts this data into electrical pulses which are transmitted to the computer. Card readers using photoelectric cells to determine the location of the holes can read over 2,000 cards per minute.

Occasionally, punched cards are also used as output media. This has been a frequent application in the past for billing and invoice purposes. The punched card was returned by the recipient (preferably in a non-folded, non-stapled, non-mutilated condition) along with payment. Though punched cards have been a familiar input medium for many years, they are becoming less visible in modern data-processing centers because they are slow (relative to other devices such as magnetic tape/disk), bulky, difficult to store, and inefficient with regard to the amount of data they can store. And, of course, the cards cannot be reused.

Figure 3.13
Keypunch Machine.
(University of Iowa,
Weeg Computing Center
Iowa City, Iowa 52242)

Figure 3.14
Punched Card Reader.
(University of Iowa,
Weeg Computing Center
Iowa City, Iowa 52242)

In summary.   Any input device allows the user to communicate with the computer in a form which is intelligible to the CPU. In many applications, input may actually be derived from several sources. In our earlier example of the semester grades, the grade data might be stored on punched cards, on optical-mark source documents or other storage medium. The instructions for the program which computes the statistics might be entered via a terminal. This program could be stored on a magnetic disk or tape (which will be discussed later in this chapter). However the input is derived, the data (student grades) and program (instructions as to what is to be done to the data) will eventually be put into the computer's main memory. Figure 3.15 depicts this somewhat enlarged situation schematically.

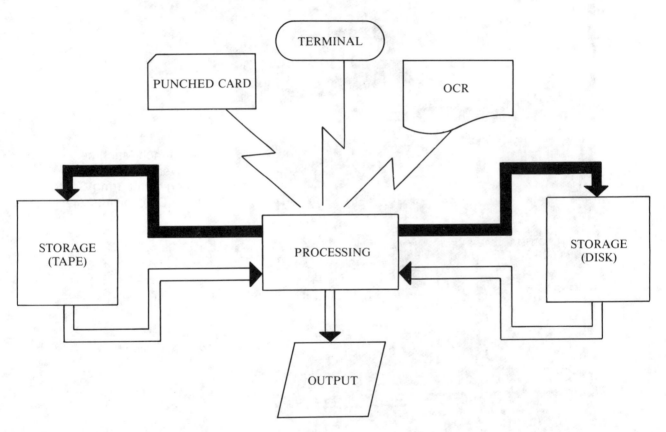

Figure 3.15
Data Processing Using Multiple Input Devices

Considerable advances in computer input technology have led to a number of other devices such as graphics tablets, game paddles, music and voice synthesizers, and the mouse. These have greatly enhanced the user's ability to interact with the computer, especially when input data are other than numbers or text. A graphics tablet can be the electronic counterpart and extension of the artist's paint brush. Synthesizers open incredible new dimensions for the

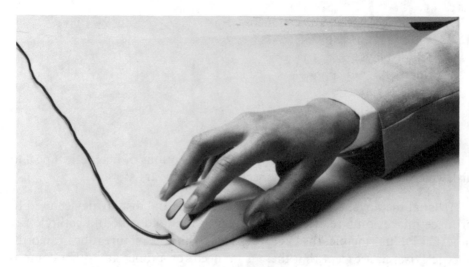

Figure 3.16
Hand-Held
Mouse for
Data Input.
(Microsoft
Corporation,
10700
Northrup Way,
Box 97200,
Bellevue, WA
98009)

musician. The *mouse,* a small hand-held device which is rolled or pushed along the desktop, moves a cursor or pointer on the screen (see figure 3.16). Unquestionably, many other such devices will become available in the not too distant future. One of the ultimate inputs is, of course, voice input. Effective voice recognition systems, however, are still a few years away.

Output Devices

Generally, an output device communicates to the user the processed data in a form that can be understood by the person using the system or by another system. Output devices can also generate output data in permanent form to be retained for future use. Just as input devices will vary from system to system, so will output devices. Furthermore, many input devices can also serve as output devices. Before this becomes confusing, let us examine a few situations. Then, we will explore several output devices in more detail.

The teacher in our earlier example may wish to produce printed reports for record-keeping purposes. In this case the output would be (you guessed it) a printer. If a permanent document isn't required, the output could be displayed on the CRT. The teacher might also want to preserve the output in some form that can be used directly as input to another computer program. For example, since the output or processed data are student semester grades, the teacher may want to produce a graph of the grade distribution. In this case, the semester grades might be saved on magnetic tape or disk for future access. The magnetic tape or disk becomes an output medium even though it cannot be immediately read by the human user. It will also be an input medium to the computer when the data are next read to produce the graph. In another situation, the teacher may want to preserve the output on tape or disk for future analysis. Next semester, he/she may plan to compare two semesters of grade averages. By storing the output from this semester on tape or disk it will not be necessary to manually reenter the data.

Output devices and media can include:

- CRT displays
- Printers
- . Magnetic tape
- Magnetic disk
- Voice or sound synthesis

These will be discussed individually with the exceptions of magnetic tape and disk which will be addressed in the section on secondary storage.

CRT/visual displays.   A *CRT,* or *monitor,* is a visual display device used to produce images on a television-like screen using (and called) a cathode ray tube (CRT). In principle, the CRT works much like the picture tube in an ordinary television set except that there is no need for a tuner and other components for receiving a TV station. Electrons are emitted from a hot filament in a vacuum tube, accelerated and focused through magnetic fields, and beamed onto a fluorescent screen. When these electron beams hit the screen, light is produced, permitting the display of images.

CRTs vary in design, some being primarily for alphanumeric display (low-resolution), and others for producing high-resolution graphics. The higher the resolution of a display, the greater the detail that is possible in an image or picture. For example, most of the popular computer arcade games employ high-resolution graphics. Some CRTs produce color displays while others are monochromatic. Probably the most common CRT uses a black and white display, though green and amber monochrome displays are rapidly gaining in popularity. CRTs come in several sizes. Popular screen sizes are nine inches and twelve inches. Larger screens are, of course, necessary for classrooms and lectures.

To a great extent, the choice of a CRT is a matter of personal preference unless the application demands certain features such as color or high-resolution graphics.

The selection of a video display will often be dependent upon the characteristics of a particular computer. Some computers, for instance, do not have color output. Also, some monitors require a R-G-B (red-green-blue) signal from the computer on three separate connector pins as opposed to a composite color output signal. A few microcomputers provide only RF (radio frequency) modulated output which is fed to the antenna terminal of a television set. In such an arrangement, the television is tuned to the RF signal on some vacant channel much as a TV station would be selected. Other computers may permit the use of a separate RF modulator. This is a device which will convert the computer video output signal into a signal which can be received by a television. Generally, a television set fed by a RF modulated signal will not produce the clarity and definition obtainable with a monitor.

The resolution capability of a monitor or TV is measured by its bandwidth in Hertz (cycles per second). Television sets, even the more expensive ones,

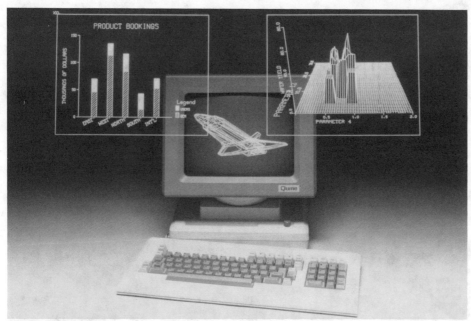

Figure 3.17
High-Resolution Graphics Display Terminal. (Qume, A Subsidiary of ITT, 2350 Qume Drive, San Jose, CA 95131)

typically do not have the bandwidth of even the cheaper monitors. This is why computers with eighty column output for word processing produce blurred and hard-to-read images when connected to a television. This text was composed on a system using an inexpensive (about $100) green-screen monitor which has a 15 MHz (megaHertz) bandwidth. Its resolution and clarity is most satisfactory.

Printers.   Almost all data-processing systems use some type of printer to produce hard copy output. Electronic signals from the computer are converted into print via several different and distinctive systems. Printers fall into a number of different categories, each of which will be discussed briefly:

- Serial printers
- Line printers
- Impact printers
- Nonimpact printers
- Dot matrix printers
- Solid character printers
- Pin or tractor paper feed
- Sheet/friction paper feed

Serial printers print characters on the paper one character at a time much like an ordinary typewriter. Some serial printers may be bidirectional, which simply means they can begin the serial printing from either side of the page.

Bidirectional capability can save printing time since the printing head does not have to return the width of the page before starting each new line.

Most small-scale data-processing systems and personal computer systems use the serial printer. They are affordable and can produce high-quality hard copy. Larger computer operations such as those in business, industry, colleges, etc. will also use line printers. Line printers, as the name suggests, print entire lines at a time rather than one character at a time. This technique can enable the printer to produce over 3,000 lines per minute. A typical serial printer may operate at 110 to 120 characters per second (CPS) so the difference in speed is quite significant. Most line printers rely upon a belt or chain which contains several complete character sets. This belt travels across the page printing many characters during each pass.

Figure 3.18
High-Speed Line Printer. (University of Iowa, Weeg Computing Center, Iowa City, Iowa 52242)

Serial printers may be of the impact or nonimpact type. Since most popular printers today are of the impact variety, we shall examine them first. Impact printers can be subdivided into two types: dot matrix and solid character. Dot matrix printers form characters by selecting certain dots from an array. The print head contains pins which will produce this array of dots. The density of the array varies from printer to printer. Some print heads form characters

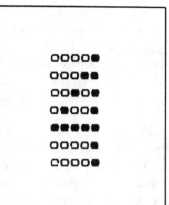

Figure 3.19
A 5 × 7 Dot Matrix Showing How
the Number 4 Would be Printed.
(Richardson and Gilchrist,
INTRODUCTION TO COMPUTERS AND
COMPUTING: A HANDS-ON
APPROACH, Gorsuch Scarisbrick,
Publishers, Scottsdale, Arizona)

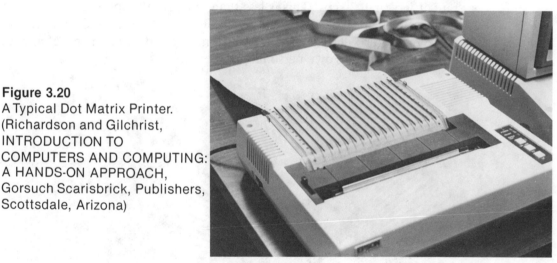

Figure 3.20
A Typical Dot Matrix Printer.
(Richardson and Gilchrist,
INTRODUCTION TO
COMPUTERS AND COMPUTING:
A HANDS-ON APPROACH,
Gorsuch Scarisbrick, Publishers,
Scottsdale, Arizona)

from a 5×7 array of pins; others may use a 7×7, 7×9, or other array. Individual solenoids can drive each pin separately out of the print head against an inked ribbon and the paper, where the impact of each pin prints a single dot on the paper. Figure 3.19 shows how the number 4 would be printed on a dot matrix printer, and figure 3.20 illustrates the dot matrix printer itself.

Dot matrix printers have improved tremendously in quality in the past few years and have simultaneously decreased sharply in price. In 1980, one might have paid $600–$800 for an impact dot matrix printer. Now, a similar or better printer can be purchased for half that price.

The usual complaints about dot matrix printers concern the general quality of appearance and readability. If the density of the dots is low and the ribbon happens to be a bit dry, the type can be difficult to read. Some dot matrix printers do not produce true descenders or tails on the letters "p," "g," "q," and "y." Some of the new dot matrix printers use high-density arrays and can produce characters almost identical to the solid character produced by a typewriter.

This brings us to the second type of impact printer—the solid character printer. These solid or fully-formed character printers are often called *letter-quality* or *daisywheel printers.* The important characteristic that these printers share is that they produce documents which appear to have been typed on an electric typewriter. Most of these printers use either an "IBM golfball" type print element or a daisywheel, which name derives from the fact that the characters reside on "petals" which spin (see figure 3.21). While solid character printers produce a letter-quality document, they run at a slower rate than the dot matrix. Most of the lower-priced printers (less than $1,000) print at a rate of less than 20 cps. This is less than one-fifth the speed of a dot matrix printer which probably costs less. Again, just as in the case of CRTs, the selection of a printer will be determined by the nature and requirements of applications as well as one's own personal preference.

Figure 3.21
Qume 130-Character Daisywheel.
(Qume, A Subsidiary of ITT,
2350 Qume Drive,
San Jose, CA 95131)

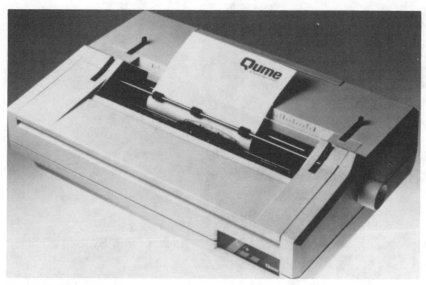

Figure 3.22
Daisywheel Printer. (Qume, A Subsidiary of ITT, 2350 Qume Drive,
San Jose, CA 95131)

Recall that serial printers may also be of the nonimpact variety. These printers usually employ thermal printing on a heat-sensitive paper or an ink-jet printing technique. The latter is more expensive and usually is found in commercial or business applications. Thermal printers, however, are commonly found in small systems or in home/school applications because of their low cost. They are also very quiet because there is no type element striking the paper. Instead, the print head simply passes over the paper and produces a dot matrix character by heating the appropriate pins. The usual complaints about thermal printers are the cost of the paper (rolls of special heat-sensitive paper must be used) and the general appearance (the paper doesn't look or feel quite like ordinary paper).

The last classification and characteristic we will consider in printers relates to the manner in which the paper is fed through the printer. There are two general mechanisms: tractor (or pin) feed and friction feed. Tractor systems require the paper to be a continuous ribbon, with sheets separated by perforations. Separable strips along the sides of the ribbon are punched with holes something like a larger version of 35mm film. Pin-studded sprockets fit into these holes and provide for continuous feeding and printing. Friction feed is the type used in an ordinary typewriter. The print roller draws the paper through the printer, allowing the printing of single sheets and envelopes. See figure 3.23.

There are several additional characteristics which will not be explored in detail here but should be considered in the selection or acquisition of a printer. These include: (a) amount of memory in the printer itself (*print buffer*); (b) variable pitch selection (e.g., ten, twelve, or fifteen characters per inch); (c) ability to back space to permit underlining or overstriking; (d) serial or paral-

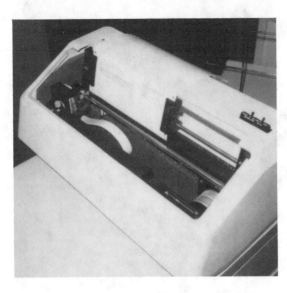

Figure 3.23
Tractor Feed System

lel interface with the computer (i.e., whether the printer receives data a bit at a time or a byte at a time); (e) type and costs of ribbons (some use a standard IBM Selectric ribbon which costs about one-half as much as some other computer printer ribbons); and (f) costs and type of paper used (especially thermal printer paper).

So, you see the printer in a computer configuration may require as much investigation and study as some of the less familiar components. It can be, and usually is, one of the more critical components, especially when word processing, report generation, and graphics are frequent applications. The available products change almost weekly, so the reader is advised to stay continually abreast of new product offerings.

Voice and sound synthesis.   Voice and sound synthesis applications in computing promise to be among the more exciting forms of output in the near future. Actually, neither form is exactly new. Speech synthesis systems which enabled handicapped persons to communicate sets of certain basic words were in use years ago. Unfortunately, they relied upon large computers and were expensive. In recent years, small, low-cost microprocessor-based systems such as the Texas Instrument Speak & Spell have been developed and produced. Chrysler uses a similar system as an option in its automobiles to alert the driver to certain conditions. Radio Shack sells a talking clock. A soft drink is dispensed from a talking pop machine. No doubt, in the very near future, many appliances and devices will be talking to us.

There are two basic types of speech synthesizers. One uses a digital representation of speech stored in its memory. While the details of the process are somewhat complicated, the process essentially involves the conversion of a voice into a digital code. A special algorithm reduces this digital representation into a form which can be stored in a chip. When the voice or word is to be reproduced, the code is fetched from memory and processed, producing an audible sound. In a sense, this is like a random-access record or a tape with a group of prerecorded words. A distinct disadvantage is the inability to expand the vocabulary.

A second method synthesizes voice using the phonemes that compose our speech. This method has the advantage of an almost unlimited vocabulary but does not, however, produce the quality that is possible through digitally stored speech. Phoneme transitions, usage, and combinations are quite complex in normal speech and are difficult to model. Inflection of natural voice and the timing of words in sentence also contribute to natural-sounding speech. As a result of these problems phonemically synthesized speech may sound like the robot from a science fiction movie.

The applications of phonemic speech synthesis to education are numerous and have barely been explored. Systems are becoming affordable and easy to use. Votrax, for example, produces a system which allows users to simply type words into a BASIC program. Instead of the words being printed, the output is voice (figure 3.24).

Quality of phonemic speech synthesis is improving. New speech-synthesis chips are reported to have increased intonation, inflection, and filtration.

Music synthesis or computer music is an area of computer output whose popularity is growing but yet is almost untapped. Anyone who has listened to the radio in the past twenty-four hours has probably heard the latest in music synthesis, possibly without even realizing it. Computers, if properly programmed, and given the appropriate hardware, can generate sound amazingly similar to a piano, clarinet, or almost any instrument or even collection of instruments.

This is possible because musical sounds are physical phenomena. The note played on the piano is a rich and complex collection of harmonics, attack, sustain, decay, and other characteristics which accompany the vibrating string. Though the technology is in its infancy, the progress is notable.

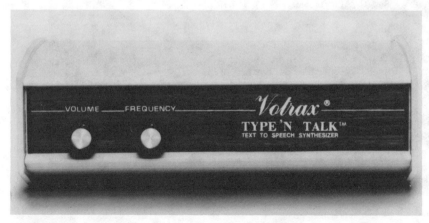

Figure 3.24
Voice Synthesizer. (Votrax, Inc., 1394 Rankin, Troy, MI 48083-4074)

Central Processing Unit

In the initial discussion of the data-processing cycle, we referred to the "brains" of the computer—the *central processing unit* or CPU. This is the system that receives inputs (both data to be processed and instructions), stores the inputs, executes the prescribed functions or commands, and prepares the data for transmission to an output device. The CPU has two principal components: the arithmetic/logic unit and the control unit. The functions of these parts are essentially what their names suggest. The arithmetic/logic unit handles calculations, arithmetic, and logical operations such as comparisons. The control unit is the executive in charge of retrieving instructions and data at the proper time and controlling other parts of the computer. In short, the CPU does all the "thinking." It makes all the decisions, does all the arithmetic, and directs all the components of the computer system.

All computers have a CPU. The early computers of the first and second generation had large CPUs based on tubes or transistors and wires. Integrated circuitry and microprocessor technology permitted these large circuits to be tremendously reduced in size and placed on silicon chips. The technologies which permit this micro-miniaturization, and the production of microprocessors are called large-scale integration (LSI) and very large scale integration (VLSI). This tiny chip made of silicon, one-quarter–inch on a side, can contain a million electronic components—ten times as many as the CPU of ENIAC. By 1990, it is expected that ten million components can be placed on a chip. Not only has this VLSI technology produced a very powerful and extremely small CPU, but also a comparatively inexpensive one.

Figure 3.25
(Courtesy Intel Corporation, Intel Corporation, 3065 Bowers Ave., Santa Clara, CA 95051)

Figure 3.26
Central Processing Unit of a
General Purpose Interactive
Minicomputer. (University of
Iowa, Weeg Computing Center,
Iowa City, Iowa 52240)

Different manufacturers may use different CPUs in their systems just as different automobile manufacturers may use different ignition systems. All CPUs share many fundamental operating concepts and purposes but may vary with regard to speed, power, and capacity. Most have rather strange names and numbers, many of which you will see frequently in journals, advertisements, and manuals. Tandy Corporation's TRS-80 uses the Zilog Z-80 CPU. The Apple and Atari computers use the 6502 microprocessor. The IBM PC uses the Intel 8088 microprocessor. While these are the more popular microprocessors now, the race is clearly on toward more and more powerful CPUs. Increasing interest is being shown, for example, in the sixteen-bit and thirty-two–bit architecture. The power of these CPUs is awesome with respect to their speed, instruction sets, and abilities to address large amounts of memory.

Storage Devices

All of us are familiar with data storage in some form. Our checkbook stores data on checks which have been written. We keep information (store data) in file cabinets. The teacher's gradebook is a form of a data storage device. From time to time we retrieve this data for processing such as in the balancing of the bank account or calculation of grades for reports. As we shall see, computers also store and retrieve data. Let us return again briefly to our earlier example of the teacher using the computer to calculate semester grades. If you recall, the teacher loaded a program or set of instructions into the main memory of the computer. This program was stored on a magnetic tape or disk. Additionally, the grade data itself were entered into memory from the keyboard as part of the input. These activities illustrate the use of two important classifications of computer storage memory: main memory and secondary storage. Since they differ in many respects, the two will be discussed in separate sections.

Main Memory

Much of the computer's working time is devoted to retrieving data, processing it, and then storing the results, all under the direction of CPU. The memory the CPU uses in these operations is called *main memory* (or random-access memory). In a sense, main memory is a temporary residence for data and instructions during the computing process.

One of the classic analogies of main memory is the post office box. Imagine for a moment the wall in the post office which is filled with boxes, each having a box number or an address. Each of these boxes can contain data—the contents of the box. When we wish to examine the contents, we simply need to know the box number or its address, go to the box, open it, and retrieve the data (i.e., a number or character). Furthermore, if we were sufficiently fast on our feet, we could reach any of the boxes in the same amount of time, regardless of the box location.

Obviously, the computer doesn't use boxes, but it does use semiconductors or integrated circuits to store data. And, just as in the case of our post office box, each of these semiconductor memory locations has an address. By using this address, the CPU can retrieve the contents of a given memory location or store a number in a specific location. Since the computer can go directly to any location (instead of counting through sequential addresses, for example), this type of memory is called a *random-access memory,* or RAM. Because they can move directly to any address, and because the signals move nearly at the speed of light, random-access memories offer exceedingly short *access time* (the time required to locate a given address and store or retrieve data in that location). Occasionally, texts may use the term "core memory" for RAM or main memory. This term is drawn from the technology used a few years ago to construct main memory. Computer memory consisted of thousands of tiny rings of a ferromagnetic material which were threaded into a matrix-like configuration on wires. By magnetizing these rings or cores, a zero or one could be represented.

Computers can have thousands or even millions of memory locations, depending on the architecture of the specific system. Usually we describe the memory size in kilobytes (K) or thousands of bytes. Hence, a 48K computer is an abbreviated description of a system with 48,000 bytes of memory (actually one K = 1,024 bytes but 1,000 is close enough).

Main memory or RAM is volatile. Volatile memory requires a constant electrical current to maintain the contents. Whenever the power is turned off, the contents will disappear or be erased. This is the case in the familiar inexpensive pocket calculator. When switched off, all the numbers entered are lost.

Main memory in a modern computer is a very active place. CPUs execute instructions at unbelievable speeds ranging from 4 million to 10 million per second! Therefore, in operation much of main memory is constantly changing as new data enter and as data are calculated and stored.

While most of the general-purpose storage for data and instructions in main memory is provided by RAM chips, the computer may often require ROM (Read Only Memory) chips. Data are permanently stored on ROM chips during their manufacture. These unchangeable, nonvolatile memory devices are especially valuable for storing data or programs which are used frequently. Programs, and the ROM in which they reside, have become known as *firmware*. This term is derived from the fact that firmware possesses characteristics of both hardware and software. A common application of firmware in microcomputers is for storage of the BASIC interpreter program. If it resides in ROM, BASIC does not have to be loaded from tape or disk.

Another type of memory associated with main memory is PROM (Programmable Read Only Memory). PROM are very similar to ROM chips except that they can be programmed or data can be stored in them after their manufacture.

In summary, main memory is a critical component in the data-processing equipment. It serves as a place where both data and instructions can reside in a form immediately accessible to the CPU. In the final analysis, all data in main memory are stored in bits (zeros and ones) even though the CPU may handle some groups of bits simultaneously (i.e., a byte at a time). The cost factors associated with capacity of memory have decreased enormously in the past few years. Only three or four years ago, it was valid to ask how much memory is needed when buying a system. Now, one generally buys all that is available. The ancillary question is "How much memory is enough?" The answer is "You never seem to have enough."

Secondary Storage

Secondary storage or *auxiliary memory* can serve several important functions but its principal purpose is to store data or programs until they are required in the data-processing cycle. Secondary storage is also known as *mass storage* because of its large memory capacities in comparison with main memory. The two principal devices for secondary storage are magnetic tape and magnetic disk. These methods of storage are the subject of the next two sections.

Recall again the computer application example at the first of this chapter. In order to compute the semester grades, the teacher loaded the instructions, or program. This is an application of secondary memory as well as input. The program had been stored on disk or tape until it was required in the data-processing cycle.

Consider another example. Suppose the principal wishes to have an alphabetic list of students in the school sorted by grade. If a student directory file were maintained and stored on disk or tape, the principal would load, or enter, the file on the disk or tape into the system along with the program to generate the desired output listing. In other words, the student file resided in secondary storage, until needed. It was copied into main memory for processing. Note here that we say "copied" into main memory. The original file on disk or tape remains unaltered unless it is updated or replaced.

Magnetic tape and disk can be distinguished as sequential- and random-access storage devices respectively. The following sections will discuss the importance of this distinction and their general operational characteristics.

Magnetic tape storage.   Magnetic tape has been, and continues to be, one of the principal media for storing data in computer systems. The techniques used with magnetic tape for data processing are almost identical to those used on the common audio tape recorder, whether it be a reel-to-reel or cassette. Basically, a plastic or mylar tape is coated with a metal oxide compound which can be magnetized. In the case of audio recorders, music or voice is converted into electrical impulses which are transferred to the tape by the recording head. To reproduce the sound, the tape is passed over a playback head which reconverts the magnetic pattern on the tape into electrical impulses which can be amplified and heard. The magnetic patterns are placed in tracks which vary with the type of recorder. Cassettes have four tracks, two of which can be recorded on or played back at a given time depending on the tape's direction. These two tracks provide the signal for the left and right stereo channels. More expensive studio recording machines may have eight, sixteen, or even thirty-two–track reel-to-reel tapes.

Magnetic tapes for computers come in several forms: reels, cartridges, or cassettes. Large computer systems such as might be found in a bank, business, or college typically use one-half–inch wide tape stored on reels. The tape is available in several lengths—such as 600, 1200 or 2400 feet. These reels of tape are stored in cabinets or tape racks. When the tape is required, an opera-

Figure 3.27
Storage Shelves for Reels of Magnetic Tape. (University of Iowa, Weeg Computing Center, Iowa City, Iowa 52242)

tor or possibly a tape librarian retrieves the tape from the rack and mounts it on a tape drive (see figures 3.27–3.29).

Data are stored on these larger reel-type tapes in channels or tracks. Depending on the type of computer and the byte size of data, tapes contain seven or nine parallel tracks. Data are recorded vertically across the tracks, one character or byte at a time as zeros and ones. Figure 3.30 shows the coding format for data on a nine-track tape. Eight bits or tracks can be used for data representation and the ninth track is used for the parity bit or error detection.

The parity bit is an extra bit. It is used in addition to the bits which are required to represent a character or number. The concept of parity for error detection is a simple but elegant one. To understand this, consider first that any binary code used to represent a number or character must contain either an even or odd total number of ones. For example, in our earlier discussion of ASCII codes, an "A" was represented by the following binary code:

1000001

There are an even number (two) of ones. A "C," however, is represented by:

1000011

Here there are an odd number (three) of ones.

Figure 3.28
Magnetic Tape Units or Tape Drives. (University of Iowa, Weeg Computing Center, Iowa City, Iowa 52242)

Figure 3.29
Operator Mouting Reel of Magnetic Tape on Tape Drive. (University of Iowa, Weeg Computing Center, Iowa City, Iowa 52242)

The object of parity is to add an additional bit (either a zero or a one) to force the total number of ones to be even. This is called *even parity.* Rewriting the ASCII code for an "A," with the additional parity bit, we have:

01000001

In this case, the parity bit is zero (or not turned on) since there was already an even number of ones. The "C" does require the addition of a one in the parity bit position to force an even number of ones:

11000011

The functioning of this system depends on probabilities. If a system malfunction should occur, a zero could become a one or a one could become a zero. As the saying goes, "a bit may flip." If this does happen, it is quite probable that the even count would be lost, signifying a problem. In summary then, we see that the parity bit allows for a check for data errors or system malfunctions. It doesn't indicate exactly what is wrong or what caused the problem—only that an error exists. Parity systems are commonly used in other computer applications besides magnetic tape storage, especially in data communications.

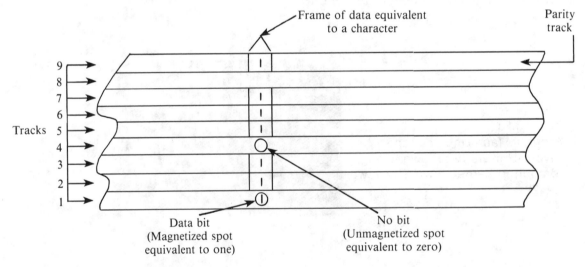

Figure 3.30
Magnetic Tape Data Format (Nine Track)

Each byte or character on magnetic tape resides in a frame. The compactness of the frames (how close they are together) is a measure of the density of the tape. This recording density of magnetic tape is measured in bits per inch (bpi). Typical densities are 556, 1600, and 6250 bpi. As you can imagine, a large amount of data storage can be achieved at the higher densities. For example, a 2400-foot reel of magnetic tape may contain over 125 million bytes (125 megabytes). Compare this storage capacity with the punched card. It would require over 1.5 million cards to store the same amount of data (given that each card can store 80 characters).

The many advantages of magnetic tape account for its long-standing popularity. The high density we just discussed permits millions of characters to be stored on a single reel. For example, the budget information for all the school districts in a state could be stored on one reel of tape. The data can be read or transferred quite rapidly, and the tape can be reused many times. Given its relatively low initial cost (about $15 for a 2400-foot reel), tape provides a very cost-efficient method of storage. In addition to being fast and cheap, magnetic tape is a reliable means of retaining records for a long period of time. Most companies rely heavily upon tape to maintain back-up files of important information. For added security, two or three back-ups may be used (sometimes called *grandfather* and *great-grandfather* tapes).

The main disadvantage to magnetic tape is that it is a sequential-access storage device. This means that in order to locate a particular record (e.g., budget data for given school district), the tape must be read sequentially until the record is found. This sequential or serial processing can present a critical time or delay factor, particularly if the desired record happens to be in the middle or toward the end of the tape. If you have used a tape recorder in your home or car to listen to music, you've probably experienced a similar problem on a smaller scale. If the song you wanted to hear was near the end of the tape, it required some time to reach it and locate the beginning. Such is the case with tapes in computer applications. Given the advantages discussed above and the sequential-access disadvantage, it turns out that tapes have found special-purpose applications such as back-up and security storage, long-term storage, and storage of files that do not require high-speed or immediate access.

Most personal computer systems use cassette tape systems. The principles discussed herein apply to them also although the actual operating characteristics are different. The storage capacity is much smaller, the transfer rate is slow, and reliability leaves something to be desired. The result is that, while cassettes continue to be used in microcomputer systems, they can be aggravating and troublesome. Nevertheless, they are cheap and will probably continue to be used for some time.

As stated earlier, magnetic tape is a sequential-access device. This characteristic results in the inability to have immediate access to particular sets of data or files. The importance of quick access to data in certain computer applications cannot be understated. Consider the example of an airline reservation system. Reservation clerks have access to computers from many remote points via terminals. Seat availability, reservations, cancellations, and stand-by lists are maintained on computer files. But not all the data on all flights can reside in main memory at once. Nevertheless, the immediate information requirements associated with such a system demand that the computer be able to locate a given file (e.g., data on a certain flight) in seconds.

A similar situation exists in financial institutions. Most banks can now provide immediate checking and savings account balances. Customers can even obtain their own balances, make deposits and withdrawals, and transfer funds at remote electronic teller stations. This type of on-line service requires immediate access to a customer's computer record or account file. Long waiting periods would defeat the system.

Clearly, there is not time in applications such as these for an operator to find a tape, mount it on a tape drive, and then locate a particular record. Even the last step, locating the file on the tape, would require too much time. These types of storage applications are better suited for magnetic disk storage.

Magnetic disk storage.   An alternative to magnetic tape as a mass storage device is magnetic disk. Whereas the main disadvantage of magnetic tape is its sequential-access characteristic, the advantage of magnetic disk is the ability to access records directly, without passing through unwanted records. For this reason, magnetic disk is considered a *direct-access storage* device (DASD). It is also sometimes referred to as a *random-access storage* device.

Magnetic disks and systems are of two basic types—hard and floppy. Large computer systems generally use hard disks. Smaller computer systems, especially home or personal computer systems, generally rely upon floppy disks for mass storage. This section will briefly examine both systems.

Probably the device most familiar to the reader which is somewhat analogous to the magnetic disk is a long-playing phonograph record. Imagine an LP with ten songs on a side. If you wish to listen to a particular song you place the tone arm on that band of the record. Within the constraint of how fast one can move his or her arm, any selection on a side can be reached in roughly equivalent time. This, in a sense, is an example of direct-access capability. Contrast this with our previous example of the album on cassette which would require passing over and even listening to unwanted selections until the desired one was reached.

Basically, a magnetic disk is a flat, circular platter coated with an iron oxide compound similar to that used on magnetic tape. Hard disks are 14 inches in diameter and look much like a phonograph record. Floppy disks are smaller—either 3½ inches, 5¼ inches, or 8 inches in diameter. The floppy disk is enclosed in a protective plastic or paper jacket to help prevent contamination by foreign particles, finger prints, and dirt.

Inside a disk drive, the disk rotates at some factory-specified speed. By comparison to a phonograph, this speed is quite fast; most hard disks spin at 3600 RPM. A read/write head similar to a tape recorder head moves over the disk. Data are recorded in concentric circles or tracks on the surface of the disk much like a phonograph except that the tracks do not spiral toward the center.

How does a disk store data? As mentioned before, data are recorded on a disk in tracks or concentric bands. The read/write head of the disk drive can move in and out to positions over each of these tracks, again, much like the

Figure 3.31
Magnetic Disk Drives in a Large Computer Center. (University of Iowa, Weeg Computing Center, Iowa City, Iowa 52242)

arm of a phonograph. Each of these tracks is divided into segments called sectors (see figure 3.32). When data are *written to disk,* or stored on a disk, the disk operating system (DOS) finds an empty sector on a track and fills it with data. As the track passes beneath the read/write head, bits are magnetized and the sector is filled with data. When a sector is filled, the disk operating system then looks for another empty sector. This process continues until there are no more data to be recorded or until the disk is full.

From the description one might expect that the result of this storage in numerous and scattered sectors would be a hopeless mess! Fortunately, the operating system maintains a directory of exactly where everything is located, and the storage process is totally transparent to the user. It all happens very rapidly also. Positioning of the head over a particular track (the *seek time*) requires less than a hundredth of a second or perhaps even just a few milliseconds.

The number of tracks of data on a disk varies among different systems. The number of possible tracks per inch (along the diameter of the disk) determines the density of the disk. Obviously, the higher density disks are able to store more data. Capacity is increased even more when both sides of the disk are used (i.e., double-sided disk storage). Recent developments and improvements in disk systems have resulted in higher and higher densities by enabling the disk system to read/write increasing numbers of tracks per side of the disk. Storage capacities are measured in kilobytes (thousands of bytes) and

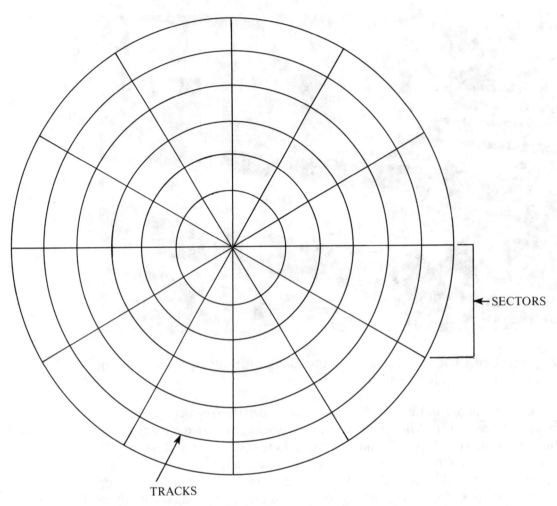

Tracks and Sectors in a Magnetic Disk
Figure 3.32

megabytes (millions of bytes). Often these measures will be abbreviated KB and MB respectively.

Large computer systems will generally use a disk pack as pictured in figure 3.33. These disk packs are collections of several platters stacked together. Each disk in the pack will have its own read/write arm and head. This multi-platter arrangement reduces the amount of head movement necessary while providing very large storage capacity. For example, the Digital Equipment Corporation (DEC) RM05 disk pack with 12 platters for the VAX-11 computer can store 256 megabytes per pack.

Unless you are using a large system such as might be found in an academic computer center, data storage will probably be on a floppy disk system such as the one in figure 3.34.

Figure 3.33
Disk Pack with Protective Cover
Removed. (University of Iowa, Weeg
Computing Center, Iowa City, Iowa
52242)

Let's now examine how a floppy disk stores data. We shall see that the technology isn't all that different than the hard disk systems. Before examining the disk itself, it may be interesting to note a few external characteristics. In figure 3.35, we have an illustration of a floppy disk in its protective cover. This protective cover is never removed from the disk. Notice that there are several openings in the cover. At the center, a circular opening exposes the hub of the disk permitting the drive to turn the disk. A small notch on the edge of the cover permits the disk to be "written on", that is, to have data electronically entered and stored on it. Covering this notch with a small piece of tape will "write-protect" the disk. Write protection prevents the user from accidently "writing over" or erasing programs or data on the disk.

The small hole close to the hub permits indexing (i.e., tells where sectors are located with reference to the position of the disk in the drive unit). In this system, called *hard sectoring,* a ring of holes are punched in the disk in a circle around the hub. A light shines through the index hole enabling the drive to locate sectors. Some systems such as the Apple II do not use this indexing feature. Disks which do not use the index hole are called *soft-sectored* disks. The operating system software in *soft-sectoring* systems locates tracks and sectors without assistance from the hardware.

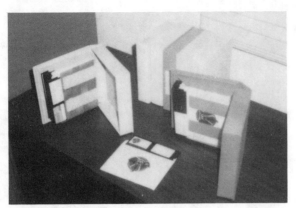

Figure 3.34
Floppy Disk Storage in a Personal Computer
System

The data storage technology used in floppy disks is quite similar to hard disks. The disk contains concentric tracks which are divided into sectors. As an example, the Apple II disk operating system (DOS) version 3.3 operates in 16 sectors with 35 tracks. Each sector can store up to 256 bytes of data. This provides a storage capacity of over 143,000 bytes on a 5 ¼-inch disk. The IBM personal computer disk drive uses 40 tracks per side and will store approximately 160,000 bytes. The Tandy TRS-80 Model 2000 personal computer offers 720,000 bytes on two floppy disks.

Floppy disks are not rigid, hence the name "floppy." The disks themselves are quite susceptible to damage from improper handling, foreign particles (even as small as cigarette-smoke particles), and warm temperatures. Stray magnetic fields (even those from a pencil or keys which might be placed on the disk) can also "garbage" a floppy disk. Because the capacity of a floppy disk is less than a hard disk, computer systems will often use multiple floppy disk drives. Even then, *disk swapping* (i.e., use of numerous disks) may be required in certain applications.

Summarized below are some of the comparative features of soft and hard disks:

1. Floppy disks are smaller and less expensive but are less reliable and do not last as long.
2. Hard disks store more data and read/write data more rapidly.
3. Floppy disks are more likely to be contaminated and damaged by foreign particles since they are not totally enclosed or sealed.
4. Because of their physical size, floppy disks provide a convenient method of delivering data or programs.

A system which is becoming more and more popular in schools is the Winchester disk. Winchester technology incorporates a sealed unit complete with hard disk, access arms, and read/write heads. One of the popular units is the Corvus Disk System (see figure 3.36) which can provide up to 20 megabytes of

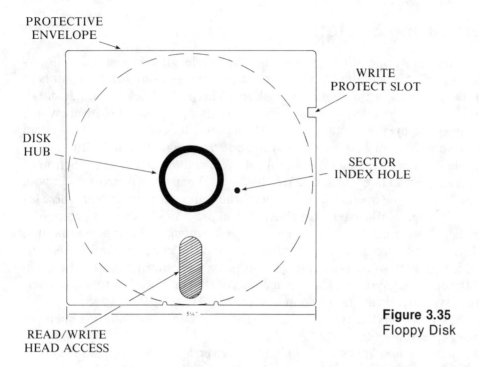

PROTECTIVE
ENVELOPE

WRITE
PROTECT SLOT

DISK
HUB

SECTOR
INDEX HOLE

5¼"

READ/WRITE
HEAD ACCESS

Figure 3.35
Floppy Disk

storage. With such a system, a number of microcomputers can share the disk system and do not require their own individual floppy disk drives. The Corvus Constellation, for example, will allow a number of microcomputers to be configured into a local network. As the prices of Winchester disks continue to decrease, economies will favor this type of storage in applications such as classrooms and computer-resource areas.

Decisions regarding disk storage systems can be difficult. Often product specifications are written in a way that makes comparisons difficult. The storage capacity advertised may be a bit misleading if a significant amount of the disk space is required for disk format data (sometimes this is referred to as *housekeeping*). Data access time is always a prime consideration. System reliability and capability to easily record and store back-up data may also be critical concerns in certain applications. Usually the question which most influences decisions, however, relates to the amount of data storage that is required.

Closely related to the technology of mass or secondary data storage is the concept of an operating system. Even though we have briefly mentioned this topic, the next section will explore operating systems in more detail.

Operating Systems

The concept of operating systems can lead to a lengthy and complex discussion—probably including more information than the average reader wants or needs to know. For this reason, we will try to keep it simple and fundamental. To begin with, an *operating system* is defined as a program or software which controls the overall operation of the computer. It is responsible for system start-up or system *booting* (short for *bootstrapping*). It handles the input/ output devices including mass storage devices and the associated function of file management (storing and retrieving data). When certain errors occur with these devices, the operating system helps the computer recover from these errors. The operating system can allow several programs to share the computer (in larger systems). This is called *multiprogramming*. Multiprogramming, which permits two or more programs to run at the same time, allows for the implementation of time-sharing systems (see next section). Another function of the operating system is the management of the computer's resources. Operating systems have strange-sounding names: HASP, VAX/VMS, OS/VSl, MVS, CP/M, UNIX, and so on. Fortunately, it's not important to remember these, at least not for now.

Smaller computer systems will have some version of disk operating system or DOS. Tandy, for example, offers TRSDOS on the TRS-80 microcomputer. The IBM PC supports both MS-DOS and CP/M. These systems perform many of the above general operating system functions, but especially those related to file management, data storage and retrieval, and housekeeping tasks.

Consideration of the operating system is an important criterion in the selection of both hardware and software. Software will only operate under the operating system for which it is written. In other words, a program written to run under CP/M won't run on an Apple with Apple DOS.

Why isn't there one common operating system for all computers or at least for given classes of computers? Answering that is like trying to explain why a Ford wheel will not fit the Chevy! It just is not the nature of the products of a competitive free enterprise system.

Some efforts have, however, been made in that direction. CP/M (Control Program for Microcomputers), a product of Digital Research, Inc., is an operating system which has been around for many years. Many persons consider it to be a "standard" operating system for microcomputers. CP/M systems are available for most microcomputers and enable the running of hundreds of different programs by many different software producers.

Notwithstanding products systems such as CP/M, do not expect any universal standards any time soon. Data processing is not a new industry. The industry has never supported totally interchangeable products and probably never will. It's the nature of the business.

Time Sharing

Early computers were designed to serve a single user at a time, processing one job at a time. The procedure somewhat resembled the mode in which we use personal computers today. However, as computers came to be more extensively used during the 1960s, it was quickly realized that these expensive systems, dedicated to single users, were not always economically feasible and did not always provide efficient use of computer resources. These considerations led to the development of operating systems which would permit the distribution of computer resources and services to many users "simultaneously." This distribution of computer resources is central to the concept of *time-sharing-systems*. Because this is practical only on very fast machines, the development of time sharing is associated with the third-generation computers of the early 1960s. Time-sharing systems enhance the efficiency of computer systems by allocating the computer's resources to many users at the same time. In other words, time sharing allows several persons to use the computer simultaneously. Because of hardware requirements, time-sharing systems are typically found only on the larger computers.

In a sense then, time sharing creates an illusion that a given user is the sole user of a computer even though there may be many other users. Dozens of persons could be connected to the same computer via terminals and still operate independently of one another.

While operating systems of software which provide time sharing are complex, the principle is simple. A given user is allocated a short portion of CPU time. Then another user is allocated some time. Since the CPU operates at a very high execution speed (millions of cycles and instructions per second), many different processes appear to be executed at once. The users share the time of the CPU, hence the term "time sharing."

Most colleges offer access to computer resources through time sharing, permitting many students to use a main computer via terminals. The University of Iowa, for example, has over one thousand terminals located throughout the campus connected to the academic computer center. One of the center's computers (a Prime 850) can support ninety-six users at a time. Time sharing is also very common in business organizations, banks, airline reservations facilities, etc. for data base query, interactive programming, and so on.

The advent of stand-alone microcomputers has drastically changed the appearance of multi-user systems. Whereas, in the past, time sharing was the most cost effective and efficient means of delivering computer services, now personal computers may be a better means. These considerations have made decisions related to hardware and services even more difficult. Many organizations have opted for a combination of stand-alone computers and time sharing as an approach. The best way to make such decisions, as we said earlier, is to determine first actual service needs and software requirements, and then decide upon the hardware appropriate to those needs and requirements.

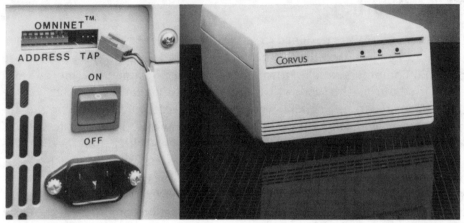

Figure 3.36
Corvus Systems' Winchester Disk Drive. (Corvus Systems, Inc., 2100
Corvus Drive, San Jose, CA 95124)

Data Communications

Throughout our discussion of the components of a computer, we have referred to the linkages between peripheral units (e.g., terminals, printers, secondary storage units) and the central processing unit. Even in the simplest data-processing model (input-processing-output), communication was a requisite element. Computer components do not function in isolation but rather as a total system. The purpose of this section is to provide an introduction to the technology of data communications between the various components. To help simplify our discussion, we shall deal with this topic as it relates principally to microcomputer systems.

Serial Interface

To begin, there are two basic modes of data communication: serial and parallel. As the name suggests, *serial communication* involves the transmission of data serially or sequentially, one bit at a time. If we transmit an ASCII character, the seven bits which constitute the character are sent and received bit by bit. Serial data transfer can be likened to a one-lane street which permits only one car to proceed at a time.

Because of the popularity and widespread use of serial data communications, a standard way of transmitting serial data has been agreed upon—the RS-232 standard. The simplest version of an RS-232 connection consists of three wires. One wire is for data transmission, one is for data reception, and the other wire is a ground connection. Essentially, this system works like a two-lane street for traffic travelling in opposite directions.

Parallel Interface

Another mode of data transfer is the *parallel interface*. Unlike serial transmission which transfers one bit at a time, parallel interfaces move an entire byte at a time. For example, an eight-bit byte system would use eight wires—one for each bit in the byte. All the eight bits would be transferred simultaneously. A sixteen-bit byte would require sixteen wires, and so on. Because data are being transferred a byte at a time, the possible speed of transmission or *transfer rate* is much higher.

Speeds of Data Transmission

Serial transfer rates are usually measured in bits per second (bps). Parallel transfer rates are measured in characters per second (cps). These different measures are reasonable since the two systems transfer bits and characters respectively. If we know the number of bits per character, we can easily convert one measure to the other. For instance, if a character or byte contains 8 bits and the rate of transmission is 2400 bits per second, this equals (including a "start" and "stop" bit):

$$\frac{2400 \text{ bits per second}}{10 \text{ bits per character}} = 240 \text{ characters per second}$$

The term *baud* is also used as a measure of the speed of data transmission in bits per second. Technically speaking, the baud rate is the number of signal changes per second. Typical baud rates are 110, 300, 600, 1200, and 2400 baud. Division of the baud rate by 10 provides a quick approximation of the number of characters per second being transferred. Some understanding of baud rates is important to computer users as they connect various devices in a system (such as a printer or terminal). Many such devices provide for the se-

Figure 3.37
Terminal Cluster at The University of Iowa's Weeg Computing Center.
(University of Iowa, Weeg Computing Center, Iowa City, Iowa 52242)

lection of a given baud rate. If incorrectly selected, errors occur and the device will not function properly.

Telecomputing

Not so long ago, computers, especially microcomputers and their users, existed in isolation from one another. Now the computer that exists in such isolation is rapidly becoming the exception rather than the rule. This is due to the growing popularity and need for telecomputing—probably the most exciting and important area of personal, business, and educational computing to come along in some time.

Telecomputing is a term derived from the combination of "telecommunications" (the transmission of information over long distances) and "computing." Most telecomputing involves the use of telephone lines—either local or long-distance. Transmission of data via telephone requires the use of a *modem*.

The term "modem" is an abbreviation for modulator-demodulator. Basically, a modem converts the data signals from the computer into a form which can be transmitted over the telephone line. This transmission process involves two steps: (1) the conversion of the data into a serial form and (2) modulation of the data or conversion into an electrical signal within the audible frequency range. Just as the telephone transmits voices, it can transmit data, bit by bit. The reception process is the reverse of the transmission process. Incoming signals over the phone line are demodulated or decoded and sent to the computer in a serial form.

Modems fall into two categories: acoustic and direct-connect modems. Acoustic modems are the older variety and employ a cradle which holds the handset of the phone.

Figure 3.38
Modem for Transmission of Data Over Telephone Line. (U.S. Robotics, Inc., 1123 W. Washington Blvd., Chicago, IL 60607)

Data are converted into sounds or whistles which are then transmitted. The problem with acoustic modems is the signal-to-noise ratio which can introduce errors. Direct-connect modems (see figures 3.38 and 3.39) plug into the standard phone jack. They provide more reliable data transmission and can also perform additional functions such as answering the phone or dialing a number.

Telecomputing opens many doors to the user. A modem used in conjunction with the appropriate software will allow a microcomputer to emulate either a dumb terminal or a smart terminal. Files can be sent from computer to computer. Computer bulletin boards provide a valuable form of information exchange. Time-sharing networks provide enormous on-line data bases (see chapter 5).

In summary, telecomputing is probably in the future of almost every computer user. The potential applications have hardly been tapped—especially in education. The possibilities are almost unbounded except by one's imagination.

Suggested Readings

Adams, D.R., Wagner, G.E., & Boyer, T.J. (1983). *Computer information systems: An introduction.* Cincinnati: South-Western Publishing Co.

Bates, W. (1983). *The computer cookbook.* Englewood Cliffs: Prentice-Hall, Inc.

Bitter, G.G. (1984). *Computers in today's world.* New York: John Wiley & Sons.

Bohl, M. (1984). *Information processing.* Chicago: SRA.

Dock, V.T., & Essick, E. (1978). *Principles of business data processing with BASIC.* Chicago: SRA.

Figure 3.39
Transmission of Data Over Telephone Line. (Hayes Microcomputer Products, Inc., 5923 Peachtree Industrial Blvd., Norcross, GA 30092)

Eliason, A.L., & Kitts, K.D. (1979). *Business computer systems and applications.* Chicago: SRA.

Gear, C.W. (1973). *Introduction to computer science.* Chicago: SRA.

Healy, M., & Hebditch, D. (1981). *The microcomputer in on-line systems.* Cambridge, MA: Winthrop Publishers, Inc.

Hopper, G.M., & Mandell, S.L. (1984). *Understanding computers.* St. Paul, MN: West Publishing Co.

Isshiki, K.R. (1982). *Small business computers.* Englewood Cliffs: Prentice-Hall, Inc.

O'Brien, J.A. (1982). *Computers in business management.* Homewood, IL: Richard D. Irwin, Inc.

Stair, R.M. (1981). *Principles of data processing.* Homewood, IL: Richard D. Irwin, Inc.

Wagner, G.E., Crawford, J.B., & Gruver, D.R. (1984). *Computer center operations.* Cincinnati: South-Western Publishing Company.

Wu, M.S. (1979). *Introduction to computer data processing.* New York: Harcourt Brace Jovanovich, Inc.

4
Computer Programming

Introduction

Many educators and data-processing professionals agree that some knowledge of computer programming is an essential component of computer literacy and of understanding the fundamentals of data processing. It is also the position taken by this text. At the very least, one must have an elementary knowledge of programming if one expects to make intelligent decisions regarding the evaluation, acquisition, and integration of computing into our schools. It is not true that every educator needs to become an expert programmer; this is neither necessary nor desirable. One does not have to become a concertmaster or an accomplished musician to appreciate music. However, it would probably not be wise to spend several thousand dollars for a fine musical instrument without acquiring some fundamental knowledge of the instrument.

Computers can perform many seemingly amazing tasks, but they cannot perform these tasks by themselves. They cannot solve problems, make decisions, or formulate solutions without human intervention. The computer is a machine and must be told exactly and explicitly what to do. Usually, when the computer is in error, it is the result of human error. The machine only performs the operations it was instructed to execute (assuming there was no equipment malfunction). There is an old acronym associated with data processing—GIGO (garbage in, garbage out). One can only expect valid output if correct data and instructions are provided in the first place.

Computer programming is an intellectual or "thinking" task; it is a science; and the development of a good program demands considerable skill. A computer program which will solve even a moderately complex problem can require hundreds of hours to develop. Even with the so-called authoring languages which permit the development of educational courseware without the use of a conventional computer language, time investments can be significant. Just as study and practice are required to become a good musician, so it is with programming.

Most users of computers today are not highly skilled or trained programmers. Fortunately, they don't have to be. The need for computer resources and the popularity of low-cost personal computers has spawned a multi-million dollar software industry which produces many needed programs. This trend in software production will likely continue for many years.

Just as learning to play a musical instrument can be an arduous and frustrating task, it can also be an enjoyable and rewarding experience. So it is with computer programming. Hopefully, the latter will be your case.

This is not a computer science or programming text. The introduction to programming offered in this chapter is an introduction and nothing more. Many excellent texts with more detail already exist. The readers are encouraged to look over a few and consider them for future study.

Programming Languages

People require a language in order to communicate information, concepts, directions, relationships, and facts. Our everyday languages contain symbols, accepted rules of order and syntax, and a certain structure. Language is also necessary for communication with a computer so that it can carry out its functions.

The particular computer language selected for this chapter is BASIC, an acronym for Beginner's All-Purpose Symbolic Instruction Code. BASIC was developed in the mid 1960s by Kemeny and Kurtz at Dartmouth College for use in an academic environment. BASIC is well-known for its ease of use and English-like commands. It is also the language used in most microcomputer systems.

There are many other high-level programming languages besides BASIC which could be presented. In fact, there are probably over 200 different programming languages in existence. Many of these languages are considered high-level languages or procedural languages. Such languages are independent of particular machine characteristics.

Pascal, for example, is a newer high-level language which is rapidly gaining popularity and acceptance, because it lends itself well to structured programming concepts (structured programming is a concept which will be discussed later in this chapter). An early programming language dating back to the late 1950s is FORTRAN (FORmula TRANslation). It is a widely used language, especially in applications related to mathematics, science, and engineering. COBOL (COmmon Business Oriented Language) is a popular programming language for business applications or the handling of large files. It is also a language widely used by the federal government.

Another high-level language is PL/1 (Programming Language One) which possesses many features of both FORTRAN and COBOL. Ada, a new language, is a product of the Department of Defense and was designed to increase software reliability, programmer efficiency, and to reduce costs. APL (A Programming Language) is an interesting language which employs a special character set. APL performs calculations and mathematics very efficiently, especially matrix algebra.

There are also many advantages to the BASIC programming language. It is supported by almost all computers, especially the personal computers. It is easy to learn and does not require extensive and intensive study. The vocabulary of BASIC is simple, contains only about a hundred words, and many of these are English-like words. It should be pointed out at the onset that there are many "dialects" of the language BASIC. Though there is an ANSI (American National Standards Institute) standard BASIC, many versions of BASIC exist today, most of which are extensions of this standard.

Most computer systems that use BASIC use an *interpreter* or, stated another way, BASIC is generally implemented as an interpreted programming language. The role of the interpreter in a computer is somewhat like the role of an interpreter of a spoken language. The BASIC language, which is a high-level language designed for ease of use by people, must be translated into a binary code or machine language. This translation is handled one line at a time when the program is run. This is a liability if speed of execution of a program is of concern. It is, however, an asset to the student because many problems related to syntax (e.g., a typographical error or an incorrectly formed statement) will be detected as the lines of the BASIC program are being entered.

There are also compiler BASICs or versions of BASIC which are implemented using a *compiler*. The function of a compiler is similar to an interpreter, with one important difference. A compiler translates an entire program at once into a machine language which is understood by the CPU or microprocessor. An advantage of a compiler is that a program need be compiled only once. The compiled version (i.e., the machine language code) can then be used whenever the program is run. This can result in considerable program execution time savings. If the user is paying for computing in a time-sharing environment, for example, a compiled program will also reduce costs of computing as less machine time is required.

In summary, BASIC is a powerful language and an excellent language for an introduction to computer programming. There are arguments against BASIC as the best introductory language, but its power and flexibility outweigh these objections.

Concept and Use of Algorithms

Central to the study of computers and programming is the concept of an algorithm. Basically, an algorithm is a set of steps leading to the solution of a problem or the accomplishment of some task. Usually an algorithm contains well-defined rules and employs a given set of steps.

Most of us use algorithms in our daily lives, perhaps without even thinking about them. A recipe is a good example. Suppose a host or hostess wishes to serve fresh broccoli with hollandaise sauce. An initial decision is required. Is the rich version (which takes a little more time to prepare) desired or a blended version? Our decision leads us to two alternate recipes.

One method of presenting the procedure is with a *flowchart*. A flowchart is a schematic or pictorial representation of the operations and sequence of activities which are required to solve some problem or accomplish a task. The flowchart shown in figure 4.1 provides most of the necessary information for the preparation of the sauce. It could, of course, be enhanced by including

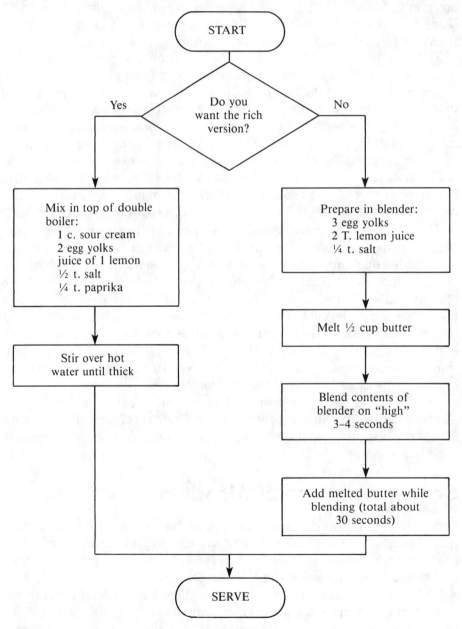

Figure 4.1
Flowchart for Preparation of Hollandaise Sauce

such specifics as the exact serving temperatures, desired consistency, type of butter. If we left no room for misunderstandings, we would have a true algorithm.

The characteristics of an algorithm are:

1. Well-defined rules, steps, or procedures
2. Generalizability (usefulness for more than one problem)
3. Use of input to generate some output

The ability to conceptualize a problem or task as an algorithm is an important step toward the development of a computer program. When we begin writing programs, we shall devote more attention to this activity.

Data Types and Variables

Before beginning our discussion of programming in BASIC, it is necessary to discuss two important types of data: *numeric* and *string*. Numeric data, as the name suggests, are numbers—symbols for use in mathematic calculations. They are generally expressed as integers (whole numbers), floating point (integer plus a decimal portion), or numbers in a scientific notation or exponential format. The first two are familiar types and require no explanation. Scientific notation, however, may be less familiar. Essentially, scientific notation involves the rewriting of a number as floating point number less than 10 and greater than negative 10, multiplied by 10 raised to a power. A few examples in the table below will clarify this. The third column simply indicates how it will look in the computer output.

Number	Scientific Notation	Computer Output
100	1×10^2	100
2929	2.929×10^3	2929
1234567890	1.23456789×10^9	1.23456789E + 09
.0001	1×10^{-4}	1E − 04

The other major type of data is the string. Strings are typically thought of as the set of alphabetic and numeric (i.e., alphanumeric) characters although they can also be other symbols (e.g., the ASCII set). One of the principal distinguishing characteristics of strings is that mathematical calculations cannot be performed on them. Strings are enclosed in quotation marks. The following are examples of strings:

```
"HELLO"
"$127.50"
"****"
"3.1415"
"        "
```

It is important to remember that even though a string can include numeric symbols, no arithmetic can be performed on the string.

The next important concept we need to understand before writing a program is that of data representation using *variables*. Actually, it is a very simple concept. We let a symbol or name represent numeric or string data. For example:

```
(1) A = 5
(2) Z = 12.34
(3) B$ = "HO HUM"
(4) C$ = "5678"
(5) P(1) = 64
(6) M(2,2) = 49
```

In reality, a variable names a location in the computer's memory. In the first example ($A = 5$), the numeric value 5 becomes the contents of a memory location named "A." In other words, we assign the value 5 to a memory location named "A." The six examples listed above represent three types of variables: real, string, and array. Numbers one and two are real variables and are used much as variables are used in arithmetic or algebra. Numbers three and four are alphanumeric string variables enclosed in quotation marks, and numbers five and six are examples of subscripted variables or *arrays*. The computer format for the subscript is parentheses. Therefore, A_1 would be written as A(1). X_{ij} would be written X(I,J).

The rules for variable names—A, C\$, M(2,2) in the examples above—change somewhat from computer to computer. An Apple II, for instance, permits variable names up to 238 characters long. Check the users' manual for your computer for limitations on variable name lengths.

Writing a Program

Let's write a simple program. This will provide an opportunity to illustrate data types, variables, and introduce a few BASIC statements. Here's a simple program:

```
10 PRINT "PROGRAM LISTING #1"
20 INPUT A
30 B = A * 2
40 PRINT B
50 END
```

A computer program is simply a series of instructions or statements. It is numbered in the order of execution and must conform to strict rules of logic and syntax. The importance of proper logic and syntax cannot be overemphasized. Computer programs, unlike our everyday language and communication, are very unforgiving. In the little program above, there are five components with line numbers 10 through 50. Line 10 would cause the string

PROGRAM #1 to be displayed. Line 20, when executed, will prompt the user with a "?" meaning that the computer awaits some entry (in this case, a number). Variable A will assume the value of this input provided by the user. The variable B will assume the value of A multiplied by 2 in line 30. Note that in BASIC an asterisk (*) is the multiplication operator or sign. Line 40 causes the value of variable B to be printed or displayed. Line 50 causes execution to cease. The END statement, which is optional in many systems, instructs the computer to cease processing of the program. When the program is executed, the following will be displayed. (Remember the 5 was entered by the user).

```
PROGRAM #1
?5
10
```

The program listed below is a slightly enhanced version:

```
10 REM #### PROGRAM LISTING #2 ####
20 REM #### JOHN SMITH - 6/15/84 ##
30 REM ##########################
35 REM
40 PRINT "### PROGRAM #2 ###"
50 PRINT "ENTER A NUMBER"
60 INPUT A
70 B = A * 2
80 PRINT
90 PRINT
100 PRINT "THE RESULT IS" B
110 END
```

This program is essentially the same and performs the same computation. It does, however, include an important BASIC statement—the REM or REMARK statement. (Since everything after REM in a given line is ignored by the computer, the REM syntax or abbreviation for REMARK is used here). This statement does not actually enter into the sequence of computation. It simply provides a place for the writer of the program to enter comments or explanations. The # symbols in the REM statement have no function beyond decorative marking. As programs become more complex, the importance of good usage of REM statements will be clear. The PRINT statement in lines 80 and 90 will merely print a blank line or, in effect, cause a line to be skipped. This is used solely for cosmetic purposes or to enhance the visual appearance of the program when it is executed. Line 100 will cause the text string THE RESULT IS to be printed, followed by the contents of memory location B (the value of variable B).

An additional variation on this same program will illustrate another important instruction, the transfer statement.

```
10 REM #### PROGRAM LISTING #3 ####
20 REM #### JOHN SMITH - 6/15/84 ##
30 REM #########################
35 REM
40 PRINT "### PROGRAM #3 ###"
50 PRINT "ENTER A NUMBER (999 to stop)"
60 INPUT A
65 IF A= 999 THEN 110
70 B= A * 2
80 PRINT
90 PRINT
100 PRINT "THE RESULT IS" B
105 GOTO 50
110 END
```

Line 65 uses a conditional transfer based on an "if . . . then" logic. The value of A is entered by the user and examined by the computer program (line 65). If the value of the quantity entered equals 999, the flow or sequence moves down to line 110 which, in this case, is the end of the program. If the value of A does not equal 999, the next statement (line 70) is executed.

Line 105 is called an unconditional transfer. When the sequence of execution reaches line 105, control or flow returns back to line 50. Remember that some versions of BASIC may permit extensions of these commands. Refer to your computer documentation or BASIC manual. Summarized below are the BASIC statements covered thus far:

IF . . . THEN: provides a logical basis for conditional transfer of control or sequence of program execution. When the condition following the IF is true, the rest of the line is executed.

```
EX: 10 IF A < 0 THEN 500
    100 IF B = 9999 THEN 1000
```

INPUT variable name: permits the entry of data into an executing program; the INPUT statement, when executed, will provide a "?" prompt for the user.

```
EX: 10 INPUT A
    100 INPUT X, Y
```

(Note that the values of more than one variable can be obtained using an INPUT statement)

PRINT: permits the display of the value of a variable or text enclosed in quotes.

```
EX: 10 PRINT "HAVE FUN"
    100 PRINT A
    200 PRINT "THE SUM IS "S
```

GOTO: overrides the normal sequential order of operations by unconditionally transferring control to a specified statement number.

```
EX: 110 GOTO 20
```

REMARK: allows the programmer to insert comments, remarks, and explanations; does not affect the logic, control, or execution of the program.

```
EX: 10 REM ###VARIABLE LIST###
```

Arithmetic Operators

Before we develop another program, it should be mentioned that computers often perform arithmetic a bit differently from humans. To be precise, computers invariably perform correctly or according to accepted rules of mathematics; people sometimes do not. Assuming our basic arithmetic is sound, problems arise occasionally due to the so-called order of operation.

When a series of arithmetic functions are handled, the computer follows the following order or sequence of operations:

1. Exponentiation
2. Multiplication and division
3 Addition and subtraction

For example,

$$100/2 - 8 = 50 - 8 = 42$$

Division was the first operation followed by the subtraction. Another example:

$$5^2 - 10/2 + 3 = 23$$

The exponentiation was first ($5^2 = 25$) followed by the division of 10 by 2. So we have $25 - 5 + 3$. As straightforward as this may appear, this hierarchy of operations results in many programmer errors.

Parentheses in arithmetic calculations also follow the accepted rules of mathematics; that is, contents of parentheses are handled first followed by operations outside the parentheses:

$$(8 + 4)/4 = 12/4 = 3$$

Compare the statement without parentheses:

$$8 + 4/4 = 8 + 1 = 9$$

Expressions with two or more embedded sets of parentheses are handled "inside-out":

$$6*((4-2*(3-2)/(3*2)) =$$
$$6*(2*(1)/6) =$$
$$6*(2/6) =$$
$$6*1/3 = 2$$

Developing Programs

Consider the problem of calculating the length of the hypotenuse of a right triangle given the length of two legs. To review the geometry, suppose in figure 4.2, $a = 5$ and $b = 7$.

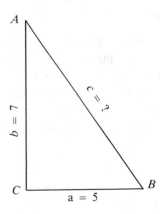

$$a^2 + b^2 = c^2$$
$$5^2 + 7^2 = 74$$
$$c = \sqrt{74} = 8.6 \quad \text{(rounded)}$$

Figure 4.2
Solution of a Right Triangle

The Pythagorean Theorem tells us that the length of the hypotenuse squared is equal to the sum of the squares of the leg lengths or

$$a^2 + b^2 = c^2 \text{ or } c = \sqrt{a^2 + b^2}$$

In this example, we have $5^2 + 7^2 = c^2$ or $c^2 = 74$. Therefore, $c = 8.6$. We now have all the pieces necessary to build a computer program in BASIC which will solve this problem. Before writing the actual code, however, we first outline the steps to be followed.

STEP #1: PROBLEM STATEMENT

Find the length of the hypotenuse of a right triangle given the length of the two legs.

STEP #2: PROCESS DESCRIPTION

1. Format screen
   a. Clear screen
   b. Print title, user information, directions
   c. Request input data
2. Input data (length of *a* and *b*)
3. Calculate length of hypotenuse (*c*)
4. Print output in appropriate format
5. Repeat program if desired
6. End program

STEP #3: SOLUTION METHOD

Obtain values for *a* and *b*. Square *a* and *b,* find the sum, and take the square root of this sum. Display results and ask user if the program is to be rerun.

At this point, one might find it useful to develop a flowchart of the solution process. This can be especially helpful in complex problems. Figure 4.3 illustrates a typical flowchart.

The three steps of Problem Statement, Process Description, and Solution Method are an important part of program development; unless you go through this process of precisely stating the problem and describing the method and solution, you cannot establish a proper foundation for program development. Obviously, these steps can be circumvented and often are omitted in part or completely. The consequence is often a program that may or may not work, is poorly organized, and possesses no structure. With this in mind, we can proceed with writing our BASIC code for this problem.

The program listing for the right triangle problem is provided in figure 4.4. A run or execution is also shown (figure 4.5). A few nonessential instructions such as commands for clearing the screen or positioning the cursor (the blinking light on the CRT) have not been included in the code. These commands will vary somewhat among different computer systems and versions of BASIC.

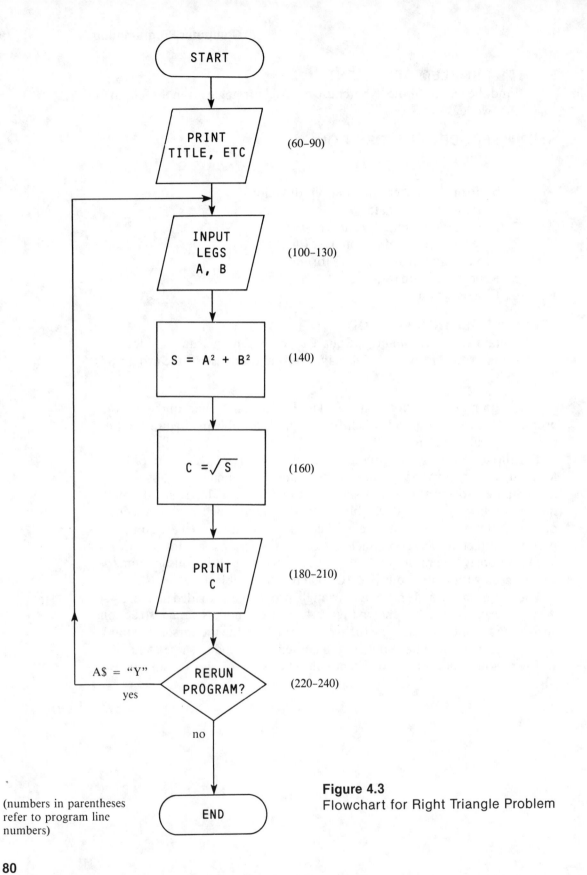

START

PRINT
TITLE, ETC   (60–90)

INPUT
LEGS
A, B   (100–130)

$S = A^2 + B^2$ (140)

$C = \sqrt{S}$ (160)

PRINT
C   (180–210)

A$ = "Y"

RERUN
PROGRAM?   (220–240)

yes

no

END

(numbers in parentheses
refer to program line
numbers)

Figure 4.3
Flowchart for Right Triangle Problem

80

```
10 REM ##### PROGRAM LISTING #4 #####
20 REM ### RIGHT TRIANGLE PROBLEM ###
30 REM #### JOHN SMITH - 6/20/84 ####
40 REM ############################
50 REM  LET A&B REPRESENT LEGS; C THE HYPOTENUSE
55 REM
60 PRINT "+++++++++++++++++++++++++++++++++++++++"
65 PRINT
70 PRINT "       RIGHT TRIANGLE PROBLEM     "
75 PRINT
80 PRINT "+++++++++++++++++++++++++++++++++++++++"
90 PRINT
100 PRINT "ENTER THE LENGTH OF ONE LEG OF THE RIGHT TR]
110 INPUT A
120 PRINT "ENTER THE LENGTH OF THE OTHER LEG"
130 INPUT B
140 S = A * A + B * B
150 REM LET S = HYP SQUARED
160 C = SQR (S)
170 REM SQR RETURNS THE SQUARE ROOT OF THE QUANTITY IN
180 PRINT
190 PRINT
200 PRINT "THE LENGTH OF THE HYPOTENUSE IS "C
210 PRINT
220 PRINT "IF YOU WISH TO USE THE PROGRAM AGAIN, ENTER
230 INPUT A$
240 IF A$ = "Y" THEN 100
250 PRINT "+++++ END OF PROGRAM +++++"
260 PRINT
270 END
```

Figure 4.4
Program Listing #4—Right Triangle Problem


```
+++++++++++++++++++++++++++++++++++++++++
         RIGHT TRIANGLE PROBLEM
+++++++++++++++++++++++++++++++++++++++++
ENTER THE LENGTH OF ONE LEG OF THE RIGHT TRIANGLE ?5
ENTER THE LENGTH OF THE OTHER LEG ?7

THE LENGTH OF THE HYPOTENUSE IS 8.60232527
IF YOU WISH TO USE THE PROGRAM AGAIN, ENTER A 'Y'
?N
+++++ END OF PROGRAM +++++
```

Figure 4.5
Sample Execution-Right Triangle Problem

So far, so good? Let's develop another program, this time a useful one. Teachers spend a lot of time averaging numbers to calculate grades. Let's write a program to do that.

STEP #1: PROBLEM STATEMENT

Find the average of a set of numbers which will be entered one at a time. It should not be necessary for the users to count how many numbers there are before putting them in the computer.

STEP #2: PROCESS DESCRIPTION

1. Format screen
   a. Clear screen
   b. Print title, user information, directions
   c. Request input data (numbers to be averaged)
2. Input data
3. Count the number of entries
4. Detect the completion of data entry (i.e., the program must know when all of the numbers to be averaged have been entered)
5. Calculate sum and average
6. Print output (sum, average, number of entries) in appropriate form
7. End program

STEP #3: SOLUTION METHOD

Obtain values (X) of numbers to be averaged. Count number of entries (N). Let 999 be a flag or sentinel to signify that all data have been entered. Calculate sum of entries (S). Divide sum by N to obtain average (A = S/N). Display results (A, S, N).

Note that in the outline, it is specified that the user should not have to count the number of entries or the number of numbers to be averaged. This requirement leads to a technique which is somewhat common in computer programs—the incrementing of a variable. A similar technique is used to build the sum of the entries.

As the flowchart (figure 4.6) indicates, the user enters a number. The program checks that number to determine if it is a *sentinel* or *flag* signifying that the user has completed data entry. If the entry isn't the sentinel, the variable N or the counter is incremented by 1. (Note: Rather than reading N = N + 1 as "N equals N plus 1" we say "N is replaced by N plus 1"). The value 999 for the sentinel was an arbitrary choice of some number which would probably not be among the numbers to be averaged. The next operation adds the value of the entry to S, the cumulative sum.

The easiest way to fully understand this process is to follow an example, step by step, through the flowchart. Three numbers are to be averaged: 12, 10, and 14. The first (X = 12) is entered. If S and N are assumed to be zero initially (lines 62 and 63 of the program set them equal to zero), the first

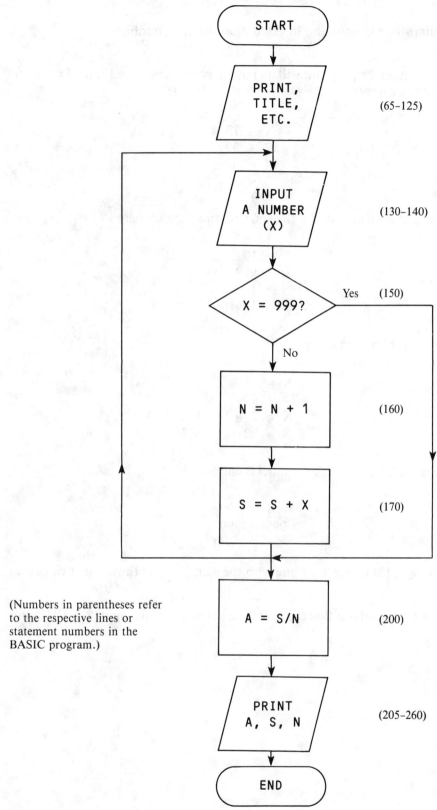

(Numbers in parentheses refer
to the respective lines or
statement numbers in the
BASIC program.)

Figure 4.6
Flowchart for Averaging Set of Numbers

"pass" through the program will increment N by 1 and S by 12, the first entry. Therefore, we have:

$$X = 12$$
$$12 \neq 999$$
$$N = 0 + 1 = 1$$
$$S = 0 + 12 = 12$$

Now the program returns for the entry of another number:

$$X = 10$$
$$10 \neq 999$$
$$N = 1 + 1 = 2$$
$$S = 12 + 10 = 22$$

Returning for the next entry:

$$X = 14$$
$$14 \neq 999$$
$$N = 2 + 1 = 3$$
$$S = 22 + 14 = 36$$

On the last entry, 999 or the sentinel is entered:

$$X = 999$$
$$999 = 999$$
$$A = 36/3 = 12$$

The average (12) is printed along with the sum (36) and the number of entries (3)

Figure 4.6 illustrates a flowchart for the problem of averaging a set of numbers.

A BASIC program and sample run are shown in figures 4.7 and 4.8.

```
10   REM ##### PROGRAM LISTING #5 #####
20   REM # AVERAGE OF A SET OF NUMBERS#
30   REM #### JOHN SMITH - 6/22/84 ####
40   REM ############################
50   REM : LET X REPRESENT THE NUMBERS ENTERED; S THE SUM OF THE X'S

55   REM
60   REM : N IS THE NUMBER OF X'S ENTERED; A THE AVERAGE OF THE X's
62   S = 0
63   N = 0
65   PRINT
70   PRINT "   PROGRAM TO AVERAGE A SET OF NUMBERS     "
75   PRINT
80   PRINT "+++++++++++++++++++++++++++++++++++++++++++"
90   PRINT
100  PRINT "THIS PROGRAM WILL CALCULATE THE AVERAGE OF A SET OF NUMBERS"
105  PRINT
110  PRINT "ENTER THE NUMBERS ONE AT A TIME, EACH FOLLOWED BY A 'RETURN'"
115  PRINT
120  PRINT "WHEN YOU HAVE ENTERED ALL YOUR NUMBERS, ENTER 999 TO STOP"
125  PRINT
130  PRINT "ENTER A NUMBER "
140  INPUT X
150  IF X = 999 THEN 200
155  REM : 999 IS SENTINEL TO END
160  N = N + 1
170  S = S + X
180  GOTO 140
200  A = S / N
205  PRINT
210  PRINT "++++++++++++++++++++++++++++++"
220  PRINT "AVERAGE = "A
230  PRINT "SUM = "S
240  PRINT "NUMBER OF ENTRIES = "N
250  PRINT "++++++++++++++++++++++++++++++"
260  PRINT
270  PRINT "END OF PROGRAM"
400  END
```

Figure 4.7
Program Listing #5 - Average of a Set of Numbers

```
    PROGRAM TO AVERAGE A SET OF NUMBERS
+++++++++++++++++++++++++++++++++++++++++++
THIS PROGRAM WILL CALCULATE THE AVERAGE OF A SET OF NUMBERS
ENTER THE NUMBERS ONE AT A TIME, EACH FOLLOWED BY A 'RETURN'
WHEN YOU HAVE ENTERED ALL YOUR NUMBERS, ENTER 999 TO STOP
ENTER A NUMBER
?88
?75
?83
?90
?98
?88
?80
?999
++++++++++++++++++++++++++++++
AVERAGE = 86
SUM = 602
NUMBER OF ENTRIES = 7
++++++++++++++++++++++++++++++
END OF PROGRAM
```

Figure 4.8
Sample Execution - Average of a Set of Numbers

As with all the programs provided in this chapter, the reader is encouraged to enter them on a computer and verify that they perform the functions described. Also the reader should not hesitate to experiment with variations on the programs.

Let us consider one more problem using the BASIC statements covered thus far before tackling any new statements. A common business-education activity concerns the calculation of monthly payments on a loan. The formula for calculating payment is:

$$P = \frac{A(1+R)^T \times R}{(1+R)^T - 1}$$

where A = amount of the initial loan
    R = interest rate *per month*
    T = the total number of months
    P = monthly payment

STEP # 1: PROBLEM STATEMENT

Find the monthly payments on a loan given the loan amount, the number of years, and the interest rate per year.

STEP #2: PROCESS DESCRIPTION

1. Format screen
   a. Clear screen
   b. Print title, user information, directions
   c. Request input data (amount of loan, annual interest rate, number of years)

2. Input data
3. Calculate payment according to given formula
4. Print output, monthly payment, number of years, interest rate
5. Rerun if requested
6. End program

STEP #3: SOLUTION METHOD

Obtain values for amount of loan (A), annual interest rate (I), and number of periods (N). Calculate payments (P) using given formula. Display results and ask if program is to be rerun.

A flowchart for the loan payment problem is shown in figure 4.9.

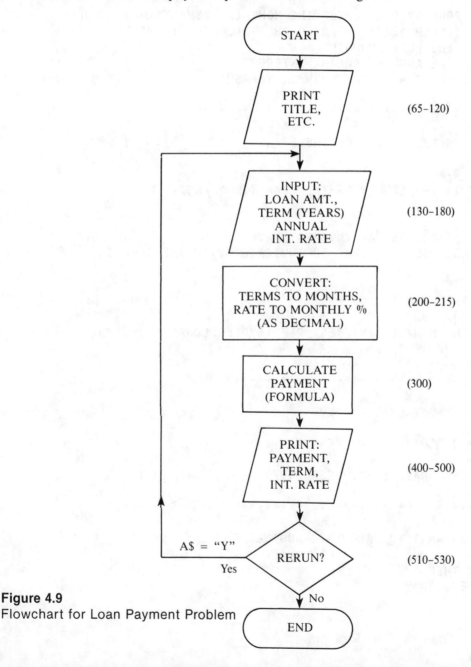

Figure 4.9
Flowchart for Loan Payment Problem

The program listing and sample execution are given in figures 4.10 and 4.11.

```
10 REM ##### PROGRAM LISTING #6 #####
20 REM ### LOAN PAYMENT PROBLEM   ####
30 REM #### JOHN SMITH - 6/25/84 ####
40 REM ##############################
50 REM LET A = AMOUNT OF LOAN; I= THE INTEREST RATE PER PERIOD
55 REM LET P = CALCULATED PAYMENT; N= THE NUMBER OF PERIODS
60 REM
65 PRINT
70 PRINT "     LOAN PAYMENT PROBLEM"
75 PRINT
80 PRINT "++++++++++++++++++++++++++++++++++++++++++++"
90 PRINT
100 PRINT "THIS PROGRAM CALCULATES THE MONTHLY PAYMENTS ON A LOAN."
105 PRINT "YOU WILL BE ASKED TO ENTER THE FOLLOWING ITEMS:"
107 PRINT "   A. THE LOAN AMOUNT"
108 PRINT "   B. THE ANNUAL PERCENT INTEREST"
109 PRINT "   C.THE TERM OF THE LOAN IN YEARS"
110 PRINT
115 PRINT "++++++++++++++++++++++++++++++++++++++++++++"
120 PRINT
130 PRINT "WHAT IS THE AMOUNT OF THE LOAN?"
140 INPUT A
145 PRINT
150 PRINT "WHAT IS THE LENGTH OF THE LOAN (IN YEARS)?"
160 INPUT N
165 PRINT
170 PRINT "WHAT IS THE ANNUAL INTEREST RATE?"
175 PRINT "(DO NOT USE A DECIMAL TO INDICATE %. IF THE RATE IS 12.8%, ENTER 12.8)"
180 INPUT I
200 T = 12 * N
205 REM : T IS THE TERM IN MONTHS
210 R = (I / 12) / 100
215 REM : R IS THE MONTHLY INTEREST RATE EXPRESSED AS A DECIMAL
300 P = (A * (1 + R) ^ T * R) / ((1 + R) ^ T - 1)
400 PRINT
410 PRINT "++++++++++++++++++++++++++++++++++++"
420 PRINT
430 PRINT "MONTHLY PAYMENTS ARE $"P
435 PRINT
440 PRINT "TERM OF LOAN IS "N" YEARS"
445 PRINT
450 PRINT "INTEREST RATE IS "I" PERCENT/YEAR"
455 PRINT
460 PRINT "++++++++++++++++++++++++++++++++++++"
500 PRINT
510 PRINT "DO YOU WANT TO CALCULATE ANOTHER PAYMENT? (Y/N)?"
520 INPUT A$
530 IF A$ = "Y" THEN 120
600 PRINT "### END ###"
700 END
```

Figure 4.10
Program Listing #6 - Loan Payment Problem

```
      LOAN PAYMENT PROBLEM
++++++++++++++++++++++++++++++++++++++++++
THIS PROGRAM CALCULATES THE MONTHLY PAYMENTS ON A LOAN.
YOU WILL BE ASKED TO ENTER THE FOLLOWING ITEMS:
  A. THE LOAN AMOUNT
  B. THE ANNUAL PERCENT INTEREST
  C. THE TERM OF THE LOAN IN YEARS
++++++++++++++++++++++++++++++++++++++++++
WHAT IS THE AMOUNT OF THE LOAN?
?1000
WHAT IS THE LENGTH OF THE LOAN (IN YEARS)?
?1
WHAT IS THE ANNUAL INTEREST RATE?
(DO NOT USE A DECIMAL TO INDICATE %. IF THE RATE IS 12.8%, ENTER 12.8)
?12
+++++++++++++++++++++++++++++++++++
MONTHLY PAYMENTS ARE $88.84879
TERM OF LOAN IS 1 YEARS
INTEREST RATE IS 12 PERCENT/YEAR
+++++++++++++++++++++++++++++++++++
DO YOU WANT TO CALCULATE ANOTHER PAYMENT? (Y/N)?
?N
### END ###
```

Figure 4.11
Sample Execution - Loan Payment Problem

The process and code should be fairly clear. Sometimes there are variations on data input which are a function of individual programmer preference. For instance, the user is prompted to enter the interest rate as a percent, not as a decimal (lines 170–175). This input is later converted to a decimal by dividing by 100 in line 210. Some programmers may decide that this could be confusing and prompt the user to enter a decimal. Of course, there's nothing wrong with either approach. Note that in line 300 the "^" symbol is used to denote the exponentiation operator. Some systems may not use the "^" and use "**" for exponentiation instead. Check your manual to be sure. Line 300 also presents an illustration of the order of arithmetic operations and use of parentheses as discussed earlier.

Structured Programming

One of the criticisms of computer-programming instruction, particularly at the high school level, has concerned the lack of adherence to principles of structured programming. One of the key concepts in structured programming is the use of *modules* or *sections* within a program. Each module is dedicated to a specific function. Usually this means that there will be a main portion of the total program or *home base* which will branch to other components or subroutines within the program.

There are many reasons for this approach to programming. For one, the programs are easier to understand. A module or set of instructions dedicated to one specific task or function rather than several will be easier to develop, code, and de-bug (*de-bug* refers to finding problems or errors in a program). Modular or structured programs generally perform better and more reliably but not necessarily faster. Writing fast, efficient programs, however, is not our goal at the present time. Learn and practice good programming techniques—then worry about things such as the reduction of execution time. For most nonprofessional programmers, this is never a serious problem anyway. In general, modular programs require more lines of code. The benefits, however, outweigh the extra time required to enter these instructions.

Before writing a modular program, we need to learn a new BASIC statement: GOSUB. The GOSUB statement transfers control of the program to the first statement of a subroutine. A subroutine, as the name suggests, is a program within a larger program. It typically contains the code related to some specific function. The subroutine may be called or used any number of times.

At the conclusion of the subroutine is another new statement: RETURN. This returns control of the program to the first statement in the program following the GOSUB. Let's examine a short program which uses the GOSUB and RETURN statements.

In program listing # 7 (figure 4.12) the first statement following the RE-MARKs is the GOSUB in line 50. This transfers control to line 1000 where execution proceeds. The statement SUBROUTINE BEGINNING AT LINE 1000 is printed at line 1100 followed by a blank line. The RETURN statement in line 1990 returns control back to the first statement after the GOSUB which called this subroutine. The GOSUB was at line 50, the next line is number 55, and that's where we are now. Line 60 follows the same procedure. The GO-SUB in line 60 transfers control to line 2000, the subroutine is executed, and then control returns to line 65. Line 70 is a PRINT statement followed by END which terminates or signals the end of the program.

The inclusion of the END statement in line 100 is not optional. If it had been omitted, the program would have continued to execute, at least for a time. Can you determine what would happen eventually if the END in line 100 had been omitted?

You now have an idea as to how subroutines in a program work. Earlier we developed a program to calculate payments on a loan. Review the listing of the code in figure 4.10. You notice that the logic or flow of the program is much like a pipeline. Things begin, data are input, processed, and printed in a nice, sequential fashion. It works and, in a sense, there's nothing wrong with the manner in which it is written. Let's re-write it anyway to use what has been learned about subroutines and modular programming. First we need a main program. That's our home base or point of departure for going off to various

```
10 REM #### PROGRAM LISTING #7 ####
20 REM #### SUBROUTINES ##########
30 REM #### JOHN SMITH - 7/1/84 ###
40 REM
50 GOSUB 1000
55 PRINT "PROGRAM AT LINE 55"
60 GOSUB 2000
65 PRINT "NOW WE'RE AT LINE 65"
70 PRINT "    THE END!!!"
100 END
1000 REM ####################################
1010 REM #######  SUBROUTINE #1  #############
1020 REM ####################################
1100 PRINT "SUBROUTINE BEGINNING AT LINE 1000"
1110 PRINT
1990 RETURN
1999 REM ####################################
2000 REM ####################################
2010 REM #######  SUBROUTINE #2  #############
2020 REM ####################################
2100 PRINT "NEXT SUBROUTINE BEGINNING AT LINE 2000"
2110 PRINT
2990 RETURN
2999 REM ####################################
9000 END


SUBROUTINE BEGINNING AT LINE 1000
PROGRAM AT LINE 55
NEXT SUBROUTINE BEGINNING AT LINE 2000
NOW WE'RE AT LINE 65
THE END!!!
```

Figure 4.12
Program Listing # 7 - Use of Subroutines

modules. The requirements of the problem (and programming experience!) suggest four subroutines are reasonable:

1. Data input
2. Processing
3. Output
4. Rerun request/transfer

Study the listing of our revised program in figure 4.13, and the execution in figure 4.14. The program works in essentially the same manner as before except that four subroutines at lines 1000, 2000, 3000, and 4000 contain the above modules. Note also the inclusion of the END statement in line 210. If you had to find a problem or bug in the program, would this structure facilitate analysis and trouble shooting? Probably so.

```
10     REM ##### PROGRAM LISTING #8 #####
20     REM ### LOAN PAYMENT PROBLEM   ####
30     REM #### JOAN SMITH - 7/7/84 #####
40     REM ##############################
50     REM LET A= AMOUNT OF LOAN; I= THE INTEREST RATE PER PERIOD
55     REM LET P= CALCULATED PAYMENT; N= THE NUMBER OF PERIODS
60     REM
65     PRINT
70     PRINT "   LOAN PAYMENT PROBLEM"
75     PRINT
80     PRINT "+++++++++++++++++++++++++++++++++++++++++"
90     PRINT
100    PRINT "THIS PROGRAM CALCULATES THE MONTHLY PAYMENTS ON A LOAN."
105    PRINT "YOU WILL BE ASKED TO ENTER THE FOLLOWING ITEMS:"
107    PRINT "  A. THE LOAN AMOUNT"
108    PRINT "  B. THE ANNUAL PERCENT INTEREST"
109    PRINT "  C. THE TERM OF THE LOAN IN YEARS"
110    PRINT
115    PRINT "+++++++++++++++++++++++++++++++++++++++++"
120    PRINT
130    GOSUB 1000
140    REM : SUB 1000 FOR INPUT
145    PRINT
150    GOSUB 2000
160    REM : SUB 2000 FOR PROCESS
165    PRINT
170    GOSUB 3000
180    REM : SUB 3000 FOR OUTPUT
190    GOSUB 4000
200    REM : SUB 4000 FOR RERUN
210    END
1000   REM ########################
1010   REM ## SUBROUT FOR INPUT  ####
1020   REM ########################
1030   PRINT "WHAT IS THE AMOUNT OF THE LOAN?"
1040   INPUT A
1050   PRINT "WHAT IS THE LENGTH OF THE LOAN (IN YEARS)?"
1060   INPUT N
1065   PRINT
1070   PRINT "WHAT IS THE ANNUAL INTEREST RATE?"
1075   PRINT "(DO NOT USE A DECIMAL TO INDICATE %. IF THE RATE IS 12.8% PER YEAR,
       ENTER 12.8)"
1080   INPUT I
1990   RETURN
1999   REM ########################
2000   REM ########################
2010   REM ## SUBROUT FOR PROCESS ###
2020   REM ########################
2030 T = 12 * N
2040   REM : T IS THE TERM IN MONTHS
2050 R = (I / 12) / 100
2055   REM : R IS THE MONTHLY INTEREST RATE EXPRESSED AS A DECIMAL
2060 P = (A * (1 + R) ^ T * R) / ((1 + R) ^ T - 1)
```

```
2990    RETURN
2999    REM ########################
3000    REM ########################
3010    REM ### SUBROUT FOR OUTPUT ##
3020    REM ########################
3030    PRINT
3040    PRINT "+++++++++++++++++++++++++++++++++"
3050    PRINT
3060    PRINT "MONTHLY PAYMENTS ARE $"P
3070    PRINT "TERM OF LOAN IS "N" YEAR(S)"
3080    PRINT "INTEREST RATE IS "I" PERCENT/YEAR"
3090    PRINT "+++++++++++++++++++++++++++++++++"
3100    PRINT
3990    RETURN
3999    REM ########################
4000    REM ########################
4010    REM ### SUBROUT FOR RERUN ###
4020    REM ########################
4030    PRINT
4040    PRINT "DO YOU WANT TO CALCULATE ANOTHER PAYMENT? (Y/N)?"
4050    INPUT A$
4060    IF A$ = "Y" THEN 130
4990    RETURN
4999    REM ########################
9999    END
```

Figure 4.13
Program Listing #8 - Loan Payment Program Using Subroutines

```
     LOAN PAYMENT PROBLEM
+++++++++++++++++++++++++++++++++++++++++
THIS PROGRAM CALCULATES THE MONTHLY PAYMENTS ON A LOAN.
YOU WILL BE ASKED TO ENTER THE FOLLOWING ITEMS:
  A. THE LOAN AMOUNT
  B. THE ANNUAL PERCENT INTEREST
  C. THE TERM OF THE LOAN IN YEARS
+++++++++++++++++++++++++++++++++++++++++
WHAT IS THE AMOUNT OF THE LOAN?
?1000
WHAT IS THE LENGTH OF THE LOAN (IN YEARS)?
?1
WHAT IS THE ANNUAL INTEREST RATE?
(DO NOT USE A DECIMAL TO INDICATE %. IF THE RATE IS 12.8% PER YEAR, ENTER 12.8)
?12


+++++++++++++++++++++++++++++++++
MONTHLY PAYMENTS ARE $88.84879
TERM OF LOAN IS 1 YEAR(S)
INTEREST RATE IS 12 PERCENT/YEAR
+++++++++++++++++++++++++++++++++
DO YOU WANT TO CALCULATE ANOTHER PAYMENT? (Y/N)?
?N
```

Figure 4.14
Sample Execution - Loan Payment Problem Using Subroutines

Repetitive Operations

Frequently a task or process requires that a certain operation or procedure be repeated a number of times. One way to approach this problem is to use the GOTO statements to create a loop. For example, suppose we wish to print "Good Morning" five times. A loop and counter could be set up to accomplish this. Examine the flowchart in figure 4.15.

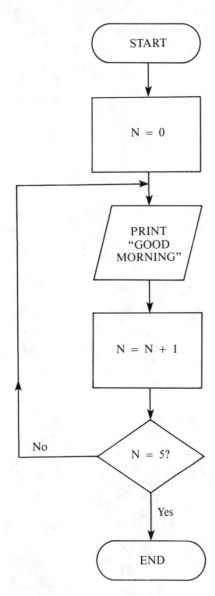

Figure 4.15
Flowchart for Repetitive Operation

The counter N is initialized to equal zero. After every print of "Good Morning," the counter is incremented by one. When five iterations have occurred, the program terminates. The BASIC code and execution of this program are presented in figure 4.16.

```
10    REM ##### PROGRAM LISTING #9 #####
20    REM # LOOP USING GOTO STATEMENT ##
30    REM #### JOAN SMITH - 7/8/84 #####
40    REM ############################
50    REM : N IS A COUNTER
60    N = 0
65    REM : INITIALIZE N TO ZERO
70    PRINT "GOOD MORNING"
80    N = N + 1
90    IF N = 5 THEN 100
95    GOTO 70
100   END
```

```
GOOD MORNING
GOOD MORNING
GOOD MORNING
GOOD MORNING
GOOD MORNING
```

Figure 4.16
Program Listing #9 - Repetitive Operations

While this loop using the GOTO statement certainly works, there is an easier method using the FOR/NEXT statements. The FOR/NEXT structure allows one to specify how many times a given portion of a program is to be executed. Stated another way, FOR/NEXT is a pair of statements which allows the repetition of a group of statements by defining a loop. The easiest way to explain this is with an example. Consider the last problem in which we wished to print "Good Morning" five times. The program shown in figure 4.17 reveals another way of approaching this problem using FOR/NEXT.

```
10    REM ##### PROGRAM LISTING #10 ####
20    REM ## LOOP USING FOR/NEXT #######
30    REM #### JOAN SMITH - 7/8/84 #####
40    REM ############################
50    FOR N = 1 TO 5
60    PRINT "GOOD MORNING"
70    NEXT N
80    END
```

```
GOOD MORNING
GOOD MORNING
GOOD MORNING
GOOD MORNING
GOOD MORNING
```

Figure 4.17
Program Listing #10 - Loop Using FOR/NEXT

The FOR statement in line 50 contains the parameters for specifying how many times the loop will be executed. FOR statements are always of the form

FOR variable name = a TO b

In our example, the variable name is N. This is an arbitrary selection and could have been any letter. The bounds on the loop are specified by the values of a and b. Unless certain conditions are changed, the system will increment the value of a by 1 after each iteration until it reaches the value specified by b. Therefore, in this case, N begins with a value of 1 and takes on the successive values of 2, 3, 4, and 5, respectively. At that point the loop is satisfied and the program proceeds with its operation beginning with the line after the NEXT statement. The program shown in figure 4.18 contains a slight modification—the PRINT statements in lines 64 and 75 indicate the values of N as the program executes.

```
10   REM ##### PROGRAM LISTING #11 ####
20   REM ## LOOP USING FOR/NEXT #######
30   REM #### JOAN SMITH - 7/8/84 #####
40   REM ############################
50   FOR N = 1 TO 5
60   PRINT "GOOD MORNING"
63   PRINT
64   PRINT "N NOW EQUALS "N
70   NEXT N
75   PRINT "THE FINAL VALUE OF N IS "N
80   END


GOOD MORNING
N NOW EQUALS 1
GOOD MORNING
N NOW EQUALS 2
GOOD MORNING
N NOW EQUALS 3
GOOD MORNING
N NOW EQUALS 4
GOOD MORNING
N NOW EQUALS 5
THE FINAL VALUE OF N IS 6
```

Figure 4.18
Program Listing # 11 - Loop Using FOR/NEXT

Now examine program listing # 12 (figure 4.19). This program calculates and prints a short table of square roots and cube roots. The FOR statement in line 50 tells the program that the variable I will assume values of 1, 2, 3, . . . 10. Line 60 replaces X with the square root of C. Line 70 replaces Y with the value of the cube root of C (the cube root of a number is the same as a number raised to the 1/3 power). Line 80 prints the current values of C, X, and Y. Line 90 returns the control to line 50, the top of the loop; C is incremented by 1, and the process is repeated.

```
10  REM ##### PROGRAM LISTING #12 ####
20  REM # TABLE OF SQUARE & CUBE ROOTS
30  REM #### JOAN SMITH - 7/10/84 ####
40  REM ############################
50  FOR C = 1 TO 10
60  X = SQR (C)
70  Y = C ^ (1 / 3)
75  REM : 1/3 POWER = CUBE ROOT
80  PRINT C,X,Y
90  NEXT C
100 END
```

1	1	1
2	1.41421356	1.25992105
3	1.73205081	1.44224957
4	2	1.58740105
5	2.23606798	1.70997595
6	2.44948974	1.81712059
7	2.64575131	1.91293118
8	2.82842713	2
9	3	2.08008383
10	3.16227766	2.15443469

Figure 4.19
Program Listing #12 - Table of Square and Cube Roots

Before leaving the topic of FOR/NEXT, let's use these statements to develop a program for calculating an amortization schedule for a loan. Remember, in the loan payment problem a program was developed which would calculate the payment amount associated with a given principal at some interest rate over a period of time. An amortization schedule would provide a user with a month-by-month statement of the amount of the payment which was applied toward reducing the principal and the declining amounts of the balance.

STEP #1: PROBLEM STATEMENT

Calculate the amount of a loan payment which will be applied to the principal of the loan each month. Develop a table which will reflect the monthly payment, interest paid that month, the amount of the payment toward the principal, and the unpaid balance of the loan.

STEP # 2: PROCESS DESCRIPTION

1. Format screen
   a. Clear screen

  b. Print title, user information, directions

  c. Request input data (amount of the loan, interest per year, number of years, and monthly payments).

2. Input data
3. Calculate elements of schedule
4. Print output (month number, amount of monthly payment, interest paid during that month, amount applied toward principal, and unpaid balance). All information should be monthly. Also calculate total interest paid.
5. End program.

STEP #3: SOLUTION METHOD

Obtain values for amount of loan (A), length of loan or number of years (N), interest/year (I), and amount of monthly payment (P). Amount of payment can be calculated using the loan payment program. Print a table according to the following format:

MONTH / PAYMENT / INTEREST / AMT. TO PRINCIPAL / UNPAID BAL
  A flowchart for this problem is shown in Figure 4.20.

This is a bit more difficult problem than those studied thus far. Yet it is representative in many respects of the problems which are appropriate for computer processing. In this case, a set of arithmetic operations are repeated numerous times. Since this problem isn't quite as straightforward as the previous ones, it may be useful to study the flowchart and the necessary operations before moving along to the actual BASIC code.

One useful approach when studying a flowchart such as this one is to execute the operations manually—that is, "play the computer." Start with the following input data:

- $A = 1000$ (amount of loan)
- $N = 1$ (length of loan in years)
- $I = 12$ (annual interest rate)
- $P = 88.85$ (monthly payment)

Conversions:

- $Q = N \times 12 = 12$ (years to months)
- $R = (I/12)/100 = .01$ (monthly interest rate)

Iteration # 1:

 (i) $M = R \times A = .01 \times 1000 = 10.00$ (1st month interest)

 (ii) $Z = P - M = 88.85 - 10.00 = 78.85$ amount toward loan balance

 (iii) $B = A - Z = 1000 - 78.85 = 921.15$ (new unpaid balance)

 (iv) $A = B = 921.15$ (replace old balance with new balance)

 (v) $T = T + M = 0 + 10.00 = 10.00$ (total interest paid)

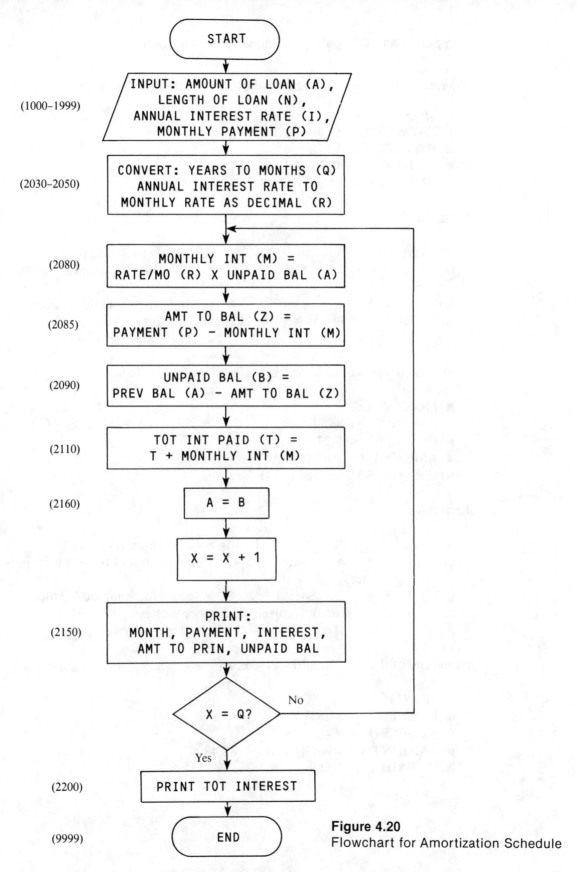

Figure 4.20
Flowchart for Amortization Schedule

Therefore, at the end of the first month or first iteration we have:

- MONTH = 1
- PAYMENT = 88.85
- INTEREST = 10.00
- AMOUNT TO PRINCIPAL = 78.85
- UNPAID BALANCE = 921.15

Iteration #2:

(i) $M = R \times A = .01 \times 921.15 = 9.21$ (2nd month interest)
(ii) $Z = P - M = 88.85 - 9.21 = 79.64$ (amount toward loan balance)
(iii) $B = A - Z = 921.15 - 79.64 = 841.51$ (new unpaid balance)
(iv) $A = B = 841.51$ (replace old balance with new balance)
(v) $T = T + M = 10.00 + 9.21 = 19.21$ (total interest paid)

At the end of the second month or second iteration we have:

- MONTH = 2
- PAYMENT = 88.85
- INTEREST = 9.21
- AMOUNT TO PRINCIPAL = 79.64
- UNPAID BALANCE = 841.51

Iteration # 3:

(i) $M = R \times A = .01 \times 841.51 = 8.42$ (3rd month interest)
(ii) $Z = P - M = 88.85 - 8.42 = 80.43$ (amount toward loan balance)
(iii) $B = A - Z = 841.51 - 80.43 = 761.08$ (new unpaid balance)
(iv) $A = B = 761.08$ (replace old balance with new balance)
(v) $T = T + M = 19.21 + 8.42 = 27.63$ (total interest paid)

At the end of the third month we have:

- MONTH = 3
- PAYMENT = 88.85
- INTEREST = 8.42
- AMOUNT TO PRINCIPAL   80.43
- UNPAID BALANCE = 761.08

Since the term of the loan is one year (12 months), the loop will execute a total of 12 times. The reader should work through a few loops comparing answers with those in figure 4.22.

The BASIC code for this problem is shown in program listing # 13 (figure 4.21). A main section plus two modules for input and output/process are used. Note that in line 2070 a parameter of the FOR/NEXT is given by the variable Q (term of the loan in months). Lines 2140, 2142, 2144, and 2195 illustrate a new command—the INT (integer) function. This function returns the integer or whole number portion of a quantity. The reader is encouraged to discover how these lines perform the rounding of the calculated values to the nearest cent (e.g., two decimal places).

In summary, we see that the FOR/NEXT commands offer the programmer a powerful tool for performing repetitive questions. Different versions of BASIC will permit extensions of the structure presented here. Some extensions will allow the user to interactively assign values to the parameters in the FOR statement. Most versions will also permit the specification of a "step variable" which simply indicates how much a variable will be incremented during each interaction. For example,

```
FOR I = 1 to 100 STEP 3
```

would cause the variable I to assume values 1, 4, 7, . . . etc. in the loop. In the next section, we'll use FOR/NEXT and a new variable type, the subscripted variable, in another program to calculate grade averages.

Subscripted Variables

Thus far in our discussion of BASIC programming we have used variable names like A, B, C, and, occasionally, A$ for a string variable. In certain cases, it may be more desirable to use another type of variable name. This brings us to a new topic—*subscripted variables*. You may recall the use of the subscript notation from a mathematics or statistics application. Basically, we use a numeric subscript to develop a set of variable names, e.g., A_1, A_2, etc. Below is a list of 100 variables using subscripts:

$$A_1, A_2, A_3, \ldots A_{100}$$

We don't need to write out all 100 since the first 3 tell us the pattern of the subscript progression. Since the computer doesn't write the subscripts like this, we would use the following equivalent set in the notation of BASIC:

```
A(1), A(2), A(3), . . . A(100)
```

```
10    REM ##### PROGRAM LISTING #13 ####
20    REM ### AMORTIZATION SCHEDULE ####
30    REM #### JOAN SMITH - 7/12/84 ####
40    REM ############################
50    REM   LET A= AMOUNT OF LOAN; I= THE INTEREST RATE PER YEAR
55    REM    LET P= CALCULATED PAYMENT; N= THE NUMBER OF PERIODS
56    REM     LET B= UNPAID BALANCE; M= MONTHLY INT ON UNPAID BAL
57    REM     T= TOTAL INTEREST PAID
60    REM
65    PRINT
70    PRINT "     AMORTIZATION SCHEDULE"
75    PRINT
80    PRINT "+++++++++++++++++++++++++++++++++++++++++++++"
90    PRINT
100   PRINT "THIS PROGRAM PROVIDES AN AMORTIZATION SCHEDULE FOR A LOAN.  "
105   PRINT "YOU WILL BE ASKED TO ENTER THE FOLLOWING ITEMS:"
107   PRINT "  A. THE LOAN AMOUNT"
108   PRINT "  B. THE ANNUAL PERCENT INTEREST"
109   PRINT "  C. THE TERM OF THE LOAN IN YEARS"
110   PRINT "  D. THE MONTHLY PAYMENTS"
111   PRINT
115   PRINT "+++++++++++++++++++++++++++++++++++++++++++++"
120   PRINT
130   GOSUB 1000
140   REM : SUB 1000 FOR INPUT
145   PRINT
150   GOSUB 2000
160   REM : SUB 2000 FOR PROCESS
165   PRINT
210   END
1000   REM #######################
1010   REM ## SUBROUT FOR INPUT ####
1020   REM #######################
1030   PRINT "WHAT IS THE AMOUNT OF THE LOAN?"
1040   INPUT A
1050   PRINT "WHAT IS THE LENGTH OF THE LOAN (IN YEARS)?"
1060   INPUT N
1065   PRINT
1070   PRINT "WHAT IS THE ANNUAL INTEREST RATE?"
1075   PRINT "(DO NOT USE A DECIMAL TO INDICATE %. IF THE RATE IS 12.8% PER YEAR,
       ENTER 12.8)"
1080   INPUT I
```

```
1090    PRINT "WHAT IS THE MONTHLY PAYMENT?"
1100    INPUT P
1990    RETURN
1999    REM #########################
2000    REM #########################
2010    REM # SUB FOR PROCESS/OUTPUT #
2020    REM #########################
2030    Q = N * 12
2050    R = (I / 12) / 100
2055    REM R IS MONTHLY INTEREST EXPRESSED AS A DECIMAL
2060    PRINT "MONTH          PAYMENT          INTEREST          AMT TO PRINCIPAL
        UNPAID BALANCE "
2062    PRINT "_____          _____          _____          ___ __ _____
        _____ _____ "
2070    FOR X = 1 TO Q
2080    M = R * A
2085    Z = P - M
2087    REM Z = AMOUNT TOWARD LOAN BALANCE
2090    B = A - Z
2100    REM UNPAID BAL(B) = PREV BAL-(PAYMENT-INT)
2110    T = T + M
2120    REM T SUMS INTEREST
2130    IF B < .01 THEN B = 0
2140    C = ( INT (M * 100 + .5)) / 100
2142    D = ( INT (Z * 100 + .5)) / 100
2144    E = ( INT (B * 100 + .5)) / 100
2145    REM : ROUND TO 2 PLACES
2150    PRINT X,P,C,D,E
2160    A = B
2170    REM A IS THE NEW UNPAID BALANCE
2180    NEXT X
2190    PRINT
2195    W = INT (T * 100 + .5) / 100
2200    PRINT "TOTAL INTEREST ON LOAN IS $"W
2990    RETURN
2999    REM #########################
9999    END
```

Figure 4.21
Program Listing #13 - Amortization Schedule Program

A sample run of the program is shown in figure 4.22

```
     AMORTIZATION SCHEDULE
+++++++++++++++++++++++++++++++++++++++++++
THIS PROGRAM PROVIDES AN AMORTIZATION SCHEDULE FOR A LOAN.
YOU WILL BE ASKED TO ENTER THE FOLLOWING ITEMS:
     A. THE LOAN AMOUNT
     B. THE ANNUAL PERCENT INTEREST
     C. THE TERM OF THE LOAN IN YEARS
     D. THE MONTHLY PAYMENTS
+++++++++++++++++++++++++++++++++++++++++++
WHAT IS THE AMOUNT OF THE LOAN?
?1000
WHAT IS THE LENGTH OF THE LOAN (IN YEARS)?
?1
WHAT IS THE ANNUAL INTEREST RATE?
(DO NOT USE A DECIMAL TO INDICATE %. IF THE RATE IS 12.8% PER YEAR, ENTER 12.8)
?12
WHAT IS THE MONTHLY PAYMENT?
?88.85
```

MONTH	PAYMENT	INTEREST	AMT TO PRINCIPAL	UNPAID BALANCE
1	88.85	10	78.85	921.15
2	88.85	9.21	79.64	841.51
3	88.85	8.42	80.43	761.08
4	88.85	7.61	81.24	679.84
5	88.85	6.8	82.05	597.79
6	88.85	5.98	82.87	514.91
7	88.85	5.15	83.7	431.21
8	88.85	4.31	84.54	346.67
9	88.85	3.47	85.38	261.29
10	88.85	2.61	86.24	175.05
11	88.85	1.75	87.1	87.96
12	88.85	.88	87.97	0

```
TOTAL INTEREST ON LOAN IS $66.18
```

Figure 4.22
Sample Execution - Amortization Schedule

Subscripted variables are blocked in groups known as *arrays*. The variables above would compose an array (or matrix) A. The subscripts distinguish among the numbers or elements of the array.

Before using an array, it is necessary to specify the largest size the group may be. This size is called the dimension of the array and involves the use of the DIM statement. In our previous example, the A array included 100 members. Therefore, the dimension specification would be A(100). This dimension size does not imply that 100 subscripted A's must be used. It simply means that we may use up to 100 subscripted A's in our program. To help clarify subscripted variables, examine program #14 in figure 4.23. This program illustrates the use of an array.

```
10  REM ##### PROGRAM LISTING #14 ####
20  REM ####### USE OF AN ARRAY ######
30  REM #### JIMMY SMITH - 7/20/84 ###
40  REM ###########################
50  DIM X(10)
60  REM : THIS LOOP FILLS THE X ARRAY
100 FOR I = 1 TO 5
110 PRINT "ENTER A NUMBER"
120 INPUT X(I)
130 NEXT I
150 PRINT "++++++++++++++++++"
200 REM : THIS LOOP PRINTS THE X ARRAY
210 FOR J = 1 TO 5
220 PRINT X(J)
230 NEXT J
500 END

ENTER A NUMBER
?2
ENTER A NUMBER
?5
ENTER A NUMBER
?7
ENTER A NUMBER
?9
ENTER a NUMBER
?13
++++++++++++++++
2
5
7
9
13
```

Figure 4.23
Use of an Array

Notice that in line 50, the dimension of the X array is 10. This means that the array can contain up to 10 elements. The first loop (lines 100 to 130) allows the user to enter a value for the subscripted variables $X_1, X_2, \ldots X_5$. The next loop (lines 210 to 230) will print those values.

Earlier in this chapter we studied a program which would calculate the average of a set of numbers. We shall now modify that program so that an array of subscripted variables may be used. As we'll see, this can be very important if we should wish to use these numbers again for some purpose. Before proceeding, it is recommended that the reader review the flowchart in figure 4.6 and program listing #5 (figure 4.7). The same principles will be used in this problem.

In the earlier solution, the numbers to be averaged were input as the variable X. The respective X's were summed, counted, and averaged. As X's were entered, however, their individual values were lost. We could not, at the end of the program, print the respective X's or perform any other calculations which would require them. In turn, the same memory location was used by each X. By using subscripted variables, however, the programmer can easily have distinct or unique variables (distinguished by the subscript) which remain available to be accessed individually for later use.

```
10    REM ##### PROGRAM LISTING #15 ####
20    REM ## AVERAGE PROG WITH ARRAY ###
30    REM #### JOHNNY SMITH - 7/22/84 ##
40    REM #########################
45    REM : X(I)=NOS. AVERAGED; N=NUMBER OF ENTRIES; S=SUM; A=AVERAGE
50    DIM X(100)
60    REM : X(I)'S REPRESENT NUMBERS ENTERED TO BE AVERAGED
100    PRINT "+++++++++++++++++++++++++++++++++++++++"
105    PRINT "+                                     +"
110    PRINT "+ PROGRAM TO AVERAGE A SET OF NUMBERS +"
112    PRINT "+                                     +"
115    PRINT "+++++++++++++++++++++++++++++++++++++++"
117    PRINT
120    PRINT "THIS PROGRAM WILL AVERAGE A SET OF UP TO 100 NUMBERS"
125    PRINT
130    PRINT "ENTER THE NUMBERS ONE AT A TIME FOLLOWED BY A RETURN"
135    PRINT
140    PRINT "WHEN YOU HAVE ENTERED ALL YOUR NUMBERS, ENTER A NEGATIVE NUMBER
       (E.G., -1) TO QUIT.
150    GOSUB 1000
160    GOSUB 2000
170    GOSUB 3000
199    END
1000    REM #######################################
1010    REM ##### SUB FOR DATA INPUT #############
1020    REM #######################################
1030    FOR I = 1 TO 100
1040    PRINT
1050    PRINT "ENTER A NUMBER"
1060    INPUT X(I)
1070    IF X(I) < 0 THEN  GOTO 1900
1080   N = N + 1
1090   S = S + X(I)
1100    NEXT
1900    RETURN
1999    REM #######################################
2000    REM #######################################
```

```
2010   REM ##### SUB FOR CALC OF AVERAGE #########
2020   REM #####################################
2030 A = S / N
2990   RETURN
2999   REM ####################################
3000   REM ####################################
3010   REM #####  SUB FOR PRINTING  ###########
3011   PRINT
3012   PRINT
3013   PRINT
3015   PRINT
3020   PRINT "     THE NUMBER OF ENTRIES = "N
3025   PRINT
3030   PRINT "     THE SUM = "S
3035   PRINT
3040   PRINT "     THE AVERAGE OF THE NUMBERS = "A
3090   RETURN
3999   REM ####################################
9999   END
```

Figure 4.24
Program Listing #15 - Calculation of Averages Using Arrays

```
++++++++++++++++++++++++++++++++++++++++
+                                      +
+ PROGRAM TO AVERAGE A SET OF NUMBERS  +
+                                      +
++++++++++++++++++++++++++++++++++++++++

THIS PROGRAM WILL AVERAGE A SET OF UP TO 100 NUMBERS
ENTER THE NUMBERS ONE AT A TIME FOLLOWED BY A RETURN
WHEN YOU HAVE ENTERED ALL YOUR NUMBERS, ENTER A NEGATIVE NUMBER (E.G., -1) TO QUIT.
ENTER A NUMBER
?95
ENTER A NUMBER
?97
ENTER A NUMBER
?100
ENTER A NUMBER
?88
ENTER A NUMBER
?91
ENTER A NUMBER
?-9
THE NUMBER OF ENTRIES = 5
THE SUM = 471
THE AVERAGE OF THE NUMBERS =94.2
```

Figure 4.25
Sample Execution - Calculation of Averages

As you can see in program listing #15 (figure 4.24), there are no significant differences in the general operation of this program and the earlier number-averaging program except for the use of subscripted variables. Using subscripted variables, however, provides capability of printing the respective entries if desired. This could be valuable to check for entry errors. The addition of this routine is left to the student as an exercise.

Now let's add a little power to our program. From time to time, teachers wish to describe a set of test scores or report certain descriptive statistics. There are a number of descriptive statistics for this such as the mean, median, mode, standard deviation, range of scores, graphs, histograms, and so on. Almost always one will find the standard deviation reported.

The standard deviation is a measure of the variability of a set of numbers. It is an indication of the degree to which scores cluster around the mean. Stated another way, it is an average of all the score deviations from the overall (distribution) mean. The standard deviation is calculated using the following formula:

$$\text{Standard Deviation} = \frac{\Sigma(X-M)^2}{N}$$

where Σ = summation or "add the values of"
X = test score
M = mean of the test scores
N = total number of scores

For example, suppose we have five numbers: 10, 8, 13, 15, and 4. First calculate the mean.

$$\text{Mean} = \frac{\Sigma X}{N} = \frac{50}{10} = 10$$

The squared differences between this mean and the respective scores are:

X	$(X\text{-}M)$	$(X\text{-}M)^2$
10	0	0
8	−2	4
13	3	9
15	5	25
4	−6	36
		74

$$\text{std. dev.} = \frac{74}{5} = 14.8 = 3.847$$

Program listing #16 (figure 4.26) includes a subroutine for the calculation of the standard deviation. This subroutine begins at line 2500 and uses the above formula. Note that the remainder of the program is virtually untouched except for a few minor print and remark modifications. This is one of the advantages of structured programming! The execution of this program is displayed in figure 4.27

```
10    REM ##### PROGRAM LISTING #16 ####
20    REM ## AVERAGE AND STD DEV       ###
30    REM #### JOHNNY SMITH - 7/24/84 ##
40    REM ###############################
45    REM : X(I)=NOS. AVERAGED; N=NUMBER OF ENTRIES; S=SUM; A=AVERAGE; D=STD DEV
50    DIM X(100)
60    REM : X(I)'S REPRESENT NUMBERS ENTERED TO BE AVERAGED
100    PRINT "++++++++++++++++++++++++++++++++++++++++"
105    PRINT "+                                      +"
110    PRINT "+        PROGRAM FOR CALCULATING        +"
111    PRINT "+     MEAN AND STANDARD DEVIATION       +"
112    PRINT "+                                      +"
115    PRINT "++++++++++++++++++++++++++++++++++++++++"
117    PRINT
125    PRINT
130    PRINT "ENTER THE NUMBERS ONE AT A TIME FOLLOWED BY A RETURN"
132    PRINT "UP TO 100 NUMBERS MAY BE ENTERED"
135    PRINT
140    PRINT "WHEN YOU HAVE ENTERED ALL YOUR NUMBERS, ENTER A NEGATIVE
       NUMBER (E.G., -1) TO QUIT.
145    PRINT
150    GOSUB 1000
160    GOSUB 2000
165    GOSUB 2500
170    GOSUB 3000
199    END
1000    REM ########################################
1010    REM #####  SUB FOR DATA INPUT ##############
1020    REM ########################################
1030    FOR I = 1 TO 100
1050    PRINT "ENTER A NUMBER"
1060    INPUT X(I)
1070    IF X(I) < 0 THEN GOTO 1900
1080 N = N + 1
1090 S = S + X(I)
1100    NEXT
1900    RETURN
1998    REM ########################################
1999    REM
2000    REM ########################################
2010    REM #####  SUB FOR CALC OF AVERAGE  ########
2020    REM ########################################
2030 A = S / N
2100    RETURN
2198    REM ########################################
2199    REM
2500    REM ########################################
2510    REM #####  SUB FOR CALC OF STD DEV  ########
2520    REM ########################################
2530    FOR I = 1 TO N
2540 B = (X(I) - A) ^ 2
```

Figure 4.26 (continued on p. 110)

109

```
2550 C = C + B
2552  REM  C SUMS THE SQUARED DIFFERENCES
2560  NEXT I
2570 D = SQR (C / N)
2990  RETURN
2998  REM #####################################
2999  REM
3000  REM #####################################
3010  REM #####  SUB FOR PRINTING  ##############
3020  REM #####################################
3021  PRINT
3022  PRINT
3025  PRINT "    THE NUMBER OF ENTRIES = "N
3027  PRINT
3030  PRINT "    THE SUM = "S
3035  PRINT
3040  PRINT "    THE AVERAGE OF THE NUMBERS = "A
3050  PRINT
3060  PRINT "    THE STANDARD DEVIATION = "D
3090  RETURN
3999  REM #####################################
9999  END
```

Figure 4.26
Program Listing #16 - Mean and Standard Deviation

```
+++++++++++++++++++++++++++++++++++++++++
+                                       +
+       PROGRAM FOR CALCULATING         +
+     MEAN AND STANDARD DEVIATION       +
+                                       +
+++++++++++++++++++++++++++++++++++++++++
ENTER THE NUMBERS ONE AT A TIME FOLLOWED BY A RETURN
UP TO 100 NUMBERS MAY BE ENTERED
WHEN YOU HAVE ENTERED ALL YOUR NUMBERS, ENTER A NEGATIVE NUMBER (E.G., -1) TO QUIT.
ENTER A NUMBER
?10
ENTER A NUMBER
?8
ENTER A NUMBER
?13
ENTER A NUMBER
?15
ENTER A NUMBER
?4
ENTER A NUMBER
?-1
    THE NUMBER OF ENTRIES = 5
    THE SUM = 50
    THE AVERAGE OF THE NUMBERS = 10
    THE STANDARD DEVIATION = 3.84707681
```

Figure 4.27
Sample Execution - Mean and Standard Deviation

BASIC Programs for Drill and Practice

Before concluding our discussion of BASIC programming, let's examine another application—a simple arithmetic drill and practice routine. One of the most familiar modes of computer-assisted instruction is the presentation of problems or questions in a "flash-card" format. Program listing #17 (figure 4.28) presents the nucleus of such a program. Essentially, this program uses random numbers to produce arithmetic fact problems, specifically, the multiplication of one-digit numbers. Figure 4.29 shows a sample execution of this program.

```
10   REM ##### PROGRAM LISTING #17 ####
20   REM ### DRILL AND PRACTICE #######
30   REM #### FRED SMITH - 7/30/84 ####
40   REM ############################
100  FOR I = 1 TO 5
110  A = INT (10 * RND (1) + 1)
120  B = INT (10 * RND (1) + 1)
130  PRINT A" X"B
140  INPUT C
150  IF C = (A * B) THEN  PRINT "CORRECT"
160  IF C < > (A * B) THEN PRINT "WRONG"
165  PRINT
170  NEXT I
200  END
```

Figure 4.28
Program Listing #17 - Simple Drill and Practice Program

```
8 X 6
?48
CORRECT
4 X 4
?16
CORRECT
1 X 6
?6
CORRECT
1 X 2
?2
CORRECT
9 X 8
?76
WRONG
```

Figure 4.29
Sample Execution - Simple Drill and Practice Program

This drill and practice program (which was written in Applesoft BASIC) uses the RND function for generating random numbers. This particular RND(1) function will return a random real number greater than or equal to zero and less than one. Be advised that RND functions vary considerably among the dialects of BASIC! The FOR/NEXT statements in lines 100 and 170 cause the program to execute five times. Lines 110 and 120 use the INT function discussed earlier to return the whole number part of the argument. The code inside the parentheses provides a random number less than ten and greater than or equal to zero. How could you modify lines 110 and 120 to provide two-digit numbers? Line 160 uses the pair of symbols " < > " to signify "is not equal to."

Obviously, this isn't a very elegant program or one which you would use for instruction. No instructions are provided, the format is not appealing or interesting, and insufficient response feedback is provided to the user. As an exercise, take the code provided in figure 4.28 and develop a more useful and pedagogically sound program. You now have all the necessary programming tools at your disposal. You might even include a subroutine to keep track of the number of correct responses, or a means that allows the user to specify how many problems it should generate and the level of difficulty (i.e., how many digits in the problems). The user might also be given the option of specifying addition, subtraction, multiplication, or division practice. Use your imagination and experience as a teacher! That's one of the keys. Don't let the software dictate how you teach. You, not the software, must decide how you use the computer to augment your instruction.

For our last BASIC program, we will use a different form of data input—the DATA and READ statements. In the previous examples, data were entered into the program using the INPUT statement. An alternate method is the DATA statement (used in conjunction with the READ statement). When the computer program encounters a READ statement, it looks for a DATA statement. Values are assigned to variables from the DATA statement in the order which they occur.

Examine the program listing in figure 4.30. The READ statement (line 2040) assigns values to the string variables S$ and C$ from the DATA statement (line 500). The first time through the loop the variable S$ equals "GEORGIA" and C$ equals "ATLANTA." This assignment process continues for the six iterations. The length of the drill and practice session could be extended by increasing the value of the loop parameter in line 2030 and by increasing the data in line 500. For example, changing the 6 to 10 would result in 10 questions. The data in line 500 would, of course, have to be changed (e.g., four more states and capitals would have to be added). New presentations can be created by changing the content of line 500. A sample execution of this program is presented in figure 4.31

```
10   REM ##### PROGRAM LISTING #18 #####
20   REM ## DRILL & PRACTICE - CAPITALS
30   REM ##### BETTY SMITH - 8/1/84 ####
40   REM ##############################
50   REM
100  REM : QUESTIONS/ANSWERS IN DATA STATEMENT - LINE 500
110  REM : C$=CAPITAL      S$=STATE
120  REM : R$=RESPONSE        N=CORRECT ANSWER COUNTER
130  REM
500  DATA    "GEORGIA","ATLANTA","WISCONSIN","MADISON","NEBRASKA","LINCOLN",
     "ALABAMA","MONTGOMERY","TEXAS","AUSTIN","OREGON","SALEM"
1000  PRINT
1010  PRINT
1030  PRINT "          STATE CAPITALS "
1040  PRINT
1050  PRINT
1060  PRINT "I'M GOING TO TEST YOUR KNOWLEDGE OF STATE CAPITALS "
1070  PRINT
1080  PRINT "I'LL SUPPLY THE STATE AND YOU ENTER THE CAPITAL"
1100  GOSUB 2000
1200  PRINT
1201  PRINT
1202  PRINT
1204  PRINT "THAT WAS FUN!!!!"
1205  PRINT
1208  PRINT
1210  PRINT "YOU ANSWERED "N" CORRECTLY."
1999  END
2000  REM ##############################
2010  REM  ## SUBROUTINE FOR QUESTIONS ##
2020  REM ##############################
2030  FOR J = 1 TO 6
2040  READ S$,C$
2045  PRINT
2050  PRINT "THE STATE IS "S$"."
2060  PRINT "WHAT'S THE CAPITAL?"
2070  INPUT R$
2075  IF R$ < > C$ THEN PRINT "NO. THE CORRECT ANSWER IS "C$
2080  IF R$ = C$ THEN PRINT "CORRECT!"
2090  IF R$ = C$ THEN N = N + 1
2095  REM : LINE 2090 COUNTS THE NUMBER OF CORRECT RESPONSES
2100  NEXT J
2900  RETURN
2999  REM ##############################
```

Figure 4.30
Program Listing #18 - Drill and Practice - Capitals

```
               STATE CAPITALS
I'M GOING TO TEST YOUR KNOWLEDGE OF STATE CAPITALS
I'LL SUPPLY THE STATE AND YOU ENTER THE CAPITAL
THE STATE IS GEORGIA.
WHAT'S THE CAPITAL?
?ATLANTA
CORRECT!
THE STATE IS WISCONSIN.
WHAT'S THE CAPITAL?
?MADISON
CORRECT!
THE STATE IS NEBRASKA.
WHAT'S THE CAPITAL?
?OMAHA
NO. THE CORRECT ANSWER IS LINCOLN
THE STATE IS ALABAMA.
WHAT'S THE CAPITAL?
?MONTGOMERY
CORRECT!
THE STATE IS TEXAS.
WHAT'S THE CAPITAL?
?DALLAS
NO. THE CORRECT ANSWER IS AUSTIN
THE STATE IS OREGON.
WHAT'S THE CAPITAL?
?SALEM
CORRECT!
THAT WAS FUN!!!!
YOU ANSWERED 4 CORRECTLY.
```

Figure 4.31
Sample Execution - Drill & Practice - Capitals

Summary

Thus concludes our brief excursion into computer programming. It was a short venture for, as was mentioned in the beginning, a complete and comprehensive study of programming is far beyond the scope or intent of this text. We have, however, used many of the more frequently needed BASIC statements. Once the reader feels comfortable with these problems he/she should experiment with new problems. There are many excellent texts available which provide an excellent program of study in this area. Don't hesitate to study other languages. Pascal is rapidly gaining favor in schools. Some knowledge of this language may prove quite productive as well as interesting. Regrettably, there is no substitute for study, practice, and diligent effort. Programming is an art, a science, and an intellectual task.

Suggested Readings

Cassel, D., & Swanson, R. (1980). *BASIC made easy.* Reston, VA: Reston Publishing Co.

Culp, G. H., & Nickles, H. (1983). *An apple for the teacher.* Monterey, CA: Brooks/Cole Publishing Co.

Doerr, C. (1979). *Microcomputers and the 3 R's.* Rochelle Park, NJ: Hayden Book Co.

Dwyer, T. A., & Critchfield, M. (1980). *A bit of BASIC.* Reading, MA: Addison-Wesley Publishing Co.

Graff, L. E., & Goldstein, L. S. (1984). *Applesoft BASIC for the Apple II and IIe.* Bowie, MD: Robert J. Brady Co.

Hirsch, S. C. (1980). *BASIC programming: Self-taught.* Reston, VA: Reston Publishing Company, Inc.

Hopper, G. M., & Mandell, S. L. (1984). *Understanding computers.* St. Paul, MN: West Publishing Co.

Knecht, K. (1983). *Microsoft BASIC.* Beaverton, OR: Dilithium Press.

Landa, R. K. (1984). *Creating courseware.* New York: Harper and Row Publishers.

Vockell, E. L., & Rivers, R. H. (1984). *Instructional computing for today's teachers.* New York: Macmillan Publishing Co.

Waller, H. M. (1980). *Problems for computer solutions using BASIC.* Cambridge, MA: Winthrop Publishers, Inc.

Suggested Exercises and Problems in BASIC Programming

These are exercises which you should be able to complete given the introduction to BASIC programming provided in chapter 4. Develop each according to the process you have studied. Once the BASIC program has been written, enter it into the computer and satisfy yourself that it works properly.

1. Write a BASIC program which will:
    a. Print your name, street address, city, state, and zip code on three separate lines.
    b. Convert your height in inches to centimeters (1 inch = 2.54 centimeters).
    c. Calculate rectangular area in square yards given the length and width in feet.
        Area = length × width
        One square yard = nine square feet
    d. Determine the cost of carpeting the area in the previous problem given that the cost of carpet per square yard is $8.50.
    e. Calculate the area and circumference of a circle given the radius (r).
        Area is πr^2 (π = 3.14159)
        Circumference = $2\pi r^2$
    f. Print a table of numbers (1–20) and their respective square roots.

g. Calculate a person's age in the year 2000, given his/her present age.

h. Convert quarts to liters (1 liter = 1.057 quarts)

2. Write a BASIC program which will convert temperatures expressed in degrees Fahrenheit to degrees centigrade and vice versa. The user should be able to select the mode of conversion (i.e., which conversion) from a menu of the two selections.

$$F = (9/5)C + 32$$
$$C = (5/9)(F - 32)$$

3. The principal's office is responsible for calculating the weekly wages of the building custodial staff. Each custodian earns $6.90 per hour based on a 40-hour work week. For each hour over 40 hours they earn $9.50 per hour. In the unusual event a person's hours total more than 60 hours in a given week, they earn $12.50 for each hour over 60.

Write a BASIC program which will permit the user to enter the employee I.D. # and the number of hours worked in a given week. The output of the program should indicate the I.D. #, number of hours worked, and the corresponding weekly earnings.

Use the sample data as given below.

I.D. #	Hours
5768	38
6789	41
3765	56
2435	61
3245	17
5768	23
4766	17
3877	28

4. The EZEE Brokerage Company charges commissions at 18% per transaction. However, if the transaction is greater than $10,000, the commission is reduced to 16%. For example, the commission on $5,000 would be $900 whereas, the commission on $20,000 would be $3,200. Write a program which will compute commissions.

5. Assume that you have given three tests to your class. Write a program which will allow you to enter the grades on the tests for each student and calculate their respective averages. The program should also calculate the class average on each of the tests. For added flexibility, include as part of the input the number of students in the class.

6. Students in a computer-programming class earn points for their final grade based on a weighted average of tests, the midterm exam, and the final exam. The grading procedures take into account the average of all

the tests, the midterm grade, plus twice the final exam grade. For example, a student has the following grades:

Test #1 - 90
Test #2 - 85
Test #3 - 95
Test #4 - 75
Midterm - 88
Final - 92

The final grade is calculated as follows:

Average of tests = 86.25
Midterm = 88.00
Final × 2 = 184.00

358.25 ÷ 4 = 89.56

Write a program which will allow the teacher to enter grades and determine the final grade.

7. Professor N.O. Lead has won an all expense paid trip to Iowa City, Iowa. He plans to drive his Corvair from Atlanta and wishes to maintain a record of his mileage and miles per gallon. Below are his beginning and ending odometer readings recorded during his trip and the gas required at each fill-up:

Location	Odometer	Number of Gallons
Atlanta	30,000	-
Chattanooga	30,125	4.9
Nashville	30,260	5.1
Cairo	30,435	5.9
Champaign	30,675	9.1
Moline	30,863	6.5
Iowa City	30,938	2.8

Write a BASIC program which will calculate the miles per gallon at each fill-up as well as the total miles per gallon for the trip.

8. You have agreed (reluctantly) to be a Little League baseball coach for the summer. Write a program which will calculate batting averages.

$$\text{Batting Average} = \frac{\text{Number of Hits}}{(\text{Times at Bat}) - (\text{Number of Walks})}$$

9. The utility company charges for electricity using the kilowatt-hour (KWH) as the unit of measure of electricity used. The first 500 KWH cost $.0717/KWH. The remaining electricity used costs $.05490/KWH. In addition, there is a $.0102/KWH charge for "energy cost adjustment" (whatever that means). Write a program which will allow the user to enter the total number of KWH used and will calculate the cost.

10. Finding the ordered pairs (x, y) which will satisfy a given mathematical expression can be a tedious part of graphing the expression. Write a program which will calculate the corresponding y values for a given set of x values for the relation below:

$$y = 2x^2 + 5x + 8$$

where x = -10, -9, -8, . . ., 0, 1, 2, . . . 10

11. Write a program which will calculate the sum, difference, product, or quotient of two numbers entered by the user. The program should permit the user to select which of the four operations is desired.

12. Modify the BASIC program presented in figure 4.30 so that a different drill and practice activity is presented (for example, nations and capitals or nations).

13. Develop a form letter. Using a program with PRINT statements and string variables, allow the user to enter the name of the recipient ("Dear------") in order to personalize the letter.

14. Enhance the form letter in the above exercise to include some variable in the body of the letter (for example, number of days absent from school, library fine owed, etc.).

15. Write a BASIC program which will solve a quadratic equation for its two roots. The formula is given below:

$$x = \frac{-b \pm \sqrt{b^2 - 4ac}}{2a}$$

where *a, b, c* are the coefficients of the general expression

$$ax^2 + bx + c = 0$$

5

Applications In Education

Introduction

Thus far we have taken a brief look at the historical origins of computing, what makes a computer work, and how we converse with a computer. Since this text is written principally for the education professional, the next logical question is "How can computers influence education or be of value to me as an educator?" This question will be addressed in this chapter. In order to pursue the topic in some orderly fashion, we will examine computing with respect to the following educational applications:

- Computer literacy
- Computer-assisted instruction
- Computer-managed instruction
- Computer science
- Administrative data processing
- Information retrieval
- Vocational education

In most cases, we will see that the lines of distinction among the above areas are not well defined, but these broad topics provide a starting point for our study.

Computer Literacy

The term *computer literacy* is becoming more and more a part of the educator's vocabulary and designates a concept which many, if not most, educators espouse and endorse. Computers as an integral part of the curriculum are now actively supported by parent groups and civic organizations as well as educators in many communities. In fact, recognition of the urgent need to introduce students to computing has instigated a much more rapid influx of computers into the curriculum than might have occurred otherwise. Regrettably, this has not always resulted in the most judicious integration of the new technology into the classroom. Perhaps this can be attributed to the fact that those in charge of the intelligent integration of the technology were not computer literate.

There is no question that our nation's schools must provide the instructional framework for students to become "computer literate." However, although many educators are quite interested in providing computer literacy for our students, there is no firm consensus, and probably never can be, as to exactly what constitutes computer literacy and how it can best be achieved. Lacking such a consensus, the best approach is to survey the range of definitions and implementations that have been suggested. In the end, each educator must decide for him or herself the concept and operational plan best suited to their particular educational environment. It is important to recognize that sophistication in regard to computers naturally varies widely among students beginning any course of computer studies today, and further, that in the future, as computer use becomes more general, the level of sophistication among entry-level students will generally and continually rise. This continuing variability alone rules out any single, fixed formula for teaching computer literacy.

A quick examination of the literature reveals many definitions of the term computer literacy. Anderson and Klassen (1981) define it to be "whatever understanding, skills, and attitudes one needs to function effectively within a given role that directly or indirectly involves computers." Their concept of literacy is a broad one, extending far beyond the narrow limitations presented by a few other writers who equate computer literacy with computer programming or the role of the computer in society. Eisele (1980) offers five areas within which curricula should be developed to provide literacy: (1) effective use of computers in real-life problem solving; (2) computing proficiency, including programming skills; (3) ethical production of computer services for others' consumption; (4) ethical consumption of computer services provided by others; and (5) understanding the role of computers in present and future society. Molnar (1978) considers the literacy issue a crisis in American education and states that:

> A student who graduates without being exposed to computers has had an incomplete education. To retrain after graduation creates an unnecessary human waste and incurs a high social and psychological cost . . . we must ensure that high school graduates have an understanding of the uses and applications of the computer in society and its effect upon their everyday lives. (p. 11)

Molnar further suggests that computer literacy courses should provide students with enough information about the nature of a computer so that they can understand the roles computers play in our society.

Arthur Luehrmann (1981), in a discussion of computer literacy in higher education, raises many questions regarding the effects and impact of the rising levels of computer literacy. Persons with knowledge and skills in computing will have an advantage over those without skills in information-processing technologies. Clearly this raises many questions regarding equality of educational opportunity. This concern is consistent with Coburn, et al. (1982) who define computer literacy to include the general range of skills and understanding needed to function effectively in a society increasingly dependent on information technology.

These concepts represent both the restrictive and comprehensive definitions and conceptions of computer literacy. As educators, we can debate the meanings and definitions, or we can proceed to formulate a prescriptive framework which corresponds with our own sense of the role of computers in education. Of course there is no one "best" definition or concept—rather the concept of literacy resides along a continuum which represents the scope and magnitude of insights, knowledge, skills, and experience in computing requisite for literacy. As curriculum policy evolves, the informed educator must seek the point along this continuum where local needs are most appropriately satisfied. The evolutionary and revolutionary nature of computing requires and demands that this policy be dynamic and ever changing to keep pace with the technology.

An excellent example of a computer literacy program is the Minnesota Educational Computing Consortium (MECC) project titled "Instructional Materials for Computer Literacy." Goals and objectives for learning are categorized into eight areas:

1. APPLICATIONS. This area covers the multitude of social and organizational areas into which computers have been integrated. It also covers the general considerations for applying computers to new situations.
2. HARDWARE. This domain deals with the basic vocabulary of computer system components including equipment such as mechanical and electronic devices.
3. IMPACT. Computer literacy also encompasses knowledge of the social effects of computerization, including both the positive and negative impacts of computers on society.
4. LIMITATIONS. This domain is distinguished from the applications domain in that it focuses on developing a general sense of the capabilities and limitations of computing machines. Examples of computer limitations include the fact that computers do not have feelings and consciousness, nor are they able to make value judgments.
5. PROGRAMMING/ALGORITHMS. This domain deals with the ability to read, modify, and construct algorithms and programs.
6. SOFTWARE AND DATA PROCESSING. This area includes vocabulary relevant to software, information processing, and data.
7. USAGE. While the foregoing areas are largely cognitive in emphasis, this domain involves motor skills for sequencing and execution of certain tasks on the computer or computer terminal.

8. VALUES AND FEELINGS. The affective domain centers on developing positive attitudes toward personal use of computers as well as balanced attitudes toward computers as a social force. (Anderson & Klassen, 1981)

If computer literacy is so important for students, one might question at what point in the curricular structure learning about computing should begin. Both advocates and critics of the computer as a tool in education seem convinced that the computer can have an effect on how people think. The question then becomes "How should students begin using computers?" At the risk of oversimplification, there are three basic patterns or options that can be followed:

1. Using computers to augment our traditional instructional practices (these computer applications are typically in the area of computer-assisted instruction as described in the next section);
2. Studies of the computer (i.e., studies in which the computer is the *object* of instruction) and phenomena associated with computing (this will likely include some of the literacy topics suggested in this section);
3. Use of the computer to enhance, as Papert (1980) suggests, the power of students as epistemologists—addressing the origin, nature, and acquisition of knowledge.

In this latter mode, Papert and others agree that students can learn about computing by learning and using the fundamental logical processes associated with computing.

A growing body of educators would agree with Papert that students can and do enhance their thinking skills through the use of a computer, especially with programming language such as Logo. Logo was designed to include many of the traditional computer language concepts and capabilities while also integrating the learning theories of Piaget. The concepts of "turtle geometry" (the *turtle* is a triangular shape manipulated by Logo commands) employed in Logo permit the user to explore not only the world of programming, but also to play and experiment with problems without the constraints of languages such as BASIC.

> Logo was developed to create an interactive environment, a mathland, in which students could set their own pace, problems and goals. It is a comfortable way for me to enter the future. It is a challenging way and it is a way that I can understand, choose and control (Watt, 1982, p. 129).

With Logo, as with other computer languages, including BASIC, Pascal, and FORTRAN, the programmer communicates with or instructs the computer—only this is much more easily done with Logo. Logo commands include statements such as FORWARD, BACK, RT 50, LT 50, etc. Proponents argue that creativity, problem solving, and the student's computer literacy are greatly enhanced through Logo usage without having to spend the requisite time teaching a conventional data-processing language.

Unquestionably, our nation's schools must provide the framework for students to become computer literate. The structure and delivery system is, to a great extent, contingent upon situation-specific needs, values, resources, and personnel. In the final analysis, the educator must be able to formulate the operational plan which makes sense for each educational environment. There is no one correct route to programs of computer literacy.

Computer-Assisted Instruction

While there are many definitions of computer-assisted instruction (CAI), it is generally considered to be a curricular program where there is interaction between the student and the computer for the purpose of instruction. Usually one student communicates with the computer system via a terminal or personal computer. The computer supporting the CAI system could be a large or medium-sized time-sharing system delivering instruction to multiple users at different locations or a stand-alone microcomputer serving an individual student. Learning activities can be provided in the form of drill and practice, tutorials, games, or simulations.

CAI is often thought to be a new teaching innovation, but actually we find applications dating back to the 1950s. This period, and the 1960s even more so, were times in which educators were especially interested in programmed instruction and, to some extent, teaching machines. CAI incorporates many of the philosophical and pedagogical principles and ideas found in programmed instruction such as:

- Specification of instructional objectives in behavioral terms
- Orderly and logical presentation of materials
- Feedback based on responses and performance
- Provision for student to proceed at his or her own speed

One should not, however, infer from this that CAI is nothing more than programmed instruction enhanced by computer-based technology. The computer can base presentation and sequence of information on student performance in a fashion not possible with earlier systems of programmed instruction. Furthermore, the computer can provide remediation, many modes of feedback, and varying levels of difficulty, as well as present audio and graphic materials, and control audio-visual devices (e.g., tape recorder, slide projector, movie projector, etc.). As intelligent videodisc technology becomes more readily accessible, modes of presentation will be expanded even more.

Throughout the 1960s and into the 1970s, a number of important CAI research and development activities were conducted. Three notable projects were the Stanford University CAI project under the direction of Patrick Suppes, Mitre Corporation's TICCIT, and PLATO at the University of Illinois. Projects such as these were conducted in close cooperation between the computer manufacturers and universities. In addition to these civilian systems, the military was quite active in development and utilization of CAI. Subsequent to these pioneering efforts, the private sector has become increasingly involved in the development of CAI programs. Commercial courseware is becoming increasingly available from textbook publishers as well as from newly formed companies, both large and small.

As mentioned earlier, there are several different modes or subcategories of CAI. An understanding of CAI may best be gained from a discussion of each of these.

Drill and Practice

Drill and practice was one of the early forms of instructional computing. It may be compared to the flash card method of teaching math, spelling, or other facts. The student is presented with a question, problem, computational item, etc., and must respond by entering the answer at the keyboard or through some device coupled with the system (such as a light pen). As in the case of conventional drill and practice media, the routine is generally a supplemental activity to instruction provided in the classroom.

The program or CAI lesson may be enhanced by adding diagnostic tests or pretests to determine the appropriate difficulty levels of items to present and posttests to assess mastery. Other features such as feedback, praise, critical analysis, and record keeping may be included in addition to the straightforward presentation of items.

An example of a CAI drill and practice program is ARITHMETIC (Rugg & Feldman, 1981). This program permits the user to request sample problems in addition, subtraction, or multiplication at three levels of difficulty (easy, medium, or hard). The problems are constructed using random numbers which provide new sets of problems each time the program is run. After a displayed set of problems has been completed, right and wrong answers are noted in addition to the presentation of the correct solutions. (See figure 5.1).

Another example of CAI drill and practice courseware is Milliken Publishing Company's MATH SEQUENCES program. MATH SEQUENCES provides exercises in elementary math topics including number readiness, basic operations, fractions, decimals, percents, and other related arithmetic functions. In addition to the drill and practice content, an instructional management package is available. Basically, the program allows the teacher to augment the existing mathematics instructional programs at the elementary (grades 1–8) level and includes remediation. MATH SEQUENCES exemplifies many of the advances in CAI as it not only allows repetitive drill activities but also permits performance monitoring and government of student progress by mastery of the topics.

A slight variation on the usual CAI drill and practice format is presented in TYPING TUTOR produced by Microsoft Consumer Products. This program teaches students how to use the standard typewriter and provides typing

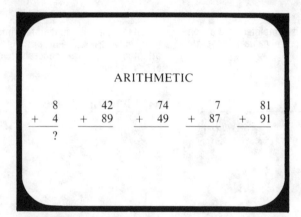

Figure 5.1
ARITHMETIC Frames

exercises. TYPING TUTOR appears to have considerable potential for use in a learning station in typing class or as a means for increasing student speed and accuracy. An important attribute of this program which capitalizes on one of the many strengths of CAI is the provision of a nonthreatening environment. The student can practice typing at a station and receive feedback on progress without a teacher or other human monitor present. Such a situation has been shown to be quite important to many learners who become anxious or threatened when the teacher observes during practice. The computer is, of course, able to time the student's keyboard input and display the number of words per minute typed.

Spelling is a well-suited and popular application for computers, whether in a microcomputer mode such as we are concerned with or in a "calculator-size" package such as Texas Instruments' SPEAK AND SPELL. SPELLING BEE from Edu-ware is a spelling package for elementary students. The program contains words in categories (one syllable, etc.). Pictures corresponding to the word to be spelled are displayed on the screen, and the student enters the word on the keyboard. The system maintains a record of words spelled incorrectly. Other programs have been developed which permit

Student Interaction

Each of the Math Sequences is divided into several small, well-defined problem levels. Students move up and down these levels based on how well they perform. The higher the problem level, the greater the difficulty.

The following example is from the Fractions Sequence. The student enters his name, class, and password; and the program begins working where he left off during his last session.

Problems Generated

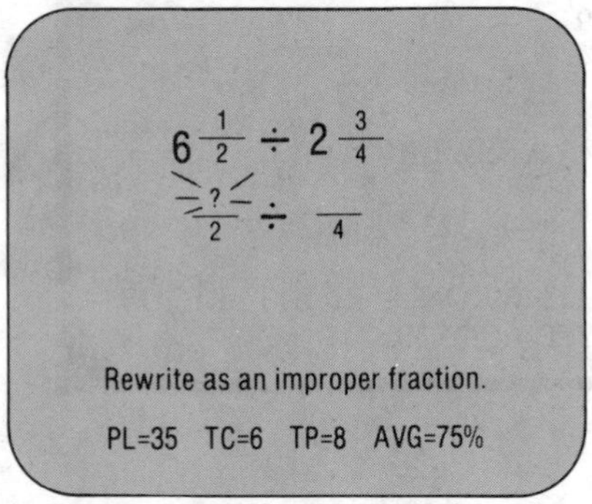

$$6\tfrac{1}{2} \div 2\tfrac{3}{4}$$
$$\frac{?}{2} \div \frac{}{4}$$

Rewrite as an improper fraction.

PL=35   TC=6   TP=8   AVG=75%

1. The flashing "?" tells the student where the next entry will go. The line at the bottom maintains the student's score. He is at problem level (PL) 35, with a total correct (TC) of 6 out of 8 total problems (TP) worked. His score is 75%.

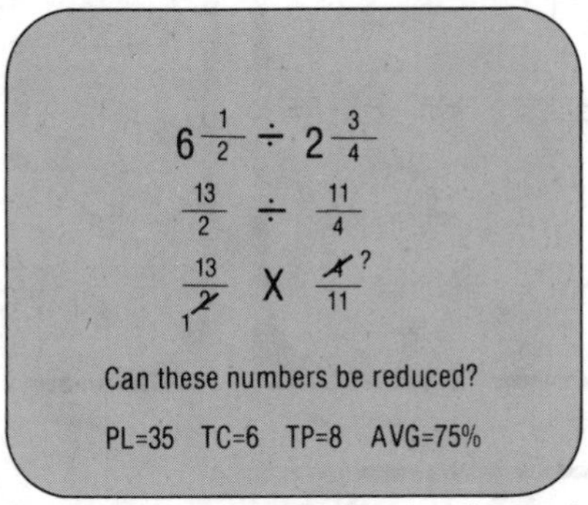

$$6\tfrac{1}{2} \div 2\tfrac{3}{4}$$
$$\frac{13}{2} \div \frac{11}{4}$$
$$\frac{13}{2} \times \frac{?}{11}$$

Can these numbers be reduced?

PL=35   TC=6   TP=8   AVG=75%

2. All of the work is completed on the monitor screen. There is rarely a need for scratch paper and pencil.

Immediate Feedback ...

3 is wrong.
Try again.

$$6\tfrac{1}{2} \div 2\tfrac{3}{4}$$
$$\frac{13}{2} \div \frac{11}{4}$$
$$\frac{13}{2} \times \frac{2}{11} = \frac{3}{11}$$

PRESS RETURN TO GO ON.

3. The student is immediately informed of incorrect entries. The program is "success-oriented" so there are generally two tries for each problem.

... And Reinforcement

Well done, Mike!

$$6\tfrac{1}{2} \div 2\tfrac{3}{4}$$
$$\frac{13}{2} \div \frac{11}{4}$$
$$\frac{13}{2} \times \frac{2}{11} = \frac{26}{11} = 2\tfrac{4}{11}$$

PRESS RETURN TO GO ON.

4. When the problem is solved, a correct answer produces one of several positive reinforcements. Younger students may be given animated reinforcements.

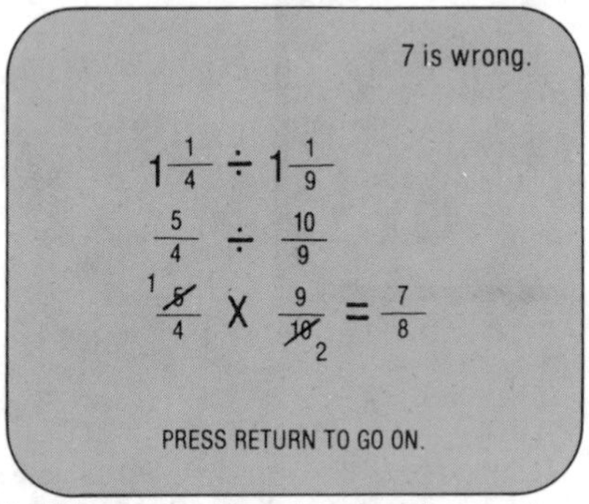

7 is wrong.

$$1\tfrac{1}{4} \div 1\tfrac{1}{9}$$
$$\frac{5}{4} \div \frac{10}{9}$$
$$\frac{5}{4} \times \frac{9}{10} = \frac{7}{8}$$

PRESS RETURN TO GO ON.

5. When a problem is missed more than once, the wrong answer will flash on the screen. The student will be scored for an incorrect answer.

"HELP" When Needed

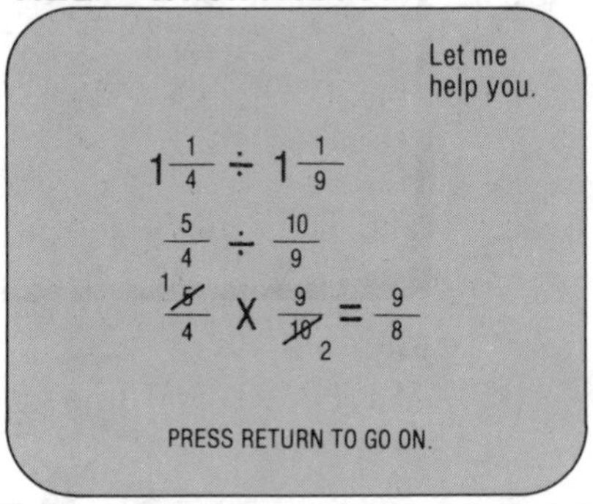

Let me help you.

$$1\tfrac{1}{4} \div 1\tfrac{1}{9}$$
$$\frac{5}{4} \div \frac{10}{9}$$
$$\frac{5}{4} \times \frac{9}{10} = \frac{9}{8}$$

PRESS RETURN TO GO ON.

6. The correct answer is then displayed, step-by-step, in the proper sequence.

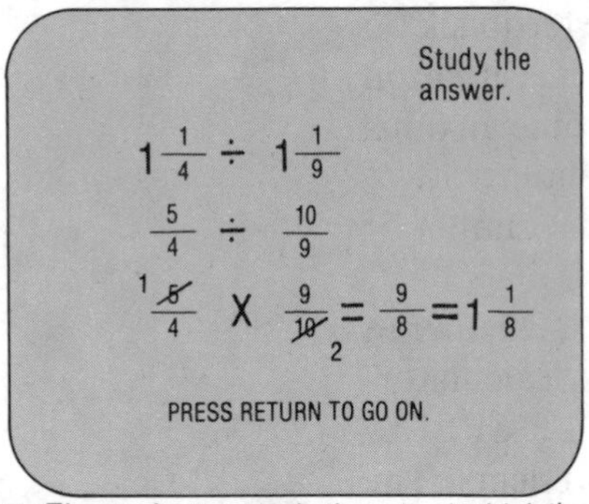

Study the answer.

$$1\tfrac{1}{4} \div 1\tfrac{1}{9}$$
$$\frac{5}{4} \div \frac{10}{9}$$
$$\frac{5}{4} \times \frac{9}{10} = \frac{9}{8} = 1\tfrac{1}{8}$$

PRESS RETURN TO GO ON.

7. The student controls the rate at which the solution is displayed and may study the answer as long as desired.

Moving Through Levels

Good news, Mike.
Your problem level went up to 36.
Good job!!

PRESS "RETURN" TO GO ON OR
PRESS "ESC" TO STOP

8. When a student achieves the individualized mastery criterion set for him, he is congratulated and moved up a level. Conversely, if he falls below his assigned failure level, he is moved down a level and asked to try harder.

Ending the Session

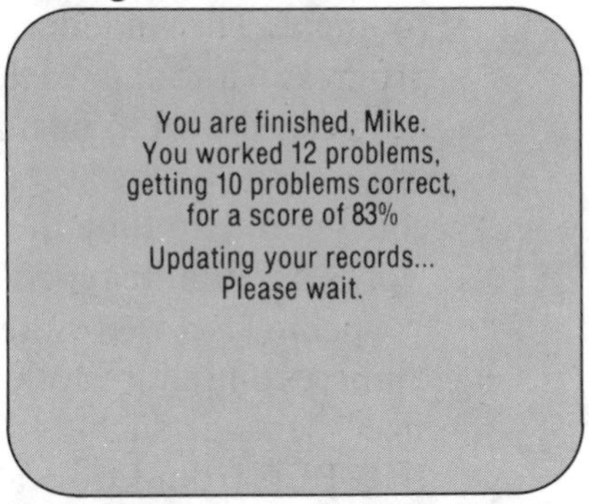

You are finished, Mike.
You worked 12 problems, getting 10 problems correct, for a score of 83%

Updating your records...
Please wait.

9. When the session is finished or when the assignment is completed, the student receives a summary of performance. This is automatically recorded in the student's file.

Figure 5.2

Frames from Computer Program *Math Sequences*. (Milliken Publishing Company, 1100 Research Blvd., P.O. Box 21579, St. Louis, MO 63132-0579) the computer to control a cassette tape recorder. The tape provides an audio presentation of a word list. The student then enters the spelling on the keyboard. In this system, the computer can be used for spelling drill and practice or as a test administrator. As voice synthesizers become more readily available and clearer in enunciation, presentation of the words in a spelling program can be produced in this manner.

Tutorial

Tutorial programs, as the name suggests, emulate the private teacher or tutor. Their frame-by-frame format resembles conventional programmed instruction materials in that text is presented along with questions which in turn permit branching to other text based upon the student's response. Tutorial CAI can provide a great part of the actual instruction as compared to drill and practice which is used to supplement other teaching methods.

Material is presented to the student in a fashion similar to a teacher's presentation. At various intervals, questions are asked and, based upon the response, additional material is offered. The program determines when new concepts or information are appropriate and when review is needed. In a sense, the interaction between the computer and student resembles a dialogue or conversation.

Examples of tutorial CAI are the software packages available to help students prepare for the Scholastic Aptitude Test (SAT). For years, publishers have offered books which help students prepare for the SAT. Likewise, private tutors have coached students in preparation for the test. The advent of personal computers has offered yet another alternative—software designed to help the students. Several SAT preparation packages are commercially available which provide information about how the tests are designed, suggestions and strategies for test taking, test items, explanations, diagnostics, and skill-building activities. An example of the feedback provided is shown in figure 5.3. One such program is "COMPUTER SAT" (Harcourt Brace Jovanovich, Inc., 1982). This package includes four practice tests which can be scored automatically. The student is then told which items were answered correctly and incorrectly. Based on test performance, a list of topics needing additional study is provided. For each of these topics, the system will outline a study plan. Additionally, drill items and vocabulary "flash cards" are offered.

Many other tutorial programs are available which teach mathematics, science, social studies, and language arts concepts. While these traditional applications of CAI are certainly important, another type of tutorial is rapidly gaining popularity—computer tutorials for learning how to use certain software packages. Stated another way, the computer is used to teach how to use the computer. Tutorial applications may range from introductory programming concepts to the use of popular systems such as VisiCalc. The programs generally include lessons, examples, and exercises.

Tutorial CAI is not offered as a substitute for the human teacher. It can, however, assist the teacher by providing creative and individualized instruc-

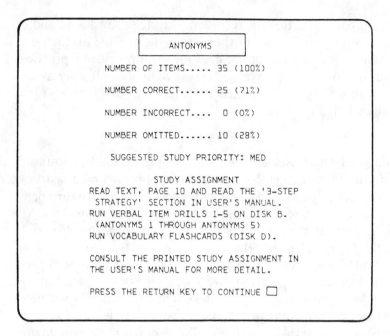

Figure 5.3
Examples of Student Feedback Provided by *Computer SAT*. (Reprinted from *Computer SAT,* Copyright 1982, Harcourt Brace Jovanovich, Inc., New York.)

tion. The student can participate in an active role rather than simply receive information. The concept of a dialog between the student and the computer is also important and cannot be overemphasized. Herein is one of the oldest approaches to teaching and learning—the conversation. We have only scratched the surface of the potential for such a Socratic situation.

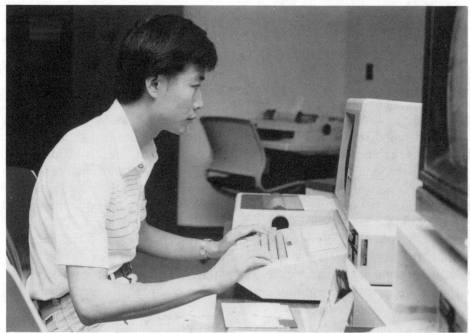

Figure 5.4
CAI Can Provide Truly Individualized Instruction. (University of Iowa, Weeg
Computing Center, Iowa City, Iowa 52242)

Figure 5.5
Tutorial CAI Offers the Possibility for Dialogue Between the Student and the
Computer. (University of Iowa, Weeg Computing Center, Iowa City, Iowa
52242)

Simulation

Simulations are computer programs which model reality or real systems. Stated another way, a computer-based model (usually mathematical) is used to represent a real-life system or situation; i.e., the computer program mimics a system as closely as possible. Use of simulations is especially valuable when actual experimentation or real experiences may be impossible or dangerous. For example, astronauts may "land" the space shuttle many times using a computer-based simulation system before attempting the real thing. Flight simulators enable pilots to sharpen their flying skills. Business students make simulated corporate decisions facing the consequences of a real management situation. A dangerous chemistry experiment can be conducted without the usual concerns for safety or the excessive cost of supplies and equipment.

The computer is capable of creating an artificial environment—one which can be controlled or manipulated depending on the situation. This method permits the demonstration of processes in action including cause and effect relationships through "experience." In addition to modeling the physical environment or phenomenon, time can be compressed (or expanded) to allow a complex occurrence to be shown.

The computer simulation CATLAB (Kinnear, 1982) is an example of this capability. This program allows students to mate domestic cats selected on the basis of coat color and pattern. CATLAB produces genetically valid litters of kittens based on the students' choices of parents. Without the trouble, expense, and delay of setting up a laboratory and breeding stock, students can learn about interpretation of experimental results, analysis of data, understanding of genetic ratios, probability, hypothesis testing, and organizing/recording data.

Other popular examples of computer simulations useful in the classroom are "Civil War," "Odell Lake," and "Oregon Trail." "Civil War" presents a re-creation of a number of Civil War battles. In addition to learning many facts and gaining valuable historical knowledge, students can achieve outcomes based on their own military decisions. "Odell Lake" allows students to learn about food chains by assuming the identity of fish in a lake and by making decisions about their behavior. "Oregon Trail" simulates a trip to Oregon in a covered wagon. During the trip decisions must be made regarding how much money to spend on food, ammunition, clothes, etc.; whether to shoot at riders approaching the wagon train; and whether to stop periodically for supplies or continue travelling. "Oregon Trail" is a powerful simulation in that it provides a "feel" for life in that era as well as historical facts and information.

Simulations are a natural product of the recent explosion of low-cost computers. Once they were only possible using large and expensive mainframes or at least super minicomputers. Now advanced simulations are possible using personal computers. Applications of simulations are rapidly expanding to include such areas as consumer-behavior patterns, urban and regional planning, financial forecasting, vehicle design, air traffic control, waiting/serving lines, client scheduling, and even the simulation of the computer itself.

Advantages of CAI

One of the advantages readily apparent in CAI systems is the ability to have students proceed through a sequence of instruction at their own pace. A student who has demonstrated mastery of some topic or set of objectives can move to new material without having to wait for others to catch up, and possibly become bored. Likewise, a student experiencing some difficulty may move at a slower rate until the lesson has been satisfactorily completed. During this time she/he will not suffer the embarrassment or anxiety that often accompanies "being slow" or requiring more time than others in the class.

In certain learning situations, it might be appropriate to have the computer pace the student through a set of activities or exercises. This is easily accomplished since the computer has its own clock and can permit a predetermined length of time per item, or can report to the student or teacher the amount of time required to complete the activity.

Feedback and reinforcement can be provided immediately to the student during a CAI lesson. Learning theory suggests that there is considerable merit in this principle. The student can know as soon as a question is answered whether the response was correct, or even why it was not correct. Computer graphics and audio systems can generate interesting and entertaining feedback in the case of right and wrong answers.

Regrettably, CAI systems are often compared to other (and older) modes of instructional technology and teaching devices (e.g., audio-visual aids, language labs, teaching machines, etc.). The many advantages of CAI systems make this type of comparison misleading and meaningless for many reasons. For one, the computer can do much more than present information or questions in a frame-by-frame sequence. Order of activities can be directed by a decision-making algorithm. For example, if a student is moving through an activity with little or no problem, the system can modify the activities and increase the difficulty of the instructional material.

Recent advances in low-cost microcomputer-based hardware have provided color, audio (including voice synthesis, music, and sound effects), and magnificent graphics. These innovations enhance the presentation of instructional materials as well as diversify feedback. The clarity of voice synthesis devices such as the Votrax "Type and Talk" provides countless options for augmenting CAI delivery capabilities. The programmer essentially enters PRINT statements in a BASIC program. When the program is run the statements are enunciated by the system. Such possibilities were never a part of the earlier teaching machines.

Perhaps even more important than electronic devices which provide color, sound, and graphics is the existence of a truly interactive environment. The student is actually involved in a dialogue. This represents a considerable departure from more primitive modes of programmed instruction.

What effects (or effectiveness) is gained as a result of this mode of instruction? A fair question, one which is addressed in the next section.

CAI Effectiveness

An important but difficult issue concerns the effectiveness of CAI as compared with traditional modes of instruction. The literature is replete with research related to CAI effectiveness including student achievement, student attitudes, time savings, learning retention, and costs. Unfortunately, some studies are contradictory, and some are inconclusive in their findings. Most studies, however, generally conclude that an instructional program supplemented with CAI is at least as effective as, and frequently more effective than a program using only traditional instructional methods (Magidson, 1978).

Several attempts have been made in recent years to pull together the findings of research related to CAI effectiveness. In a review by Jamison et al. (1974) it was concluded that no uniform conclusions about the effectiveness of CAI could be drawn, particularly with regard to achievement. Savings in student time, however, were reported which could be viewed as a measure of efficiency. Furthermore, it was reported that small amounts of CAI supplementary instruction led to improved achievement, particularly for slower students.

A review of research literature by Edwards, et al. (1975), concluded that CAI-supplemented instruction led to higher performance levels than normal instruction alone. Furthermore, less time was required for learning through CAI than through other methods. The review also indicated, however, that learning retention levels of CAI students may not be as high as for students taught in a traditional manner.

Thomas (1979), in a study focused toward the effectiveness of CAI in secondary school settings, determined that CAI utilization typically increased achievement over traditional teaching methods. In addition, retention was found to equal that obtained through conventional teaching methods and attitudes toward CAI were generally favorable. The review was consistent with previous studies in that the research seems to point toward a compression of time required for learning mastery.

A recent study by Burns (1981) analyzed and integrated research relative to the pedagogical effectiveness of computer-assisted mathematics instruction as compared to traditional mathematics instruction at both the elementary and secondary levels. This investigation employed the meta-analysis technique for research purposes.

Primary findings were the following:

1. A mathematics instructional program supplemented with either CAI drill/practice or tutorial computer-assisted instruction was significantly more effective in fostering student achievement than a program utilizing only traditional instructional methods.
2. CAI drill/practice programs were significantly more effective in promoting increased student achievement at both the elementary and secondary instructional levels, for both high achievers and disadvantaged students, and for students whose distinct ability levels had not been dif-

ferentiated by the original researchers. The achievement of average-level students was not significantly enhanced by supplementary drill/practice CAI.

3. Instructional plans accommodating supplementary drill/practice CAI showed significantly greater achievement gains among boys at the intermediate grade level than instructional plans employing only traditional pedagogical models. An analogous conclusion relative to achievement among intermediate-level girls was not demonstrated.

4. Tutorial CAI-supplemented instruction was significantly more effective in promoting increased mathematics achievement among students at both the elementary and secondary instructional levels and among disadvantaged students.

5. There was virtually no evidence to suggest the existence of a relationship between experimental design features and study outcomes. (Burns, 1982)

A similar study (Kulik, Bangert & Williams, 1983) also employed the meta-analysis technique to synthesize the findings of research related to computer-based education. Their study integrated the findings of fifty-one independent evaluations of computer-based teaching in grades six through twelve. Six major areas were addressed: final examination performance, performance on retention examinations, attitude toward subject matter, attitude toward computers, attitude toward instruction, and time to learn. The results are summarized as follows:

1. Students from the computer-based instruction classes received the better examination scores. In a typical class, performance of these students was raised by approximately .32 standard deviations.

2. Attitudes of students toward subject matter in classes taught using computers were, in general, favorable.

3. The student attitudes toward computers in classes using computer-based instruction were more positive as compared with classes not using computers.

4. The computer reduced substantially the amount of time that students needed for learning.

The reviews of CAI effectiveness research, while promising, offer no guarantees of success. CAI, as any other instructional support system, will be influenced by many variables, some uncontrollable. The studies do indicate that the promises offered in the early days of CAI may not be empty, and that CAI, if properly structured and implemented, can enhance the learning process (Burns & Bozeman, 1981).

Costs of CAI

Cost estimates are difficult to present for any instructional technology system—especially computer-based education. This is due to the many ways in which cost figures can be developed (i.e., what expenses are included in the total dollar figure), the rapidly changing costs of both personnel and hardware/software, and the impact of economies of scale. Cost estimates can include: software design and development, personnel training and in-service programs, hardware, maintenance, instructor time, telecommunications, distribution, electricity, facilities, environmental control, and miscellaneous factors (Spuck, 1981). For these reasons, many cost estimates are quite deceiving. For example, if one assumes the cost of a microcomputer to be about $2,000 and that courseware costs are negligible (perhaps through a cooperative area service agency), the cost/pupil is very low—perhaps less than $1/hour over a three-year period. Of course, such a figure does not begin to include the factors presented above.

A more rigorous study of costs presented by Levine and Woo (1981) determined annual costs may vary from about $125 to almost $150 per year for a daily ten-minute drill and practice session. This estimate assumed a thirty-two terminal configuration in a single classroom (twenty-three sessions per day per terminal). Cost included facilities and equipment, personnel, training, curriculum rental, maintenance, and miscellaneous expenses.

Other cost estimates have ranged from less than $1 per student hour for CAI instruction to over $5 per student hour. Often such estimates relate only to actual computer time and communications and do not include courseware development, programming, maintenance, and overhead.

So, what is the cost of CAI? The question, as stated, has no meaningful or definitive answer. We can only conclude that it is becoming more and more affordable for most schools and that this trend will almost certainly continue.

In addition to cost factors already discussed, it is suggested that the educator consider a few more points when addressing this question:

1. What are the cost-savings that can be attributed to any increases in learning, morale, and general attitudes toward school?
2. Could available moneys expended for CAI return a greater educational benefit if allocated elsewhere?
3. Have the cost outlays been considered over a long period of time? When savings in instructional time and effort can be achieved at subsequent grade levels through accomplishments at a lower level, this value must be weighed.

In summary, it seems safe to say that although the economics of CAI are elusive, they can be approximated. The educator must be articulate in this area if the case for CAI is to be successfully presented to school administration, the board of education, and the public.

Computer-Managed Instruction

As we saw in the previous section, the purpose of a computer-assisted instruction (CAI) system is to deliver instructional material via a student-computer dialogue or interaction. Frequently this format includes programmed sequences of instruction delivered in an interactive manner. The purpose of a computer-managed instruction (CMI) system is somewhat different in that it assists in the control, prescription, and direction of the learning activities. CMI systems are generally considered management information systems designed to support certain management functions of instruction such as planning, scheduling, coordinating, and reporting. These functions are especially important in programs which individualize instruction. One of the problems often cited by teachers involved in individualized instruction is the burdensome record keeping and related clerical activity. While a CMI system would certainly handle record keeping of student achievement and progress, it could go far beyond this application.

Until recently, CMI systems were supported only on large and costly mainframe computers thereby limiting CMI accessibility due to equipment requirements and costs. Representative CMI systems were PLAN (Program for Learning in Accordance with Needs), WIS-SIM (Wisconsin System for Instructional Management), the U.S. Navy CMI System, MICA (Managed Instruction with Computer Assistance), and TRACER. While earlier systems were often beset with procedural, technical, and economic problems, they did provide a conceptual foundation for CMI and important proofs-of-concept. Microcomputer-based CMI systems offer the potential for reducing, and even eliminating, many of the difficulties associated with these early systems. Compared with a time-sharing system on a large mainframe, a microcomputer CMI system can also offer the user features such as system control, access, convenience, and reduced costs as compared with a time-sharing system (McIsaac & Baker, 1981).

The design, functions, and capabilities of different CMI systems vary from application to application. There are, however, several generalizations about CMI functions which can be made. Most systems offer:

1. Maintenance of student achievement records—A data base manager permits the recording of assessment information and updating of files which contain mastery or performance information. The computer file may also contain student demographic or directory information.
2. Reports—Status reports for individual students or groups of students may be prepared for review by parents, teachers, or school administration. These progress or achievement reports may be periodic or even online.
3. Testing—Many variations of testing capabilities exist within CMI systems. Item banks are possible in which sets of test questions/items are maintained along with item statistics. Test construction is possible through random or selective generation. This can permit development of parallel forms of a given test, tests for individual students, standardized tests, or practice quizzes.

4. Grading—Student grade data can be periodically entered into the computer data base in several ways. Manual entry (via the keyboard) is common and closely analogous to the posting of grades in the conventional gradebook. Sheet scanners or optical mark readers may also be used in certain applications. If the test is administered by the computer as part of CAI lesson, the score can be automatically stored in the student file. Tests administered using optical scan sheets provide even another method for updating the file.

5. Identification of instructional needs—This is an important extension of the reporting function through which teachers can examine student progress within some specified area of the curricular structure or for some specific time period. Based upon the reports, the teacher can determine what instruction, review, or remediation might be appropriate.

6. Grouping of students for instruction—Instructional grouping for specific topics or learning objectives can be recommended by the system based upon individual progress within the curricular structure. The opposite approach might also be used. The teacher could supply the names of a group of students, and the CMI system would indicate the topics for which they have met the prerequisites.

7. Search and recommendation of instructional resources—Data bases of resources and activities relative to student needs can be accessed, relieving teachers of another time-consuming clerical task.

Perhaps, the best way to gain some insight into CMI is to describe a functional CMI system. One such system is the Wisconsin System for Instructional Management (WIS-SIM). WIS-SIM is a CMI system developed at The University of Wisconsin Research and Development Center for Individualized Schooling in an effort to improve and support decision making relative to the instructional program. The following components are identified in the system:

1. Assessing Instructional Outcomes/Updating Student Records—Allows for the submission of assessment information and updating of the files which contain individual student performance and demographic data.

2. Identifying Instructional Needs—Teachers can receive lists of units or specific students with a computer-stored record of their progress. The format of the individual reports also allows them to be used in reporting to parents. Both the unit and individual reports can be tailored to report progress for a teacher-specified range of objectives within an instructional program.

3. Grouping Students for Instruction—Instructional groups can be formed on the basis of the previously identified instructional needs. This is accomplished by searching a particular group of student records (usually a unit or class) and indicating whether students are eligible for a particular instructional module, listing those who are or who are not, as

well as a summary report listing student eligibility totals over a range of modules.

Functional capabilities provided by WIS-SIM include:

1. Program data base initiation
2. Student data base initiation
3. Entering student achievement tests
4. Achievement profiling
5. Instructional grouping recommendation and implementation
6. Diagnostic reporting
7. Student data base maintenance
8. Monitoring overlap between instructional programs
9. Data base purging
10. Curriculum and program evaluation (Douglas, Belt, Owen, & Chan, 1977, pp. 12-14)

All requests for reports, file updates, grading, etc., are submitted via the school computer terminal interactively. The terminal permits communication with the central computing facility at another site via telephone. In this mode, the operator has the option of remaining on-line to receive a report directly at the terminal or directing the system to print the report at another site on a deferred basis for economy.

Part of the WIS-SIM research and development effort was a two-year intensive pilot test and evaluation. This test and evaluation did not provide strong evidence that this particular system was cost-effective. The evaluation, however, did offer support for the concept of computer support for individualized education. Teacher perceptions of the utility of the CMI system were positive. Furthermore, the data indicated that teacher time was used more effectively and efficiently in instructional management and planning. Teacher time required for clerical tasks was reduced, allowing more time for both direct instruction and planning (Spuck & Bozeman, 1978).

Studies associated with the MICA CMI system reflected a positive and supportive climate on the part of teachers and students. With regard to the economics of the system, district evaluation considered it cost-efficient and cost-beneficial. Analysis of math achievement in CMI and non-CMI schools suggests no difference in achievement patterns. However, evaluation of classroom time utilization indicated a substantial improvement in classroom efficiency (Roecks, 1976).

In summary, these and other studies appear to offer evidence that CMI, when properly implemented, enhances the total effectiveness and efficiency of the instructional program. Benefits which may accrue include:

1. Reduction of teacher time required for clerical and record-keeping tasks
2. Enhanced student record files

3. Improved instruction and planning
4. Expanded diagnosis and prescription
5. Student achievement profiling
6. Curricular evaluation

Much of the evidence, unfortunately, is not supported by hard data, especially in the area of student achievement. Furthermore, the question of cost-efficiency remains unresolved at this point. No doubt, the application of microcomputers to CMI will dramatically alter the economics of CMI applications.

A concluding note regarding computer-managed instruction may be appropriate. CMI systems have not historically received as much popular attention from either the professional educator or the public as have the more popular CAI systems. There are many explanations for this. CAI applications tend to gain popular attention and appeal because they can resemble a game, complete with color, graphics, animation. Even amateur programmers can develop elementary CAI programs. Furthermore, CAI can be rather quickly integrated (properly or otherwise) into an existing curriculum or program of study. Conversely, CMI system applications require careful analysis of the instructional program as well as possible major changes in instructional and management strategies.

Only time will reveal the outcome of the generalized implementation and utilization of computer-based instructional management systems. One scenario suggests the integration of CAI and CMI in commercially available software. This is already the case in a few packages. Such systems offer the management component for use by the teacher who feels comfortable with this option. Those who do not can use the CAI portion of the software, and handle management manually. Use of a CMI system may require the teacher to make a number of drastic changes in the instructional format. This, of course, is always the case when instruction is truly individualized. Furthermore, many teachers remember the unpleasant experiences associated with earlier programs of individualized education (without computer support) and the enormous amount of record keeping associated with these systems. Since CMI systems, once in place, actually make both record keeping and individualized instruction easier, CMI has been, and continues to be, a very important educational application of computers.

Computer Science

Computer science is a term used to describe a curricular area in which topics related to computing are the object of instruction. These topics, as we shall see, include but are not limited to programming, problem solving using the computer, data representation, and information processing. Until very recently, computer science courses were taught almost exclusively at the post-secondary level. Now it is common to find a computer science curriculum taught in many secondary schools. As the availability and access to computing machinery continues to grow and as the expectations of colleges with regard to student preparation in high schools change, it is almost certain that this trend will continue. Now, for example, advanced placement in college computer science is available to students who are able to demonstrate proficiency in this area.

The scope and nature of a computer science curriculum vary from school to school. Some of the specific components which might be included are listed below:

1. Introduction to computer applications
   a. Business data processing
   b. Computers as tools in everyday life
   c. Industrial and commercial uses
   d. Employment and career opportunities
   e. Information as a commodity
   f. Integration of computing and communication
2. Data-processing systems
   a. Data representation in computers
   b. Data and information processing procedures
   c. History of computing machinery
   d. Computer hardware (including CPU, input/output devices, media for data, and storage devices)
3. Computer programming
   a. Phases of program development/programming methodologies
   b. Text editing and formatting
   c. Structured programming
   d. Introduction to algorithms
   e. Introduction to several languages (e.g., Pascal, FORTRAN, BASIC, etc.)
   f. Documentation procedures and practices
   g. Testing and debugging
   h. Assembler language applications
   i. Data structures
   j. Machine language
4. Software applications
   a. Specification of user requirements
   b. Review and evaluation of existing programs
   c. Modification of software
   d. Documentation procedures
   e. Systems software
   f. Operating systems
   g. Data base management
5. Issues and special topics
   a. Societal implications and concerns

b. Privacy, security, theft
c. Office automation
d. Maintenance and operation of data-processing equipment
e. Advanced system concepts (e.g., multiprogramming, multiprocessing, time-sharing, distributed processing, and virtual machines)
f. Artificial intelligence

The introduction of computer science into the curriculum poses many new problems and challenges for the educator. At present, there is a critical shortage of teachers with formal preparation adequate to yield the many requisite competencies. This shortage will continue into the foreseeable future. The computer science teacher must be quite knowledgeable about the topics for which he/she is responsible. Ideally, the instructor should have a bachelor's degree in computer science. If such a person is not available, the teacher should at least have successfully completed several core courses in computer science. An inadequately prepared teacher will only exacerbate the students' problems as they enter computer science at the college or university level. A computer science curriculum at any level should go beyond the study of a computer language, computer programming, or problem-solving applications. However, before a school can determine the content of its computer science curriculum, it must first resolve a very fundamental question—"What is the purpose of the curricular program?"

If the purpose is highly vocational in nature, the overall design will be different than if the purpose is to prepare students for postsecondary computer science study. Persons hired into programmer positions may find themselves involved, to a great degree, in the revision of existing software so that it can be used in specific application areas such as accounting or data base management (as opposed to the "ground-up" development of new special purpose software). The costs of developing new programs almost prohibits their creation except in situations where no other alternatives exist. In order to be successful in such work, persons must be knowledgeable not only about a computer language and programming techniques but also about the style, design, logic, flow, and structure of a computer program.

If the purpose of the curriculum is to provide students with prerequisites for post-secondary computer science studies, a clear articulation of expectancies must be established among the various schools concerned. Also, the seemingly diverse goals of the computer science curriculum do not have to be mutually exclusive. They can be coordinated and can complement one another.

Much additional clarity of direction will emerge as computer science curricula continue to develop and expand. Principles of good curriculum design and implementation must be adhered to as in any other subject. The "fly in the ointment," however, comes from lack of experience in this area at the precollege level. Regrettably, time is not on the side of the school. Pressure in this area will increase, and progress must be shown in the very near future.

The need for computer science professionals will not diminish. The demand in business, industry, and education for persons with computer science skills will continue to increase as our entire social system becomes more dependent upon information and information processing.

Administrative Data Processing

Introduction

Any organization, including the school, or any unit within an organization, such as (in the case of schools) the classroom, requires information to function on a regular basis (e.g., from day to day, week to week, month to month, and so on). Processing of data into some form of information useful to management, administrators, or the classroom teacher is a critical component in the successful operation of the school. This conversion of *data* or unorganized raw facts into useful *information* is called *data processing*. Within the educational environment, data processing is frequently divided into two broad areas—*academic* data processing and *administrative* data processing (ADP). This chapter thus far has concentrated on academic data processing or academic computing. Academic computing typically includes instruction (including CAI, CMI, computer literacy, computer science, etc.), computing for research purposes, and computing support for instruction.

Only a few years ago administrative computing would have referred exclusively to applications associated with the business functions of the school. Now, however, with the advent of low-cost, personal computers these administrative functions can be extended to include the management functions requisite to the role of the teacher.

The distinction between traditional administrative computing and personal administrative computing is principally a matter of scale and scope of applications. The traditional applications in administration are as follows:

STUDENT APPLICATIONS

1. Student scheduling
2. Grade reporting
3. Grade and transcript information
4. Daily and summary attendance accounting
5. Student and family demographic information
6. Health records
7. Summary test information
8. Instructional management
9. Test scoring
10. Tuition and fee statements

PERSONNEL APPLICATIONS

1. Payroll checks and deductions
2. Personnel records
3. Staff assignments
4. Certification records
5. Health records
6. Tax information and W-2 reports

FINANCIAL APPLICATIONS

1. Budget/accounting
2. Accounts receivable/payable
3. General ledger
4. Purchase order generation
5. Salary schedule analysis and forecasting

FACILITIES/EQUIPMENT APPLICATIONS

1. Room locations/capacities
2. Room assignments/utilization
3. Equipment inventories
4. Maintenance scheduling
5. Energy utilization/control

RESEARCH/PLANNING APPLICATIONS

1. Budget forecasting
2. Bus routing (Charp, et al., 1982)

To a great extent, these and other administrative applications have been possible only in larger school districts which could afford the expenses associated with the hardware, software, personnel, and other necessary resources. An alternative to owning a computer has been the contracting of data-processing services through some type of consortium in which several districts share expenses. The low-cost computing power possible with microcomputers may offer more schools and districts the opportunity to enhance the effectiveness and efficiency of the school administration. Software is becoming increasingly available for the microcomputer and will likely transform the methods of data processing in many schools.

Administrator and staff training which will enable the proper utilization of microcomputers presents another problem—a problem perhaps more critical than the availability of software. Even the use of so-called turnkey systems (i.e., software and systems ready-to-use) often requires personnel with technical expertise in computing. The hand-holding offered by skilled computer professionals is essential to cope with system "crashes" or other problems which plague even the most dependable hardware and software. Recent experiences in a number of schools suggest, however, that the concept of microcomputer-based administrative data processing is possible and feasible. Time alone will provide the answer as to the extent and scope of these applications.

Classroom/Personal Administrative Data Processing: Data Base Management

The classroom or personal administrative data-processing applications are, in a sense, a subset of the traditional administrative applications. Consider, for example, a senior class sponsor or homeroom teacher. One application which comes to mind immediately is data base management. Such a system would allow the teacher to keep a record for each student on the computer. The record might contain such things as directory information (name, address, phone, parent/guardian, etc.) as well as updated posting of fee payments, etc. Lists and searches could be performed on any of these fields or combinations of fields. It would be quite simple, for instance, to produce a list of all seniors owing library fines.

File management systems and data base management systems (DBMS) are an important category of computer applications. The logical storage and retrieval of information are among the tasks that computers do best. Generally, the concept of DBMS is a method of maintaining some control over the large amount of information which accumulates in an organization. Additionally, the software facilitates user (who may or may not be a programmer) interaction with the computer system. A DBMS gives the user relatively powerful commands for creating, adding, formatting, modifying, displaying, sorting, searching, and manipulating files through English-like commands. The requisite systems functions, therefore, can become somewhat transparent or invisible to the user. With regard to control, a true DBMS should provide various levels of security (e.g., passwords) to protect against unauthorized use. More advanced systems may even encrypt the data in case security is broken. Finally, a true DBMS should offer some reasonable degree of protection against failure due to malfunction of hardware, interruption of power, or other error-generating problems. In short, the DBMS is an interface or link between a user and a file (data base).

A program which is particularly useful in file management applications is called Personal Filing System or simply PFS. Since PFS does not contain all of the features generally associated with a complete DBMS, it is more accurate to classify it as a file manager. PFS successfully integrates many qualities which users regard as being the hallmarks of a good computer software package—useful functions, clearly written documentation, appealing "cosmetic" features, and versatility. All of the above come at what should be considered a reasonable price, given the current prices of microcomputer programs.

It may be helpful to review PFS as an example of a file management package to gain an appreciation of its possible applications. Page 1 of the *PFS Us-*

er's Manual asks the question "What is PFS?" The answer to this question certainly offers an appropriate entree into our review. Generally, PFS is an electronic filing system. The program allows the user to design (on the computer screen) a form containing fields of information. After this form has been created, it is saved on disk and used whenever it is necessary to store or retrieve data. Let's consider the example of the senior homeroom sponsor. The teacher often uses a card for recording certain important facts about each student for quick and easy referral. This might include name, ID, address, telephone number, parent or guardian's name, check lists for things such as cap and gown fees, and the number of accumulated credits.

The development of such a PFS form is as easy as the design of a similar form using pencil and paper. From a menu of PFS functions (figure 5.6, the option 1, "DESIGN FILE," is selected.

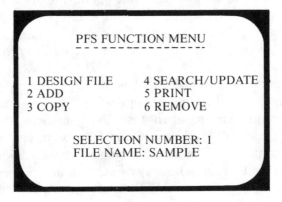

Figure 5.6
PFS Menu. (PFS, Software Publishing Company, 1901 Landings Drive, Mountain View, CA 94043)

A blank computer screen is displayed after selecting number 1 (figure 5.7).

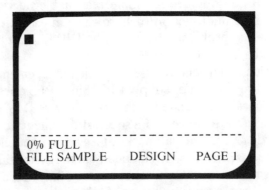

Figure 5.7
PFS Screen—Design Mode. (PFS, Software Publishing Company, 1901 Landings Drive, Mountain View, CA 94043)

Then it is merely a matter of defining the items or fields and placing them in the proper location on the screen so adequate space exists for the data (e.g., name, address, etc.). A screen containing fields of information is illustrated in figure 5.8.

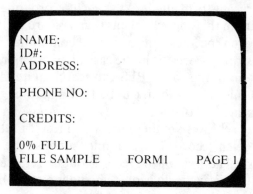

```
NAME:
ID#:
ADDRESS:

PHONE NO:

CREDITS:

0% FULL
FILE SAMPLE        FORM1        PAGE 1
```

Figure 5.8
PFS Screen with Titles of Fields. (PFS, Software Publishing Company, 1901 Landings Drive, Mountain View, CA 94043)

Once the design of the form has been completed, files can be stored, changed, retrieved, or deleted. Also, the overall form can be revised or redesigned.

Information retrieval is another exciting application of PFS. The user returns to the PFS function menu and selects SEARCH/UPDATE. Several types of searches can now be performed using the PFS form as a guide. For instance, the file page for student, W. Patrick, may be accessed by merely entering the characters "W. Patrick," ". .Patrick," or even "W. .". The latter two, however, may result in the location of other files in addition to the desired one (such as "Fred Patrick" or "W. Jones"). The two periods in the ". . Patrick" example essentially command the system to search for any string of characters containing "Patrick," ignoring preceding characters; or, in the "W. ." case, to search for any character string which begins with "W." These are examples of partial item searches and can be useful if you do not remember exactly how a name was entered. Other types of character searches are also available and are discussed in the documentation.

Searches using numeric fields can be particularly important. We may wish to search for all applicants who have less than twelve Carnegie units. To do this, we enter "<12" in the number of credits field while in the search mode. Numeric searches can be based on equality/inequality, greater than/less than, and inclusive conditions. If no search conditions are given, the user may page through every form in the file.

Combinations of logical conditions may be specified. We may wish to see all the seniors who have a desire to participate in graduation activities AND have less than fourteen credits toward graduation. At this point, it is important to offer the caveat that while PFS has a number of powerful features, it requires (as does any data base management system) the user to be somewhat thoughtful in the form design and in the entry of data. Otherwise, the search capabilities will not be as effective as possible.

The search process is sequential in that the program starts at the end of the file with the most recent form and looks at each record, one by one, until a *hit* is achieved. A "hit" in this context means that a record contains fields of data which meet the search specifications or logical conditions. The one exception to this sequential search process is in the case of an exact or full item match in the first field or item in the form. PFS can search quite rapidly through the file for content in this field (a form can be found in three to five seconds) by using an efficient search algorithm known as a *hashing scheme*.

Hash addressing schemes are methods which result in the computation of an address for a given record. For example, suppose the first field is an ID number. The physical address of the record could be created by using the last few digits of the ID (this is the division-remainder method). In other words, a key field is transformed into a record address. In the event the addresses of two files are not unique (i.e., a *collision* occurred and *synonym* addresses resulted), an alternative address must be used. The random accessibility of disk files coupled with this type of addressing system can produce very efficient retrieval. Again, PFS only uses this technique in the first key field of the form. Therefore, it is critical for the designer to carefully consider the form layout in order to maximize efficiency.

Other functions offered in the PFS menu are ADD (for storing information in previously designed form), COPY (for making duplicate or backup copies), PRINT (for printing forms or portions of forms), and REMOVE (you guessed it—for eliminating unwanted forms from the file).

The program contains reasonably good error messages which are either obvious in meaning or are explained in an appendix of the documentation. Control keys provide adequate cursor movement, page control, and certain PFS-specific functions. Printer control is not difficult, although experimentation may be necessary when generating special forms such as mailing labels.

The PFS data disk can store up to 1000 forms. The exact number is a function of the amount of data residing in each record of the file. Given the content of the form, a method of calculating the number of records to be stored on a disk is provided in the user's manual.

PFS is not a substitute for a true data base management system nor is it intended to be. The experienced or sophisticated user may find PFS too limited, and thus require a more complex program. PFS represents the result of trade-offs between elegance of data structure and ease of use or user friendliness. The designers of PFS kept things neat and simple but yet quite useful.

Another popular and useful database management package is DB Master (Stoneware Microcomputer Products). DB Master is similar in many respects to PFS with regard to features, capabilities, and options to the user. The program is, however, more powerful and offers a greater range of file management flexibility. DB Master allows for the design of a form which may be up to nine pages (screen displays) in length for a given record. A record is considered to be a collection of data related to one subject or individual. This form can contain combinations of ten different type fields or items of information. Types of fields provided by DB Master include numeric (small/large integer and floating point), dollars/cents, computed or calculated numeric, yes/no, social security number, telephone, date and auto date. In this last field type, the current date is automatically entered in the field. Social security number, telephone number, and date fields are preformatted. Spaces and dashes are set up and only numerals 0 through 9 are accepted thereby reducing data entry errors.

During the actual development of the form on the monitor, the user selects field types from a menu. The location (horizontal/vertical) and field length are also entered. As the user manual suggests, it is helpful to lay out the form in advance on the 24×39 grid sheet provided. After a page has been entered, an edit mode may be used to correct or alter the contents.

When the file is created, three levels of protection using passwords can be specified: (1) READ ONLY users may only display records; (2) READ/ WRITE USERS have full system access but may not change passwords; (3) MASTER password users have full system access and may change, add, or delete passwords.

Once a database has been created, records can be located and displayed in a manner similar to PFS. After records have been found, DB Master provides a number of options for printing via a report generator.

Data base managers and/or file managers such as PFS and DB Master are relatively easy to use and their advantages over traditional paper and pencil record-keeping systems are obvious. There are several commercial programs available, but, in general, the more sophisticated the program capabilities, the more difficult the program is to use. The user should first identify requirements and specifications, then determine if a particular program will satisfy those prerequisites.

Word Processing

Another important personal administrative computer application is word processing. Uses of word processing are limited only by one's imagination. Basically, word processing is the use of the computer system to store, manipulate, and generate text copy (the text you're reading now was developed using a word processor). Word-processing systems can range from relatively inexpensive software for a personal computer to a large mainframe system.

Regardless of the type of system, most word processors involve the use of a typewriter-like keyboard, a CRT display, a hard copy printer, and, of course, the computer. Text is entered much as it would be on any typewriter and is then displayed on the CRT. Corrections, additions, deletions, and text insertions can be easily performed, and then the text is stored for retrieval, use, or modification at a future date.

The many functions and capabilities of word processors vary among different machines and software. There are however certain features found in most general-purpose systems:

- Character and text editing
- Text/line insertion and deletion
- Moving of text ("cut and paste editing")
- Overall or global text searches or text modification
- Flush left and right margins
- Automatic centering of lines
- Page and margin control
- Automatic entry of headers and footers
- Merging and appending of documents

Through the use of a word processor, enormous gains in productivity can be realized. A document such as an article draft can be easily revised. Assignments, worksheets, tests, handouts, bibliographies, etc., can be periodically updated without retyping the entire document. To a great extent, correction fluid, scissors, and paste can be thrown away—the system serves their purposes. In a greater sense, the typewriter is now virtually obsolete.

In a matter of seconds, spelling errors can be detected with a spelling-checking program used in conjunction with the word processor. This program contains a dictionary of thousands of the more commonly used words. Additionally, the user can add a dictionary of special or unusual words. When executed, the program reads through a file noting words spelled differently from the words contained in its dictionary. The writer can then determine if the words are indeed misspelled and then make any necessary corrections.

Generation of personalized form letters is another important advantage of a word processor. A computer file of inside addresses and salutations can be linked to the body of a letter. The individual letters, when printed, are indistinguishable from letters typed one at a time. Letters or notes to parents can be produced quickly, especially when a standardized format is used.

There are numerous word-processing programs available for personal computers. Dozens of programs exist for the Apple II alone, including Apple Writer II, Screen Writer II, Zardax, Pie Writer, Executive Secretary, Wordstar, and Bank Street Writer. Prices on these word processors range from under $100 to over $500 depending on features, options, and capabilities. The various choices of software may be complicated somewhat by hardware considerations such as lower-case and eighty-column display, keyboard functions (for example, use of a true shift key rather than some substitute), and printer selections.

The selection combinations must also take into consideration the printer. Three to four years ago only two or three printers designed for use with personal computers were priced under $1,000. Now there are more than two dozen printers costing less than $1000. These printers vary considerably in quality, type of print (i.e., dot matrix or fully formed characters), speed, type of paper used (e.g., friction feed or tractor feed), noise levels, graphics capability, serviceability, and other general features.

Clearly, the choice of a word-processing system is not an easy one and requires many decisions. The many features of word processing make choosing worth the trouble to most educators. One only needs to use a word processor for a short while to appreciate the ways it can enhance total efficiency of operation.

Figure 5.9
Use of a word processor can facilitate the preparation of reports and papers for both students and teachers. (University of Iowa, Weeg Computing Center, Iowa City, Iowa 52242)

Electronic Spreadsheets

A third area which offers considerable promise for administrative as well as classroom application is the electronic spreadsheet. One such program is Visi-Calc, a product of Personal Software, Inc. The simplest way to describe a spreadsheet is to imagine a matrix or array with rows and columns. The contents of the respective cells can be user-entered values, labels, or user-defined formulas. The spreadsheet can be helpful as a gradebook because it can provide for weighting of tests and assignments in addition to simple entry and averaging of scores. It can also be used as an attendance register or to assist in bookkeeping and budgets, as well as for many other functions.

Let's briefly examine a VisiCalc application. In this example a junior class sponsor is developing a budget for the junior-senior prom. The planning committee anticipates income from three sources—car washes, a bake sale, and admission tickets. Some expenses will be associated with each of these fund-raising activities. The prom will require funds for five items—decorations, food, the band, security, and a custodian. Anyone who has ever prepared a budget knows that the initial stages represent a "what if" situation. The committee has projected $500 in proceeds from the car wash and $550 from the bake sale. They also expect to sell 1000 tickets at $2 per ticket. The band has agreed to play for a guarantee of $500 plus one-half of the door (paid admissions). Other expenses are shown in figure 5.10.

If income from the ticket sales, car washes, and bake sale meet the committee's expectations, income will exceed expenses by $770. This is an ideal situation, but there could be unforeseen expenses or unexpected income. Examination of the spreadsheet in figure 5.10 shows a line-by-line breakdown of income and expenses.

```
          A              B              C              D              E
 1               PROM INCOME
 2  # OF TICKETS        1000
 3  *********************************************************************
 4  SOURCE         CAR WASHES     BAKE SALE      DOOR @ $2        TOTALS
 5  ------         ---------      ----------     ----------       -------
 6  INCOME            500.00         550.00        2000.00        3050.00
 7  EXPENSES           50.00          20.00          10.00          80.00
 8  NET PROCEEDS      450.00         530.00        1990.00        2970.00
 9
10  *********************************************************************
11               PROM EXPENSE
12  ITEM
13  ----
14  DECORATIONS       325.00
15  FOOD              225.00
16  BAND             1500.00
17  SECURITY          100.00
18  CUSTODIAN          50.00
19                  -------
20  TOTAL EXP        2200.00
21
22  TOTAL INC        2970.00
23
24  NET DIFF          770.00 (INC-EXP)
```

Figure 5.10
Use of VisiCalc for Budget Preparation

What if only 700 tickets are sold and the car wash nets only $250 (naturally it rained)? Now the budget doesn't look so good! Income only exceeds expenses by $40. Figure 5.11 presents this budget.

```
          A              B              C              D              E
 1                  PROM INCOME
 2   # OF TICKETS         700
 3   **********************************************************
 4   SOURCE         CAR WASHES    BAKE SALE    DOOR @ $2      TOTALS
 5   ------         ----------    ---------    ----------     -------
 6   INCOME            300.00        320.00      1400.00      2020.00
 7   EXPENSES           50.00         20.00        10.00        80.00
 8   NET PROCEEDS      250.00        300.00      1390.00      1940.00
 9
10   **********************************************************
11                  PROM EXPENSE
12   ITEM
13   ----
14   DECORATIONS       325.00
15   FOOD              225.00
16   BAND             1200.00
17   SECURITY          100.00
18   CUSTODIAN          50.00
19                    -------
20   TOTAL EXP        1900.00
21
22   TOTAL INC        1940.00
23
24   NET DIFF           40.00 (INC-EXP)
```

Figure 5.11
VisiCalc Screen #2

What if 600 tickets were sold, the car washes netted $200 AND the bake sale only provided $300? The expenses exceed the income by $110. Figure 5.12 presents this unfortunate (but possible) situation.

The power of this program and how easily the results shown in figures 5.10–5.12 were achieved are difficult to appreciate unless one has actually used VisiCalc. Once the spreadsheet has been developed, the user only changes the cell in question (e.g., number of tickets sold). The rest of sheet affected by this change is automatically updated. In this example, cells D6 (door income), D8 (net proceeds from door), E6 (total income), E8 (total net income), B16 (band expense), B20 (total expenses), B22 (total income), and B24 (net difference) are all changed as a result of changing the value of cell B2—the number of tickets sold.

Spreadsheet programs permit this type of comprehensive modification by allowing cells to contain not only values (such as the number of tickets sold) but also formulas which may be linked to contents of other cells. In figure 5.13, which illustrates the content of the respective cells, we see that cell B8 (net proceeds from car washes) contains a formula, +B6–B7. This simply

```
             A              B             C            D            E
  1                    PROM INCOME
  2    # OF TICKETS          600
  3    *********************************************************************
  4    SOURCE          CAR WASHES    BAKE SALE    DOOR @ $2      TOTALS
  5    -------         ---------     ----------   ----------     -------
  6    INCOME             250.00        320.00      1200.00      1770.00
  7    EXPENSES            50.00         20.00        10.00        80.00
  8    NET PROCEEDS       200.00        300.00      1190.00      1690.00
  9
 10    *********************************************************************
 11                    PROM EXPENSE
 12    ITEM
 13    ----
 14    DECORATIONS        325.00
 15    FOOD               225.00
 16    BAND              1100.00
 17    SECURITY           100.00
 18    CUSTODIAN           50.00
 19                      -------
 20    TOTAL EXP         1800.00
 21
 22    TOTAL INC         1690.00
 23
 24    NET DIFF          -110.00 (INC-EXP)
```

Figure 5.12
VisiCalc Screen #3

means that the quantity in cell B8 will be determined by the values of B6 and B7 and will be their arithmetic difference. The formulas in cells C8 and D8 serve a similar purpose. The formula in cell E8 is a VisiCalc shorthand notation for summing cells B8, C8, and D8.

Space does not permit an extensive review of the many capabilities of a program such as VisiCalc. In some respects, this example represents only a trivial case of the problems which can be structured. Indeed, numerous articles have been written which describe very complex configurations of a spreadsheet. The user is not limited to simple arithmetic computations either. Functions for descriptive statistics, trigonometric and logarithmic calculations, logical operations, etc. are also provided. Entries can be readily edited, inserted, deleted, and replicated. Once the user is familiar with the command structure, modifications and manipulations of the grid are easily performed.

Other types of administrative programs useful to the educator include statistical packages for analysis of data (e.g., test scores, graphics programs for display of data, business management software, and so on) are readily available at affordable prices for microcomputers. Because the field is so rapidly

	A	B	C	D	E
1		Prom Income			
2	# of tickets	700			
3	***************	***********************	*********************	***********************	********************
4	Source	Car washes	Bake Sale	Door @ $2	Totals
5	-------------------------	-------------------------	-------------------------	-------------------------	-------------------------
6	Income	250.00	550.00	1400.00	2200.00
7	Expenses	50.00	20.00	10.00	80.00
8	Net Proceeds	+ B6 – B7	+ C6 – C7	+ D6 – D7	@SUM (B8...D8)
9					
10	***************	***********************	*********************	***********************	********************
11		Prom Expense			
12	Item				
13	-------------------------				
14	Decorations	325.00			
15	Food	225.00			
16	Band	500 + (.5*B2*2)			
17	Security	100.00			
18	Custodian	50.00			
19		-------------------------			
20	Total Expense	@SUM(B14...B18)			
21					
22	Total Income	+ E8			
23					
24	Net Difference	+ B22 – B20	(Inc-Exp)		

Figure 5.13
VisiCalc Formulas for Budget Application

developing, it is necessary for the serious user to stay as closely in touch with the new product lines as possible.

In summary.   What does the near future hold for administrative computing? Of course our crystal ball is as cloudy as the next writer's, but a few things seem reasonably certain. More and more software will be marketed which can be tailored by the user to his or her own unique needs. This has become, to a certain extent, the case with large systems software, and the microcomputer industry will likely follow suit. Prices of software will drop as economies of scale, increased production, and other forces continue to influence the market. Software, as well as computer systems in general, will become increasingly user friendly. Less knowledge about computer technology will be required. Clearly, there will be less and less need for a user to entertain the prospect of "ground-up" software development. The cost-efficiency of such a project will be more and more difficult to justify except in very unique applications.

The future is bright for the person with the vision and the imagination for using computers in education—whether for teaching or the administration of functions related to teaching.

Information Retrieval

At the risk of repetition, our society is truly an information society. Given the high value placed on information as a commodity, it is the responsibility of educators to teach, or at least to introduce students to the concepts of data/information access and retrieval systems. Already, commercial information systems are readily available to anyone with the necessary hardware and access rights.

One form of information retrieval which is currently gaining considerable popularity is the large time-sharing network such as The Source, Compu-Serve, Delphi, MicroNet, Dow Jones News Retrieval Service, the National Library of Medicine, NewsNet Inc., or the DIALOG Information Services, Inc. Basically, these on-line data bases are designed to serve the needs of the personal computer user. Various types of offerings are presently available.

The Source (Source Telecomputing Corporation) is the oldest and largest of the public information retrieval services. One of the main services of The Source (and a number of other time sharing services) is electronic mail which allows subscribers to send letters, files, and other information to other persons on the system. Bulletin board service is another popular feature which includes classified ads and information exchange. United Press International (UPI) is accessible to subscribers of The Source and, since the system is constantly updated, readers have access to the most current news available. Travel information, flight schedules, and hotel and airline reservations are other options provided. Business and financial information including prices of stocks and commodities are popular services of The Source. Additionally, interest is rapidly growing in the possibilities of shopping via a computer. Computer shopping is especially valuable when one is able to do comparison pricing. There are a number of other features available through The Source, but those mentioned here are among those most often used.

The Dow Jones data base provides current quotes on stocks, bonds, options, etc. as well as articles from *The Wall Street Journal* and *Barron's,* corporate financial histories, weather reports, and sports news. DIALOG, a subsidiary of Lockheed, is a collection of many data bases providing reference citations and abstracts from many professional journals. A keyword search system allows the user to access materials which match the specific descriptors provided. The selections cover a wide range of disciplines including engineering, medicine, language, and energy. In addition to reference citations and abstracts, DIALOG includes electronic yellow pages and government reports.

Electronic mail is a service provided by most large time sharing networks. Essentially, this provides for the *uploading* of a file (i.e., the transferring of a file from a sender's personal computer to the network's host computer) and the *downloading* of that file by the recipient at some later time. The file may simply be a friendly letter or it may be a lengthy manuscript. It may well be a sales representative's daily orders which are sent via the network to the main office. A special advantage of the host computer concept is the relaxation of the compatability requirements between two different types of computers. By taking advantage of evening telephone rates, the electronic mail system can be quite cost efficient for many applications. Perhaps in the not too distant future we will see student files and transcripts transmitted between schools by electronic mail. The technology exists today.

One of the potentialities of such networks is already being realized in school districts. That is the use of on-line bibliographic, article, and article abstract retrieval. Such capabilities have in the past been restricted to the larger libraries. Now educators, especially those in remote or rural areas, can obtain current and important educational literature quickly and conveniently.

A data base which has been used extensively in education for a number of years is ERIC (Educational Resources Information Center). ERIC contains over half a million citations including books, journal articles, research reports, newsletters, technical reports, and manuscripts in the field of education. The ERIC data base or content may be accessed or searched based on a Boolean logic format, i.e., a system of cross-referencing. By specifying a set of subject descriptors, one can obtain citations from the data base on a very well-defined topic of interest. For example, the descriptors "computer-assisted instruction" and "elementary education" would serve to identify all the entries which have these terms as appropriate identifiers. One could reduce the size of the set of citations even more by adding additional descriptors for increased specification (e.g., "mathematics" would limit the citations to a subject area of CAI in elementary education). The ERIC system also can provide abstracts of many entries in addition to detailed source information.

In order to take advantage of these time-sharing networks, the user must add both hardware and software to the computer to make it a communications device. This is accomplished using a *modem* (this is short for modulator and demodulator). Basically, the modem converts the signals from the computer into a form which can be transmitted through the telephone network. Most popular modems today are of the direct-connect type which means that they will plug into the standard modular phone jack. The modem can also be used to connect one computer to another remote computer. Once the communications hardware and software are in place, the user typically pays the on-line data base facility an initiation fee plus hourly use charges.

Communications equipment and computer communications are vast domains that education has barely explored. Much of the work is still in the pilot test stage but the future looks bright and promising. Computers standing alone are powerful educational devices. When this power can be shared, the possibilities really begin to expand.

Vocational Education

Computer-based education and instructional applications of computer-related technology have historically been associated with mathematics and science. This is no surprise, given the nature of computer programming and the interest that persons from a science background naturally have in computers. The trend has been toward the introduction of computing in the mathematics curriculum as an extension of topics that are addressed traditionally. One might argue that this was a natural phenomenon since the computer does support the teaching of mathematics and science quite readily. Complex functions can be quickly evaluated, graphs plotted, equations solved, hypotheses tested, and so on. Early CAI materials were often drill and practice programs to support the learning of basic math facts. Such materials were fairly easy to develop and were an extension of the flash card. Even though this is no longer the case and computer courseware and software is available for almost any area of the general curriculum, there continues to be one area overlooked in many schools—vocational education.

For many years, vocational education has been an integral part of the total public education system, particularly at the secondary and postsecondary levels. While the scope and content varies among the states and districts in the states, ranging from basic employability skills to sophisticated technologies, the vocational department remains an important and critical component of the total education program.

Why should educators be especially concerned about the role of computer-related technology in vocational education? In order to answer or even contemplate this question, we must think about the world of work in a high-technology society. One view is that everyone must develop math, science, and data-processing skills if they are to survive in the job market. Future jobs will be oriented more toward high technology and will require an ever-increasing knowledge of computing. Certainly this is a popular view and an exciting one to anticipate.

Another view offers a somewhat bleaker scenario. From this opposite perspective, many jobs will disappear and the workers replaced by automated devices. Many of the remaining jobs will require fewer job skills. The computer industry itself provides some support for this view. Only a few years ago the only user of a computer was a person who possessed programming skills and an in-depth knowledge of a particular system. The preparation that an individual received for entry into even a middle-skilled position was extensive. Now everyday users of computers for many important applications have no formal preparation in data processing, programming, or other previously requisite areas. This is a result of the advances made in both hardware and software. Much of the work performed in the past by higher-echelon professionals is now considered tedious tasks to be relegated to programmers and code writers. Turnkey and off-the-shelf systems are the direction of the industry. User friendliness is the keyword. There is little doubt that this momentum will continue.

What are the implications for vocational education given these two views of the future? Regardless of which view one chooses, it is clear that the rapid technological changes in computers and communications present a mandate to educators. Either public education will prepare young people to work in this technological environment or someone else (e.g., business and industry) will assume that function.

There are three general areas of vocational education: (1) consumer and homemaking; (2) business and office occupations; and (3) trade and industry. While the objectives of these areas may vary among states and school districts, one outcome criterion is common—placement in a job. This criterion can never be met unless the rapidly changing role of computer-related technology is considered in the development of the vocational curriculum. In this section several popular vocational courses in the above three areas will be reviewed along with the implications of computing in the various areas.

A crystal ball with images of future society isn't necessary to see the changes which will occur (and which have already occurred), for example, in the modern office. Heretofore, most information exchange has been handled by paper—written or typed correspondence. Word processors, beginning with the IBM Magnetic Tape Selectric Typewriter in 1964, have initiated a dramatic change in the ways that written material can be generated. Businesses quickly learned the improvements in productivity that word processing can bring, even in the simplest applications. Cost reductions can be achieved while correspondence, papers, and reports are made more attractive.

Costs associated with office automation suggest a number of extensions of word processing. For example, in many situations it is cheaper to store information normally contained on a page of paper on a computer disk than in a file cabinet. Also, retrieval of that page from the computer can be easier and more efficient than from the file cabinet. Additionally, once that page resides in the computer system, it can be transmitted to another office via electronic

Figure 5.14
Computer Applications in the Office. (Recognition Equipment, Inc., P.O. Box 660204, Dallas, TX 75266)

mail. Best evidence suggests that while all the changes in the office will come gradually, they will be conveniently available in the not too distant future.

Many office accounting functions are supported by microcomputers. Accounts payable, accounts receivable, payroll, invoice, tax, and inventory software are available for even the smallest operations. Many organizations also use the spreadsheet and data base management programs discussed earlier in this chapter for office functions.

As the office of the future becomes a reality (and in many ways it is a reality now), the skills expected of the work force will continually change. Persons not equipped with skills to meet the changing requirements will be at a considerable disadvantage. Business education and related vocational curricula must recognize and even anticipate the changes. Failure will mean that our classes will be as obsolete as the mechanical adding machine.

Agriculture is another part of vocational education which must be mindful of the role of the computer. Today the efficiency of farms is enhanced with programs for improving crop yields, for calculating field size and population, for formulating fertilizer, for protein balancing for cattle, for calculating cow-calf profitability, and many other functions.

Home economics programs can profit from applications of computing. Applications software for diet planning, nutrition, household and personal finances, home inventory, interior design, and filing systems are available today and will certainly be even more commonplace in the near future.

Industry and industrial technology continue to receive more and more publicity regarding the changes that can be expected. Whereas computers have been used for years in certain large industries (petroleum and chemical, for

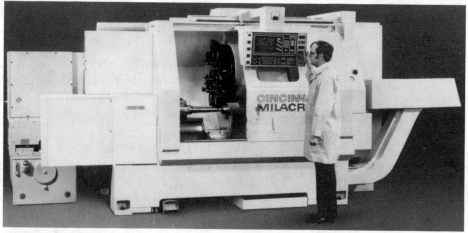

Figure 5.15
Advanced Computer Lathe. (Photograph courtesy Cincinnati Milacron,
Cincinnati Milacron Inc., 4701 Marburg Ave., Cincinnati, OH 45209)

example), cheap computers are becoming more and more common in smaller
plants. Process control is an illustration. Workers will require skills to program machines to perform certain tasks rather than the skills to actually perform a task.

For example, the industrial computer lathe shown in figure 5.15 contains a
stand-alone microcomputer, video display, keyboard, cassette recorder, peripherals interface, and 16k of user program memory. It can be programmed
manually by the operator or from programs stored on cassette. It can also be
interfaced with another computer.

Robotics has emerged as a potent force in manufacturing. Assembly line
workers will gradually be replaced by robot arms under the direction of a very
sophisticated computer. Even now, a robot for the home can be purchased
and assembled from a kit (see figure 5.16).

Figure 5.16
Heath Company's Robot. (Heath
Company, Benton Harbor, MI 49022)

The electronics industry of today bears little resemblance to that industry only ten to twelve years ago. Whereas transistors replaced the vacuum tube in television, radio, and other systems in the 1960s, integrated circuits have now replaced those transistors. Processes for component testing, repair, and replacement have also radically changed.

Computer-aided design (CAD) and computer-aided manufacturing (CAM) are commonplace in the large industrial areas and will become more and more ubiquitous as the technology progresses. Layout and drafting is often performed on a CRT. In some applications, performance of a design can then be simulated and evaluated before actual physical production is begun. Computer aided drafting systems also permit three-dimensional drawing. Once data and coordinates are entered, the drawing can be scaled, rotated, dimensioned, and repositioned.

This section has provided only a glimpse of what the present and future of computer applications in vocational education portends. There are many problems to be addressed. Costs of the hardware in some of the illustrations given here place these types of classes out of reach of most schools. For example, a programmable milling machine for the industrial arts shop may cost approximately $25,000 as compared to a nonprogrammable machine for about $5000. A computer aided drafting work station complete with microcomputer, software, and necessary peripherals may cost in excess of $10,000. Schools must be able to use equipment for a long period of time. High-technology equipment often becomes dated or even obsolete very quickly.

Finding qualified instructors and keeping them abreast of new developments is very difficult. Another major problem is keeping these instructors in education when they can usually earn considerably more money in industry. Schools must find ways to cultivate partnerships with business and industry. This association will be of value to all concerned. The persons to benefit most will be the students and, after all, the schools exist to serve them. The mandate for vocational education is clear.

The Evaluation and Selection of Software

The preceding topics in this chapter have addressed the applications of computers in education. As educators begin to incorporate these applications of computing into the curriculum, critical questions arise concerning the acquisition of good software. The purpose, therefore, of this section is to introduce evaluation and selection criteria which will assist in this process.

When microcomputers were first introduced into schools a few years ago, software selection was not a problem. There simply was very little software available from which to choose. As instructional requirements for software were determined, the programs were often written by teachers or computer center personnel. This, of course, was an expensive, time-consuming method and didn't always result in quality programs.

As "micro-mania" spread during the late 1970s and early 1980s, a veritable flood of software began to appear. Some of it was quite good, while much of it was poorly designed and written. Entrepreneurs in their basements nationwide began developing software for almost any imaginable application—including education.

Fortunately, this situation has changed in recent years. Computer users have become increasingly knowledgeable and sophisticated. As consumers, they have demanded better software. The economics of the personal computer industry have also made it lucrative for the larger companies and the established textbook publishers to enter the software field. Now there are hundreds of software publishers marketing thousands of computer-based educational programs and software packages.

The effect of this synergy between the consumer need for software and the market/economic motivation (both fueled by an exponential increase in numbers of computers) is a "good news–bad news" story. The ability to acquire quality software has increased tremendously. However, the volume of available software has resulted in a situation where it is almost impossible for educators to keep up with what is new, good, and appropriate software.

One partial solution to this problem is the use of national data on software evaluation. Several organizations have been involved in this effort including the MicroSIFT project at the Northwest Regional Educational Laboratory (NWREL) in Portland, Oregon, CONDUIT at The University of Iowa, and the EDIE Institute. Additionally, a number of journals, magazines, and professional organizations publish reviews and critiques of educational software.

Even though there are reviews and evaluations of software available, it is important that educators be able to evaluate software and make their own determinations with regard to quality and applicability.

An excellent software evaluation guide was developed by the Office of Research and Development at The University of Iowa. This guide includes two sets of evaluative criteria—one for technical issues and the other for instructional considerations. The guide is presented in figures 5.17 and 5.19. Figure 5.18 presents a summary of descriptive terms used in the instructional evaluation.

In summary. Computers, no matter how sophisticated and complex, are no better than the software. It is, therefore, critical that educators become actively involved in the review, evaluation, and selection of software appropriate for their own applications. Software which is useful for one teacher's application may not be at all useful for another teacher. Instructional requirements, in part, determine computing requirements. This is a simple but important concept. Stated another way, don't let the software, no matter how "good" it is, determine how instruction should be offered.

Software Evaluation Guide: Instructional

There are tremendous differences in software instructional design and subject matter, and there is no single list of criteria that will fit all. Use only the categories and questions you feel will fit the program you are evaluating. Responses can range from one word to a paragraph. No question on this list is intended as a prescription of what should be in a program, they are only questions to consider. Please discuss these topics in the order listed below.

Documentation

1. Is the documentation useful for the instructor and/or the students?
2. Are the objectives given?
3. Are suggested uses and activities given and effective?
4. Are prerequisites indicated?

Introductory Part of Lesson

1. Is the program interesting?
2. How are the objectives given? (Are they necessary?)
3. Does the program require prior knowledge?
4. Is a pretest given? (Is it necessary?)
5. Are the instructions clear?
6. Are the instructions complete?

Presentation of Information

1. Is the dialogue appropriately personalized?
2. Are necessary terms well defined?
3. Is the reading level in agreement with publisher's claim?
4. Is the text clear and concise?
5. Are other information sources necessary to use the program?
6. Is sufficient time provided for responses?
7. Are graphics used for important information?
8. Is color used effectively?
9. Are diagrams well labeled?
10. Are animations relevant and visually clear?
11. Are animations and graphics distracting?
12. Is the screen lay-out appropriate? (lettering, spacing, graphics)
13. Is sound used appropriately?
14. Is the information provided or taught when needed?

Program Questioning Technique

1. Are questioning intervals appropriate?
2. Are responses easy to enter?
3. Is the computer expected response format clear?
4. Are multiple responses needed?
5. Can students be caught in a question loop? (questions & responses repeated)
6. Are exercises modeled in the program?

Feedback

1. Is the feedback appropriate? (corrective, supportive, immediate)
2. Is graphic and audio feedback used?

Sequence

1. Does the program follow a logical order?
2. Is the information given in appropriate increments?
3. Are menus appropriate and clear?
4. Are the transitions between statements or lessons clear?
5. Is instruction individualized for all levels of student ability?

Motivation

1. For what grade levels is the content appropriate (interesting/motivational)?
2. If appropriate, does the program keep score?
3. Does the program provide progress reports?
4. Do the graphics increase motivation?
5. Is the program competitive against time, other students, or the computer information?
6. Is the length motivationally correct?

Content

1. Is the content complete?
2. Is the content accurate?
3. Is the content significant or relevant?
4. Are the key concepts taught well?
5. Does the knowledge presented integrate well with prior learning?

Student Control

1. Does the student have adequate control of the program?
2. Are pauses appropriate?
3. Can students take shortcuts?

Overall

1. Describe the program purpose: (See Descriptive Terms list.) Is it effective?
2. Does the program succeed in its objectives?
3. Can a student work independently? (no teacher input or help)
4. Discuss the ease of use (student and/or teacher).
5. Discuss how the program might be implemented in the classroom.
6. Discuss the levels of thinking required of the student.
7. Does the program challenge a student's creative ability?
8. Does the program utilize the computer or could the same information/learning be accomplished with another form of media?
9. Does the program provide a management system?
10. Is there cultural or sexual stereotyping?

Figure 5.17

Software Evaluation Guide: Instructional (Figures reprinted from *The Executive Review*, 4(4), 1984)

Descriptive Terms*

Authoring: assists in creating or modifying computer programs

Classroom Management: program is organized to record student behavior, responses, or scores

Creative Activity: any synthesis activity where students create and/or use their imagination

Demonstration: shows an activity such as an experiment or process

Descriptions: provides information with little or no student interaction

Drill and Practice: reviews content with no instruction, can include timed activities and controlled response time

Game: any program using a contest format which may or may not be educational

Logic and Problem Solving: requires students to analyze and/or apply reasoning

Programming: specifically designed to teach a computer language

Simulations: creates an artificial situation that requires the student to participate

Tool: programs which help students or teachers accomplish a task

Tutorial: specifically designed to teach students new information and/or skills

(*see Software Evaluation Guide: Instructional)

Figure 5.18

Software Review—Summary of Descriptive Terms. (Figures reprinted from *The Executive Review,* 4(4), 1984)

References

Anderson, R. E., & Klassen, D. L. (1981). A conceptual framework for developing computer literacy instruction. *AEDS Journal, 14*(3), 128–150.

Burns, P. K. (1981). *A quantitative synthesis of research findings relative to the pedagogical effectiveness of computer-assisted mathematics instruction in elementary and secondary schools.* Unpublished doctoral dissertation, The University of Iowa.

Burns, P. K., & Bozeman, W. C. (1981, October). Computer-assisted instruction and mathematics achievement: Is there a relationship? *Educational Technology, 21*(10), 32–39.

Charp, S., Bozeman, W. C., Altschuler, H., D'Orazio, R., & Spuck, D. W. (1982). *Layman's guide to the use of computers in education.* Washington, DC: Association for Educational Data Systems.

Coburn, P., Kelman, P., Roberts, N., Snyder, T. F., Walt, D. H., & Weiner, C. (1982). *Practical guide to computers in education.* Reading, MA: Addison-Wesley.

Software Evaluation Guide: Technical

Listed below are the items which have been tested for technical operation of the program. For the most part the responses are intended to be descriptive of the program and its use. Some space is provided at the end for specific comments about the operation of the program and ways it could be improved.

Package name:
Package #:
Routing:

Equipment Needs
Computer:
Model #:
Screen B&W: Color:
Columns:
Number of disk drives:
Language required:
Memory required:

Peripherals
Additional diskettes:
Printer:
Paddles:
Joystick:
Voice synthesizer:
Music synthesizer:
Graphics tablet:
Other:

Software Design
Entry code can be modified:
Program is protected:
Ctrl C restart:
Power-off restart:
Menu driven:
Reset protection:
Write protected:
Diskettes initialized automatically:

Start-up Procedure
Instructions available:
Self-boot with power-on:
Simple command (PR#6):

Documentation
Designed for:
Indexed:
Organized by:
Initially requires sequence:
Glossary:
Reading level:
Information mapping applied:
Overall usefulness:

Ease of Use
Consistent response modes:
Uses key conventions (Q = Quit):
Easy to end program:
Easy access to menu & earlier parts of the program:
Length of pauses controlled by:
Disk switching required:

Presentation
Letter font appropriate:
Can suppress sound:
Graphics are clear:
Use of flashing lights:
Screen scrolling:
Colors are distinct and easy to use:
Does program fail?

Physical
Jacket provided for diskette:
Packaging format:

Comments

Figure 5.19
Software Evaluation Guide: Technical

Douglas, B. G., Belt, S. L., Owen, S. P., & Chan, N. (1977). *System design manual for the unified Wisconsin system of instructional management.* Unpublished paper. Madison, Wisconsin Research and Development Center for Cognitive Learning.

Edwards, J., Norton, S., Taylor, S., Weiss, M., & VanDusseldorp, R. (1975, November). How effective is CAI: A review of the research. *Educational Leadership, 33,* 147–153.

Eisele, J. E. (1981, October). Computers in the schools: Now that we have them. . . ? *Educational Technology, 21*(10), 24–27.

Jamison, D., Suppes, P., & Wells, S. (1974). The effectiveness of alternative instructional media: A survey. *Review of Educational Research, 44,* 1–67.

Kulik, J. A., Bangert, R. L., & Williams, G. W. (1983). Effects of computer-based teaching on secondary school students. *Journal of Educational Psychology, 75*(1), 19–26.

Levin, H. M., & Woo, L. (1981). An evaluation of the costs of computer-assisted instruction. *Economies of Education Review, 1*(1), 1–25.

Luehrmann, A. (1981, Winter). Computer literacy. *EDUCOM Bulletin,* 14–15, 24.

Magidson, E. M. (1978). Issue overview: Trends in computer-assisted instruction. *Educational Technology, 18,* 5–8.

McIsaac, D. N., & Baker, F. B. (1981). Computer-managed instruction system implementation on a microcomputer. *Educational Technology, 21,* 40–46.

Molnar, A. (1978, Fall). The next great crisis in American education: Computer literacy. *AEDS Journal, 12*(1), 11–20.

Papert, S. A. (1980). Computers and learning. In M. L. Dertouzos & J. Moses (Eds.), *The computer age: A twenty year view.* Cambridge, MA: MIT Press.

Roecks, A. L. (1976, November). *CMI Project activities.* Paper presented at the Annual Meeting of the Wisconsin Research Association, Milwaukee.

Rugg, T., & Feldman, P. (1981). *32 BASIC programs for the apple,* 61–68. Beaverton, OR: Dilithium.

Spuck, D. W. (1981). An analysis of the cost-effectiveness of CAI and factors associated with its successful implementation. *AEDS Journal, 15*(1), 10–22.

Spuck, D. W., & Bozeman, W. C. (1978). Pilot test and evaluation of a system of computer-managed instruction. *AEDS Journal, 12*(1), 31–41.

Thomas, D. B. (1979, Spring). The effectiveness of computer-assisted instruction in secondary schools. *AEDS Journal, 12*(3), 103–116.

United States Department of Education, National Commission on Excellence in Education (1983, April). *A nation at risk: The imperative for educational reform.* Washington, DC: U.S. Government Printing Office.

Walt, M. (1982, October). What is logo? *Creative Computing, 8*(10), 112–129.

Suggested Readings

Administrative Data Processing

Edwards, J. (1983, July). The desktop buyer's guide to electronic spreadsheet programs. *Desktop Computing,* 38–43.

Good, P. (1982, January). Beyond VisiCalc. *Popular Computing,* 38–42.

Good, P. (1982, April). Choosing the right business software. *Popular Computing,* 33–38.

Good, P. (1982, April). Word-processing software directory. *Popular Computing, 33–38.*

Hooper, G. (1982, February). Your office—Out of the dark ages. *Electronic Education, 16–21.*

McWilliams, P. (1982, February). An introduction to word processing. *Popular Computing, 17–19.*

Marshall, D. G. (1982, Summer). Purchasing a microprocessor system for administrative use in schools. *AEDS Journal, 183–195.*

Mau, E. E. (1983, June). In search of a word processor. *Creative Computing, 12–30.*

Ross, S. (1983, June). Spreadsheet programs. *Call A.P.P.L.E., 17–21.*

Shea, T., & Chin, K. (1983, January 17). *Infoworld's* guide to word-processing programs. *Infoworld, 27–31.*

Computer-Assisted Instruction

Bork, A. (1981). *Learning with computers.* Bedford, MA: Digital Press.

Burke, R. L. (1982). *CAI Sourcebook.* Englewood Cliffs: Prentice-Hall, Inc.

Cruikshank, D. R., & Telfer, R. (1980). Classroom games and simulations. *Theory into Practice, 19*(1), 75–80.

Dick, W. (1981). Instructional design models: Future trends and issues. *Educational Technology, 21*(7), 29–32.

Doerr, C. (1979). *Microcomputers and the 3 R's.* Rochelle Park, NJ: Hayden Book Co.

Gagne, R. M. (1980). Is educational technology in phase? *Educational Technology, 20*(2), 7–14.

Gagne, R. M. (1982). An interview with Robert M. Gagne. *Educational Technology, 22*(6), 11–15.

Gagne, R. M., Wager, W., & Rojas, A. (1981). Planning and authoring computer-assisted lessons. *Educational Technology, 21*(9), 17–26.

Landa, R. K. (1984). *Creating courseware.* New York: Harper and Row Publishers.

Taylor, R., (1980). *The computer in the school: Tutor, tool, tutee.* New York: Teacher's College Press.

Computer Literacy

Becker, W. E., & Davis R. W. (1983, December). An economic model of training in an industrial setting. Can the potential become reality? *Journal of Instructional Development, 6*(2), 26–32.

Educational Equality Project (1983, May). *Academic preparation for college: What students need to know and be able to do.* New York: College Board.

Luehrmann, A. (1980, July). Computer literacy—A national crisis and a solution for it. *BYTE, 98–102.*

Magarell, J. (1981, January 19). Universal access to personal computers is urged for college students, professors. *Chronicle of Higher Education,* p. 1.

U.S. Congress, Office of Technology Assessment (1982, September). *Information technology and its impact on American education.* Washington, DC.

Computer-Managed Instruction

Baker, F. B. (1978). *Computer-managed instruction: Theory and practice.* Englewood Cliffs: Educational Technology Publications.

Bozeman, W. C. (1978). Human factor considerations in the design of systems of computer-managed instruction. *AEDS Journal, 11*(4), 89–96.

Bozeman, W. C. (1979, May). Computer-managed instruction—Is it a system for your school? *THE Journal,* 50–53.

Bozeman, W. C. (1979). Computer-managed instruction: State of the art. *AEDS Journal, 12*(3), 117–137.

Dagnon, C., & Spuck, D. W. (1977, February). A role for computers in individualizing education—and it's not teaching. *Phi Delta Kappan,* 460–462.

Spuck, D. W., Bozeman, W. C., & Lawrence, B. F. (1977). *Evaluation of the Wisconsin system for instructional management.* Technical Report No. 438. Madison: Wisconsin Research and Development Center for Cognitive Learning.

Evaluation and Selection of Software

Barden, W., Jr. (1983, January). How to buy software. *Popular Computing,* 54–57.

Cohen, V. B. (1983). Criteria for the evaluation of microcomputer courseware. *Educational Technology, 23*(1), 9–14.

Hammer, M. (1983, June 15). Software evaluation. *Computerworld,* 53–59.

Jones, N. B. (Ed.) (1983). *Evaluation of educational software: A guide to guides.* Austin, TX: Southwest Educational Development Laboratory.

Kansky, B., Heck, W., & Johnson, J. (1981, November). Getting hard-nosed about software: Guidelines for evaluating computerized instructional materials. *Mathematics Teacher,* 600–603.

Molek, R., & Switzer, D. (1984, January). Educational software: An evaluation process. *The Executive Review, 4*(4).

Northwest Regional Educational Laboratory (1983). *Administrative and instructional management package evaluation.* Portland, OR: NWREL.

Northwest Regional Educational Laboratory (1983). *Evaluator's guide for microcomputer-based instructional application.* Eugene, OR: International Council for Computers in Education.

Roblyer, M. D. (1983, in press). Reviewing the reviewers: Who's who and what's current in courseware review efforts. *Executive Educator.*

Signer, B. (1983, October). How do teacher and student evaluations of CAI software compare? *The Computing Teacher, 11*(3), 34–36.

Standards for software? *Instructional Innovator,* 1982, *27*(6), 15.

Welsh, R. (1982, October 13). Qualities of good software. *Management Information Systems Week,* 38.

General

Becker, H. J. (1982). *Microcomputers in the classroom—Dreams and realities.* Report No. 319. Baltimore, MD: The John Hopkins University, Center for Social Organization of Schools.

Becker, H. J. (1983). School uses of microcomputers: Report of a national survey. Baltimore, MD: The John Hopkins University, Center for Social Organization of Schools.

Culp, G., & Nickles, H. (1983). *An apple for the teacher.* Monterey, CA: Brooks/Cole Publishing Company.

Dennis, J. R., & Kansky, R. J. (1984). *Instructional computing.* Glenview, IL: Scott, Foresman and Company.

Eisele, J. E. (Ed.) (1980). Computers in instruction. *Journal of Research and Development in Education, 14*(1). Athens, GA: University of Georgia.

Harper, D. O., & Stewart, J. H. (1983). *RUN: Computer education.* Monterey: Brooks/Cole Publishing Company.

Hofmeister, A. (1984). *Microcomputer applications in the classroom.* New York: Holt, Rinehart and Winston.

Joiner, L. M., Vensel, G. J., Ross, J. D., & Silverstein, B. J. (1982). *Microcomputers in education.* Holmes Beach, FL: Learning Publications, Inc.

Judd, D. H., & Judd, R. C. (1984). *Mastering the micro.* Glenview, IL: Scott, Foresman and Company.

O'Neill, H. F. (Ed.) (1981). *Computer-based instruction: A state of the art assessment.* New York: Academic Press.

Papert, S. (1980). *Mindstorms: Children, computers and powerful ideas.* New York: Basic Books, Inc.

Rose, S. N. (1982). Barriers to the use of educational technologies and recommendations to promote and increase their use. *Educational Technology, 22*(12), 12–15.

Van Dusseldorp, R., Spuck, D. W., Atkinson, G. (Eds.) (1983). Applications of microcomputers for instruction and educational management (Special Issue). *AEDS Journal, 17*(1, 2).

Vockell, E. L., & Rivers, R. H. (1984). *Instructional computing for today's teachers.* New York: Macmillan Publishing Co.

Willis, J. W., Johnson, D. L., & Dixon, P. N. (1983). *Computers, teaching, and learning.* Beaverton, OR: Dilithium Press.

6
Societal Implications

Personal Privacy

Invasion of personal privacy and the possibility for oppressive governmental control of citizens have been among the most often expressed concerns related to information processing. Possible loss of privacy is not an unfounded concern when large files of personal data are collected in centralized or networked computer systems.

What is privacy? What is this domain considered by many to be so threatened by computers? C. F. Westin addressed this question at the 1983 World Computer Congress:

> Almost all definitions of privacy agree on a core concept: that privacy is the claim of an individual to determine what information about himself or herself should be known to others. This also involves when such information will be communicated or obtained, and what uses will be made of it by others. In addition, many definitions of privacy—my own included—would add a claim to privacy by groups and associations as well as individuals, and also a limited (largely temporary) right of privacy for government bodies as well. (1983, p. 733)

Certainly record-keeping systems, either by government or private organizations, are nothing new. However, the introduction of computer-based record systems in the 1950s elevated public concerns considerably. Massive data files are one thing. Rapid and economical remote access to those files is something entirely different. The spectre of an Orwellian society becomes more of a potential reality.

For example, one system which has attracted national attention for several years is the FBI's National Crime Information Center (NCIC) which began operating in 1965. This massive data base contains millions of records related to wanted persons, vehicles, license plates, firearms, boats, and criminal histories. NCIC links thousands of law enforcement agencies nationwide and in Canada. Thousands of inquiries and transactions occur daily, raising the potential for abuse by both individuals and government.

Numerous other government data bases exist on local, state, and national levels. These include such systems as health care/hospital records, psychiatric center records, motor vehicle registrations, tax and revenue files, welfare and unemployment records, and social services files. Each of these data systems may represent a minimal threat to personal privacy. However, collectively (assuming the systems could be linked), they could pose a considerable threat. Clearly, there must be a balance between the advantages of such immensely powerful applications of technology and the risks to society as a whole.

There are many other applications besides law enforcement which have the potential for misuse and abuse. Electronic funds transfer (EFT), credit cards, point-of-sale (POS) terminals, and computer-based stock exchange systems involve records of all user transactions. The nature of many such systems offers the danger of intrusion by individuals and government. For example, credit cards and point-of-sale terminals reduce or even eliminate the use of currency. When a purchase is made, the individual's bank account can be electronically debited. While this is often convenient and more efficient than a cash transaction, it leaves a "paper trail"—figuratively speaking. Electronic records are maintained which could be amassed about a given individual revealing his or her purchases, the location of the purchases, total financial transactions over some period of time, or other potentially important information. Howard (1984) reported five threats to individual privacy as identified by the National Commission on Electronic Funds Transfers.

1. EFT is creating financial records where none existed before.
2. EFT is increasing the amount of information in an individual's financial records.
3. EFT is causing financial records to be maintained in electronically readable form, thus making the records easier to retrieve and manipulate.
4. On-line real-time EFT systems can be used to locate the system's customers.
5. EFT may increase the number of organizations with access to an individual's records. (p. 16)

In a similar sense, electronic mail presents an opportunity for personal privacy invasion. Electronic mail typically involves the creation of computer files which are transmitted via telephone. These files are received by another computer. The communication (mail) is then delivered electronically (e.g., viewed at a terminal) or delivered in hard copy form. Access, legal or otherwise, may be easier because of the electronic storage and transmission.

Fortunately, the United States has enacted a number of privacy protection laws at both the federal and the state level. Two examples are the Privacy Act of 1974 and the Financial Institutions Regulations Act (1978). Many states have additional laws which regulate access and use of information. While this area continues to receive the attention of legislative bodies, public attention and scrutiny remains critical. Organizations, both public and private, enamoured with the power of information-processing technology may not foresee the pitfalls and dangers. Assurances from technologists that the system works and is safe are not sufficient. Three Mile Island serves to remind us of those promises.

As educators, we have a special concern and commitment regarding privacy within the American educational system. The rapidly emerging applications of computers for student record data bases will require increased attention to rights of individual privacy. Even though existing laws, policies, and procedures may be generally adequate, a close and continuing examination is necessary. Additional policies and standards which may be required as the applications evolve must be developed through close cooperation of educators and data-processing professionals.

Artificial Intelligence

"Can a machine think?" This is a question that many of us have probably pondered or even debated from time to time in one form or another. Usually the discussion includes some attempt to define "thinking" or to clarify what it means to say that a machine is "intelligent," and then moves toward descriptions of the capabilities of certain machines.

These certainly are not new questions. They have been debated and argued for many years. One of the earliest objections to the notion of a thinking machine was from Augusta Ada Byron, Countess of Lovelace, who worked with Charles Babbage on the Analytical Engine in the 1800s and has the distinction of being the world's first computer programmer. (The programming language, Ada, is named in her honor). Her principal objection was that a machine can never do anything really new. In other words, machines only do what people tell them to do.

In 1950, A. M. Turing, a famous British mathematician, raised the question in an important paper entitled "Can a Machine Think?" Turing, in an effort to address his own question, replaced that question by a different question which in turn described a game called the *imitation game*. The game would be played by three people: a man, a woman, and an interrogator. The object of the game was for the interrogator (who stays in another room) to determine which of the other two was the man and which was the woman. The interrogator would ask questions (voices were masked) and the responses from the two might or might not be truthful. Turing then asked the question, "What would happen when a machine takes the part of (the man) in the game?" In other words, would the interrogator decide wrongly as often when the game was played with a machine as when played between a man and a woman? This question replaced Turing's original question, "Can a machine think?" This interesting test continues to challenge the machine.

Of course, computers don't think in the usual or comprehensive sense of the word. And it is doubtful that they ever will. There are some similarities between the logic systems ("gates") and their interconnections in a computer and the networks of neurons and axons in the human brain. The human brain, however, possesses a wonderful ability to think about many things at the same time, to form associations, and to receive information through perceptions as well as the senses. It can also process these in more than one way. The psychologist Carl Jung called these alternate processing modes *thinking* and *feeling*. Most computers process data in a serial or sequential fashion. This is fine for a numerical problem but it doesn't necessarily work as well for even the most trivial everyday problem, decision, or task.

Artificial intelligence is an area of computer science which is concerned with making the computer emulate the human thought process. Stated another way, artificial intelligence enables a machine to perform some task generally considered possible only for an intelligent being.

The initial surge of interest in artificial intelligence was in the 1950s with such applications as language translation and pattern recognition. Language translation was not very successful; researchers found in every attempt that a large part of the text could not be translated because of contextual problems. Another early application was pattern recognition (letters, objects, etc.). This too was not very successful, especially in the case of spatial patterns. Given these early unsuccessful attempts to create computer hardware and software which could model human reasoning, artificial intelligence fell into disfavor in the 1960s.

Renewed and intense interest is now being shown in this area. In fact, it is often referred to as the fifth generation of computer development. Rather than being concerned with philosophical arguments about artificial intelligence and tests such as Turing's, scientists and designers are pushing toward use and application. Improved usability of computers, better human interface, and practical applications are among the present artificial intelligence goals. These goals are being realized through advances in natural language processing, reduction of requirements for numerical or coded data, and expanded input modes such as visual images.

One of the particularly exciting areas of artificial intelligence is the *expert system*. Basically, the expert system is a computer system which models the knowledge and reasoning process employed by a human expert. Essentially, these systems use decision techniques, rules, and logic in a manner similar to human experts. The expert system "thinks" the way a human expert thinks. Such systems can be extremely useful because they are applicable in routine, practical, real-world problems. The user tells the computer what the problem is in an English or natural language dialogue. The computer determines how to solve the problem using its knowledge base and mechanisms for problem solving.

Expert systems are being used with success in geology, oil exploration, medicine, business, and many other areas. PROSPECTOR is an example of an expert system. The system is given information about possible sites and it evaluates them for potential mineral deposits. A program called CADUCEUS is used in internal medicine. Information about a patient is given to the computer which, in turn, provides a medical diagnosis. A similar system, MYCIN, diagnoses bacterial infections and prescribes treatment. Other expert systems can diagnose problems in complex apparatus like oil rigs or a space shuttle, can aid analysis and synthesis of DNA, can enhance economic and corporate decisions, and can even tutor students.

Scientists are cautiously optimistic about the future of expert systems and artificial intelligence. Don't expect a computer like HAL (from the movie ("2001: A Space Odyssey") or a robot like Gort (from the movie "The Day the Earth Stood Still"). Intelligent systems will become commonplace in specialized applications just as they are now in cars, sewing machines, microwave ovens, climate control systems, and so on. Expert systems will be available for a myriad of personal computing applications such as taxes, personal finance, career decisions, games, and general automated control systems.

The integration of artificial intelligence into our society must be guided by an informed citizenry. Many of the decisions related to artificial intelligence systems are too important and too critical to be left in the hands of the "experts in expert systems." The responsibility of education cannot be over-stated.

Economic Effects and Implications

Much has been written and said about our industrial society's transition into an information society. And rightly so; this transition has affected and will continue to affect almost every individual. As John Naisbitt so accurately stated in his bestseller *Megatrends*, "It (the information society) is no longer an idea—it is a reality."

The basic notion of an information society is not at all complex. Basically, in such a society, the economy is built upon information as the principal commodity as opposed to typical manufactured goods and products. Workers in an information society are concerned with the production, handling, and communication of knowledge and information rather than the production of goods.

Consider for a moment the dramatic changes that have occurred in the composition of our nation's work force. Farmers, for example, comprised over one-third of the work force at the beginning of this century. Now they represent only about 3 percent of the nation's workers. Laborers or persons involved in manufacturing operations comprised the major portion of occupations during the middle of this century. Now only about a tenth of the work force is engaged in occupations related to the production of goods. The majority of us work in jobs related to service, information, and knowledge. These "information workers" work in a variety of occupations including clerks, secretaries, managers, teachers, lawyers, doctors, nurses, bureaucrats, politicians, government officials, librarians, computer programmers, media reporters, engineers, technicians, systems analysts, and many others. Recent research by David Birch at MIT shows that of the almost 20 million new jobs created in the 1970s, only about 5 percent were in manufacturing. Almost 90 percent were in information, knowledge, or service jobs.

Many existing occupations are requiring an increasing knowledge of computers and information processing. Corporate executives and clerks alike find themselves faced with the need to become familiar with the use and application of data-processing technologies. Automation in the office, factory, store, and supermarket is progressing at an amazing rate. Workers have been replaced by robots; typists by word processors (which may include many functions beyond entering text); bank tellers have been replaced by teller terminals. The advent of automation, in which computers play a critical role, has served to create many new occupations. These new jobs, of course, require new and different skills as compared with the jobs eliminated. This trend will probably continue into the near future—but probably not forever.

The role of our nation's educational systems in this changing economic society cannot be overstated. As stated in the National Commission on Excellence in Education Report:

> The people of the United States need to know that individuals in our
> society who do not possess the levels of skill, literacy, and training
> essential to this new era will be effectively disenfranchised, not simply
> from the material rewards that accompany competent performance, but
> also from the chance to participate fully in our national life.

The preparation of students for entry into this service, technological, and knowledge-based work force places a new set of demands and expectations on our educational institutions. These demands come at a time when our schools are being judged harshly. There is little doubt at this time that our country is lagging behind a number of other developed nations in mathematics and science education. If, in fact, our graduates are as scientifically and technologically illiterate as has been suggested, our citizenry will be deprived of the rewards and privileges which they have a right to expect.

Computer-Based Crime

As we have seen throughout our discussions, computer-based technology promises to open many new frontiers in our lives. Unfortunately, one of the products of this technology is computer-based crime or *computer crime*. White-collar crime and computer crime are regrettable realities of the information society—realities that are reaching significant proportions. Such crimes may assume many forms, ranging from fraud, embezzlement, thefts, blackmail, and espionage to illegal copying of popular software (software piracy).

In order to gain some perspective on this subject, let us begin by examining the scope of the problem and some examples. Possible types of crimes may include actual theft of inventory, theft of computer hardware services (e.g., computer time), theft of data (for re-sale, espionage, blackmail, etc.), and alteration or misrepresentation of data (e.g., tampering with election results, credit records, criminal records, or assets/earnings data).

There are many reasons for this increase in computer crime. Two prominent reasons are (a) the increasing involvement of individuals with computers and (b) the nature of storage, handling, and transmission of data in computer systems. In the first case, it is now quite common to have many persons in an organization use a computer; whereas only a few years ago usage would have been restricted to a few persons. This access is no longer confined to executives, programmers, technicians, and the like. Clerical personnel, in fact, may constitute the largest percent of users, due to increasing data entry and retrieval. In the second case, the nature of information handling is considerably different when compared with previous paper systems. Records, files, and transactions in paper systems are visible and are usually handled, at least in part, by hand. In computer systems, they are less visible and the likelihood of the detection of illicit use or alteration is reduced considerably. Computer systems encourage centralization of files through integrated data base management systems. While such systems may greatly increase operating efficiencies, they also make the work of a criminal easier.

The possible motives which lead to computer crime are numerous and complex. Such a discussion is clearly beyond the scope and purpose of this text. However, personal gain, including direct and indirect economic gain, certainly ranks high among motives. Changing a personnel record may provide direct personal economic gain. For example, suppose a school district uses a centralized data base for school employees. One element of this file might be a teacher's tenure or number of years of service. The payroll and accounting office would access this record when payroll checks are generated. A simple change of one number would change the employee's placement on the salary schedule and the amount paid. If appropriate measures in the audit trail were taken, the change might not be detected. The personnel file could be tampered with in other ways also, such as level of certification, tax-withholding claims, hours of overtime and so on. Imagination is the only limit once illegal entry is gained.

While direct personal economic gain through fraud or embezzlement is the most obvious motive for computer crime, motives related to indirect personal gain can result in crimes equally serious and costly. Examples of such crimes include:

1. *Unauthorized use of computer resources and services.* This may range from using an organization's computer facilities to play games to the use of computing resources for personal economic gain. In either case, computers are used for purposes other than those for which they were intended.
2. *Theft of data.* Usually data are not physically stolen but are copied. Such data might be an organization's records, mailing lists, confidential information, or other files of potential economic value.
3. *Falsification of data.* Crimes of this nature are both serious and often quite difficult to detect. Essentially, these crimes involve misrepresenta-

tion or alteration of data to achieve some objective. Examples include change of voting records, personal files, health records, product test data, financial records, and the like.

4. *Theft of software*. Software obtained through unauthorized copying represents a major loss of revenue to vendors. Basically, every copied program, whether a game or a complex business program, is a lost sale for the vendor.

Problems related to computer crime span an enormous scale of magnitude. At one end of the continuum, we have software piracy which may be as simple as the copying of a game for a friend. On the other end of the continuum, we have crimes involving the theft of millions of dollars. A few true cases may help illustrate the significance of the problem.

Not so long ago a bank teller embezzled over a million dollars in just a few years by making electronic transfers from inactive accounts and by diverting deposits to his own account. In another amazing case, over 200 railroad cars were diverted by computer. As they arrived at a specified location, they were unloaded, resulting in losses of over $100,000. A common swindle in many cases has involved the use of the computer to "skim" small amounts of money from payroll checks or bank accounts. This scheme is based on the fact that people usually don't miss or even question small discrepancies of a dollar or less. If enough accounts or checks are skimmed over a period of time, the theft can be quite significant. In another famous computer crime case, dummy insurance claim receipts were entered into a company's computer file. Over a relatively short period of time, several hundred thousand dollars were paid to nonexistent persons.

These are just a few of the large computer crimes. The true extent of computer-assisted crime is not really known because the crimes may go undetected or unreported. Even conservative estimates place losses in the billions of dollars per year.

Our society, interestingly and regrettably, takes a curious moral and ethical position regarding the people who commit these crimes. Many people, for instance, view theft by computer as somehow "different" from theft by burglary. This view is difficult to understand or explain. Certainly it represents a lack of ethics.

The role of educators in addressing the problem of computer crime is critical. Somehow, teachers must convey to their students that stealing is stealing. Theft by computer is still theft. Educators must also set good examples. Some of the worst software pirates are educators. How can we expect our students to respect copyright laws if they see the law violated by their schools?

The responsibility for ethics in computing must be shared by the lawmakers, law enforcement agencies and the courts. It is not "cute" when a teenager gains illegal access to an organization's data base. It is also unfair to sentence a teenager to a prison term for stealing a car when a banker guilty of embezzlement is allowed to plea bargain and receive probation.

Educators must get involved in this problem. They must take the problem seriously. The loss to society can and will be great if the illegal and unethical use of computers is ignored.

Summary

This chapter has briefly examined four aspects of the societal implications for the use of computers and information processing: personal privacy, artificial intelligence, economic effects, and computer-based crime. Clearly, there are many other aspects which should be considered as one considers the overall impact of computer technology on our social system and our individual lives. We discussed governmental uses of computers from a privacy perspective but there are other concerns that we must recognize. For example, computerized voting systems offer many opportunities for election fraud unless safeguards are carefully designed. Computer-based polls and surveys may be used to guide and formulate government policies. The potential benefits of these opinion surveys are obvious but there is also the potential for misuse by politicians and government officials.

In our look at the economic implications of computers we discussed the changing role of workers in the information society. Even while the present work force is undergoing change, we are witnessing the emergence of a new worker. The advent of sophisticated microprocessors has, in a sense, spawned another segment of the work force—the robot. Industrial robots can presently perform many tasks as well, if not better, than the human worker. Routine factory functions such as spray painting, assembly of components, moving of parts, welding, handling of hazardous materials, and so on are tasks well-suited for robots. As the technology becomes more sophisticated, other jobs may be assumed by them also. Even though automation has not resulted in a loss in total numbers of jobs at this time, it has the potential for effecting immense economic change. As economies of scale permit robots to become cost-efficient, factories have access to a work force that doesn't complain, become bored, get sick, or demand a negotiated contract. And, the robot can work twenty-four hours a day with only a little time off for maintenance. We have two choices. Automation can be fought, through labor unions and other groups, or we can accept the possible effects and try to maximize the benefits to everyone.

Our nation's schools exist, in part, for the purpose of preparing useful and productive members of our society. The assumptions, however, which form the basis for the curricula of schools are based, in large part, on the requirements of an industrial society. As changes occur in our social and economic system, educators must question the role and function of the schools. The challenges and opportunities are not only important—they are critical.

References

Howard, J. (1984). Electronic funds transfer. *AEDS Monitor, 22*(9, 10), 15–17.

Naisbitt, J. (1984). *Megatrends*. New York: Warner Books, Inc.

Westin, A. F. (1983). New issues of computer privacy in the eighties. In R.E.A. Mason (Ed.), *Information processing 83* (pp. 733–739). New York: North-Holland. (Reprinted in *AEDS Monitor, 22*(9, 10), 1984.)

Suggested Readings

Adams, J. M., & Haden, D. H. (1976). *Social effects of computer use and misuse*. New York: John Wiley & Sons.

Bohl, M. (1984). *Information processing*. Chicago: SRA.

Computer-based national information systems: Technology and public policy issues (1981, September). Washington, DC: Office of Technology Assessment.

Graham, N. (1983). *The mind tool*. St. Paul: West Publishing Company.

Green, J. O. (1984, January). Artificial intelligence and the future classroom. *Classroom Computer Learning*, 26–31.

Hirsch, A. (1984, March). Artificial intelligence comes of age. *Computer and Electronics*, 63–67, 93–96.

Krauss, L. I., & Macgahan, A. (1979). *Computer fraud and countermeasures*. Englewood Cliffs: Prentice-Hall, Inc.

Kreidler, W. J. (1984, January). Teaching computer ethics. *Electronic Learning*, 54–57.

Laurie, E. J. (1979). *Computers, automation, and society*. Homewood, IL: Richard D. Irwin, Inc.

Lenat, D. B. (1981). *Knowledge-based systems in AI*. New York: McGraw-Hill.

London, K. (1976). *The people side of systems*. London: McGraw-Hill Co.

Marchand, D. A. (1980). *The politics of privacy, computers, and criminal justice records*. Arlington, VA: Information Resources Press.

Michie, D. (1980). *Expert systems in the microelectronic age*. New York: Columbia University Press.

Spencer, D. D. (1974). *Computers in society*. Rochelle Park, NJ: Hayden Book Co.

Turing, A. M. (1956). Can a machine think? In J. R. Newman (Ed.), *The world of mathematics* (pp. 2099–2123). New York: Simon and Schuster.

Wu, M. S. (1979). *Introduction to computer data processing*. New York: Harcourt Brace Jovanovich, Inc.

7

Implementation of Computer-Based Education

Introduction

This chapter represents somewhat of a departure from the topics generally found in a text on educational applications of computing. Thus far we have explored a number of basic and fundamental concepts regarding the function and operation of a computer, the components of computers, and some ways computers can be and are being used in schools. Given this foundation, we can explore a perplexing problem faced by many educators today—how the technology can be intelligently integrated into the classroom, the school, or the school district. Therefore, this chapter will try to offer to the education professional some direction with regard to the development of a master plan for the implementation and application of computer technology in an educational system. In a sense, this chapter seeks to answer the question which pervades our nation's schools—"Now that we have computers and computer-based technology, how do we introduce this technology into the classroom?" Clearly, the rapid development of hardware and software for educational applications has far exceeded our schools' capacity for programmatic change. The successful implementation and integration of these innovations represent a major challenge to all educators.

Two principal areas will be discussed in this chapter: concepts, theory, and research related to organizational change; and a conceptual structure and strategy for planning which will lead to continuing change and improvement. It is hoped that a research and theoretical framework will provide a foundation for a practical and operational approach to planning and change. To paraphrase John Dewey, "In the end, theory is the most practical thing." The conceptual structure and planning strategy presented in this chapter, PDA (The Planning and Design Approach), stems from a wide range of research and experience in problem solving, cognitive psychology, group processes, organizational development, and systems theory.

Change in Education

There is a vast amount of literature regarding educational innovations such as computer-based education. Unfortunately, much of this literature fails to provide significant insight regarding factors associated with success or failure of planned change. Indeed, much of the literature in the popular educational periodicals reads like press releases and recounts subjective narratives about projects that "work." In general, the literature does not provide information regarding the implementation strategy and the evaluation of efforts toward programmatic change and innovation. Evidence that does exist seems to suggest apparent ineffectiveness and instability of innovative efforts (Berman & McLaughlin, p. 6).

Educators are not presented with a promising scenario for ready acceptance of change and innovation related to computer-based technology. All too often, teachers and administrators are reminded of the innovations that held so much promise but didn't work or didn't last. And, unfortunately, that list is long—language labs, individualized instruction, teaching machines, educational television, etc. Persons opposed to computer-based education take great pleasure in reminding us of these innovative misadventures. Certainly the innovation was attempted, but lasting change, for the most part, did not occur. What have we learned, then, from years of experience, study, and research?

The elements of four strategies of innovation are identified and synthesized by Havelock (1973): (1) the problem-solving strategy; (2) the social interaction orientation; (3) the research, development, and diffusion orientation; and (4) a linkage model. These models or orientations provide frameworks for understanding some of the processes inherent in knowledge dissemination/utilization and implementation of innovations. Havelock emphasized that while each of these strategies for change and innovation has its own unique merits, there is no one best approach. Situations and circumstances will influence the selection of an approach in a given setting.

The first strategy, problem solving, begins with the perception of need which is translated into a problem statement and diagnosis. This is followed by a search and selection of an innovation. The innovation must then be adapted, tried, and evaluated.

Social interaction, the second orientation, emphasizes the ways innovations are diffused through a social system such as an organization. Havelock refers to "quasi-strategies" which can be identified with this orientation: natural diffusion, natural communication networks, network building, and media approaches. An old and familiar example of a social interaction tactic is the county agent of agriculture. Another example is the salesperson. These persons contact the users or consumers making them aware of new products and innovations. This is well-illustrated in the health care field; new pharmaceuticals are often introduced to physicians by company representatives.

Figure 7.1
Courtesy of Apple
Computer, Inc.

The research, development, and diffusion (RD&D) orientation suggests a sequence of events or processes which lead to innovation. This perspective assumes a progression of basic research, applied research, development and testing, mass production, mass dissemination, and acceptance of the innovation by the end user. Many specific strategies can be associated with this model from surveys of user target audiences to complex advertising methods.

The last strategy identified by Havelock, the linkage model, represents a synthesis of many of the components of the previous models. Essentially, this model employs the concept important in the user system—resource system interaction.

To a great extent, these four orientations focus on what might be termed "preadoptive behavior" or the behavior of an organization before the adoption of some system. This adoption perspective is the topic of another important work related to change and innovation.

A Rand Corporation study (Berman & McLaughlin, 1974) of educational change identifies two perspectives that dominate the analytical literature on planned change in education. This literature, focusing on the institutional aspects of educational innovations, emphasizes (a) the adoption perspective, and (b) the implementation perspective.

From the adoption perspective, the problem of bringing about change is essentially one of selecting, receiving, and adopting an innovation.

> Underlying (the adoption perspective) of effecting educational
> innovation is a rational model of bureaucratic behavior that assumes that
> schoolmen constantly seek better practices, have reliable means of
> identifying superior procedures, and are eager and able to adopt proved
> innovations. Thus, given the existence of promising strategies, the
> primary barriers to change are seen as deficiencies in:
> *Planning, communicating, and dissemination
> *The quantity and quality of available information. (p. 7)

The implementation perspective on innovation and change presents a different set of problems and impediments when compared to the adoption perspective. This model suggests that failures of planned changes and innovations are not a result of preadoption behavior within the organization but rather with problems during the implementation.

> The innovations typically were initiated with a high level of enthusiasm and support by faculty and staff, but these innovative plans failed to achieve their objectives because of unanticipated and often prosaic difficulties and obstacles encountered during the course of project implementation. In addition, the organizational perspective on planned change contends that "resistance" to change persists after a decision to adopt is made, continuing to exert influence throughout the process of adaption and implementation. (p. 8).

Certainly, both the adoption and implementation perspectives suggest possible causes of the relative absence of lasting change.

Figure 7.2
(Courtesy of
Apple Computer, Inc.)

Hage and Aiken (1970) have hypothesized certain organizational characteristics which may affect the probability of successful program innovation. For example:

> HYPOTHESIS 1. The higher the centralization of power distribution, the lower the rate of program change.
> HYPOTHESIS 2. The greater the formalization (i.e., codification of jobs, number of rules, etc.), the lower the rate of program change.
> HYPOTHESIS 3. The higher the job satisfaction (e.g., the degree of morale among the job occupants), the greater the rate of program change.

Research indicates that these relationships do, in fact, exist. What can be said about the existence of these conditions in schools?

Figure 7.3
(Courtesy of
Apple Computer, Inc.)

Consider the first hypothesis regarding the distribution of power. At the building level, the principal is ordinarily the administrative officer. In schools with large enrollments, the administration may also include assistants to the principal, especially at the secondary level. In many situations, this administrative hierarchy and the power which is given the principal leave little opportunity for planning and decision making on the part of the teachers. Hypothesis #1 would suggest, therefore, that the rate of programmatic change in such an environment will be slower than if the administration were handled through participatory and shared decision-making systems.

The second hypothesis concerns the degree of formalization in the organization.

> Formalization refers to the degree of codification of jobs in an
> organization. The greater the number of rules specifying what is to be
> done, whether formally written or informally understood, and the more
> strictly they are enforced, the greater the formalization of the
> organization. (Hage & Aiken, 1970, p. 43)

Every educator can appreciate the need for a certain amount of formalization in a school. Without rules and guidelines, the administration would be innundated with requests for decisions regarding even the smallest day-to-day activities. While formalization can certainly enhance the efficiency of operation of a school, it can also discourage persons from being creative and innovative. The military is an example of a highly formalized organization. Conformity is encouraged and the following of certain patterns becomes a ritual. Hypothesis #2 indicates a negative relationship between the rate of program change and the degree of formalization. While the research in this area is not extensive, existing studies suggest that such a relationship does exist. The implications for the introduction of computer-based education into a school are very important.

The last hypothesis concerns the relationship between job satisfaction and the rate of program change. The concept of job satisfaction has been defined and analyzed in many ways by many scholars. Job satisfaction includes such elements as satisfaction/contentment with administration/supervision, co-workers, career future, school indentification, financial aspects, work conditions, amounts of work, pupil/teacher relations, and community relations (Speed, 1979).

It is not fair to say that morale and job satisfaction are universally low among educators. This, however, is certainly the case in many schools and districts, and where this is the case, the implementation of computing may not be easily accomplished.

Of course, change does occur in organizations. When change and innovation occur, it can be conceptualized as a process, a set of events, or stages of occurrence. One such conceptualization of the general organizational change process includes three sequential steps:

1. Recognition of some disequilibrium; unfreezing of attitudes and perceptions.
2. Development of specific recommendations.
3. Emergence of a new equilibrium or refreezing. (Nadler, 1981, p. 268)

The Rand Corporation Study (Berman, et al., 1974) described an innovation (i.e., a new practice or plan) as a three-stage process:

1. INITIATION. The period when persons conceive and plan possible innovations, look for resources, and decide which projects to support.
2. IMPLEMENTATION. The stage where the project confronts the institutional setting. Plans are translated into practice.
3. INCORPORATION. The final stage at which the project becomes part of the organizational environment. (Vol. V, pp. 8–9)

Hage and Aiken (1970) describe the change process more completely in a four-stage model:

1. EVALUATION. Organizational decision makers (a) determine that their system is not accomplishing its goals as effectively as it could, or (b) alter or amend the goals of the organization.
2. INITIATION. This stage is concerned with the choice of a solution and the search for resources that are required for the program.
3. IMPLEMENTATION. The actual attempt to integrate the innovation into the organization. Resistance and disequilibrium is greatest at this time because of conflicts, the realities associated with the new program, and the discontinuity between the new program and the existing organizational structure.
4. ROUTINIZATION. This phase follows the initial trial in the implementation stage. In routinization, the decision is made to retain or reject the new program. (pp. 94–106)

Figure 7.4
"Computer Assisted
Instruction, Circa 1965"
IBM, Armonk, NY 10504

From *Computer Preparations
for the SAT* (Harcourt Brace
Javanovich Computer Test
Preparation Series), copyright
© 1982 by Harcourt Brace
Javanovich, Inc. Reprinted by
permission of the publisher.

Interestingly, there is not an abundance of literature and research related to the process of change within educational organizations. Much of that available is of the "loose-knit" case study variety or "testimonials" from practitioners. Closer inspection of many so-called organizational changes or innovations are actually relabelings of previous practices.

One important study, however, is the Rand Study (Berman, et al., 1974) of federally funded programs designed to introduce and spread innovative practices in public schools. Conclusions from this several-year study are given below:

> Our data show that a receptive institutional setting is a necessary but not a sufficient one for effective implementation. An implementation strategy that promotes mutual adaption is essential.
>
> The main factors affecting innovations were the institutional setting, particularly organizational climate and motivations of the participants; the implementation strategy employed by local innovators to install the project; and the scope of change implied by the project relative to its setting. Neither the technology nor the project resources nor the federal management strategies influences outcomes in major ways. Thus, project outcomes did not depend primarily on outside influence but on internal factors and local decisions. (Vol. IV, p. 6)

Findings of a number of studies at the University of Wisconsin concerning educational change, leadership, and decision making are, to a great extent, consistent with the Rand study conclusions. Results from several of these studies are presented below:

1. Successful schools utilize both systematic adoption and situational adaptation to implement change effectively.
2. The direction of a major change is particularly sensitive to budgetary control.
3. The principal is the key educational agent within the school.
4. Appropriate leadership behavior is essential at the different steps in the change process.
5. A dynamic educational leader is the prime prerequisite for a significant educational change.
6. Local schools do not engage in major change in isolation but reach out to the larger educational organizations for ideas and resources.
7. Most major educational changes require several years—not months.
8. Adequate, appropriate, systematic in-service training is absolutely essential for an educational change to be implemented effectively. (Lipham & Rankin, 1982, pp. 3–7)

How then does theory and research help the educator successfully introduce computer-based educational technology into the school? We have revisited some of education's past problems and failures to change. Two perspectives on planned change adoption and implementation were reviewed. Hypothesized relationships between organizational variables and change were offered. Stages of change, when it occurs, were examined. Finally, certain conclusions about change in organizations were presented. Given this background and foundation from theory and research, a strategy for planning for change, innovation, and improvement will be discussed.

PDA: The Planning and Design Approach

The particular strategy offered herein is PDA—the Planning and Design Approach. PDA addresses the characteristics and status of organizations which may affect successful program innovation while capitalizing on the findings of research related to the sociological and psychological components of change. Furthermore, PDA embraces a timeline perspective, a purpose-oriented strategy, and a comprehensive systems framework, all of which have been shown to enhance the quality and results of planning efforts.

Educators at all levels are frequently called upon to make decisions, formulate programs, effect curricular changes and improvement, or to simply enhance the educational program. For example, the teacher searches for a better way to achieve instructional objectives; principals, curriculum directors, and other educational leaders conduct meetings and direct task forces charged with developing or improving programs; the district superintendent or his designee plans the system's organizational hierarchy of authority and responsibility. And, as is our concern, educators may seek to implement programs of computer-based education.

All educators share a common task—the improvement of the educational programs for which they are responsible. Inherent in this common task are two interrelated requirements: (a) the need for a general approach for improving programs, or what might be called a game plan, and (b) the need for specific techniques or procedures, or to maintain the analogy, plays that can be used to execute the game plan.

In this section one such game plan will be described: PDA—the Planning and Design Approach and its associated plays found useful by educators at many organizational levels and in many situations (Nadler, 1981).

The PDA strategy involves a five-phase sequence of planning. Each phase requires a different focus of attention and uses different techniques.

PDA is an approach to planning and problem solving which seeks to accomplish three primary objectives: (1) to maximize the effectiveness and efficiency of recommended solutions; (2) to maximize the probability of implementation of solutions; (3) to maximize the effective utilization of available planning and design resources. In principle, the strategy employed in PDA to achieve these objectives is simple. It involves thinking of alternative ways to achieve the desired ends and selecting the one that (a) eliminates the problem, and (b) creates as few additional problems as possible.

The five planning phases are as follows:

    I. Purpose determination
   II. Possible solution generation
  III. Target plan selection
  IV. Details and specification
   V. Implementation and evaluation

As with any game plan, PDA has a set of general principles which guide what is actually done. To be useful as guidelines, the principles listed below should be kept in mind during all phases of planning.

1. Ascertain the purpose of what is being done—continually ask "Why?"
2. Direct planning toward the development of the ideal solution rather than toward repairing what presently exists.
3. Devise a target plan.
4. Try to include in the planning as many as possible of the people who will be affected by the plan.
5. Don't worry about everything at once. Different activities have different purposes and may be treated separately.
6. Gather information and data only as needed to answer specific, necessary questions.
7. As conditions or needs change, do not patch up the plan. Replan from the appropriate point, continually asking why and thinking in terms of purpose.

These seven principles, whether considered individually or collectively, are generally accepted without argument. In actual planning situations, however, they are generally not followed. This is due in part to failing to use a well-defined sequence of planning steps consistent with the principles. The PDA strategy, however, actually encourages their use.

Phase I of the PDA, purpose determination, is possibly the most important. Work in this phase sets the stage for all subsequent planning. To be effective, all planning activities should be directed toward achieving a specific purpose; if there is no specific purpose, the planning effort tends to be diffuse, resulting in a plan which is not effective nor even adequate. A well-defined purpose is thus vital for the success of the planning effort and ultimately of the program being planned.

Often planners make the assumption that their purpose is clear and agreed upon. In most cases, this assumption is false—the purpose, or the exact meaning of the words in which the purpose is expressed, is not clear or is subject to debate. The technique recommended in Phase I to specify the purpose of the project is purpose expansion. Initially, the group is asked to brainstorm possible purposes for the program. As many purposes as possible should be elicited and recorded on a flip-chart. From these possible purposes, the most specific purpose is selected and is then expanded to encompass other broader purposes.

Expansion of purpose is accomplished by asking the question, "What is the immediate purpose of the given purpose?" By applying this question successively, levels of purpose are generated until a satisfactory purpose has been reached.

A simple example of a purpose hierarchy is given in Figure 7.5. This hierarchy was developed by a group of high school students in the process of organizing their photography club. The purpose "to help gain photographic experience" was selected as the most specific from a list of possible purposes and expanded into the hierarchy shown below. The purpose "to develop photographic creativity" was chosen as the focus or purpose for the club.

The idea upon which the use of the purpose hierarchy is founded is a basic but important one. As one approaches the accomplishment of a higher-level purpose, usually the preceding or lower-level purposes will also be addressed. The converse, however, is not true. Accomplishment of a more fundamental purpose (e.g., "to learn about photography") will not address the chosen level ("to develop photographic creativity").

An excellent activity and exercise for the reader would be the development of a purpose hierarchy for some computer-related application. For example, suppose the high school English department seeks to develop a master plan for the implementation of computer-based technology. The first question to be addressed might be "What is the purpose of using computers in the English department?" Brainstorm possible purposes, record them, and select some lower-level or obvious purpose. Then attempt to expand the purpose in the hierarchy. Results are often quite surprising.

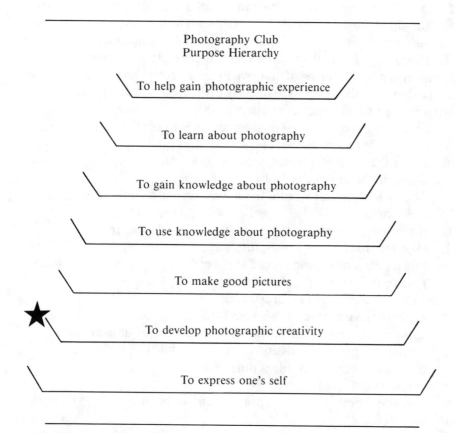

Photography Club
Purpose Hierarchy

To help gain photographic experience

To learn about photography

To gain knowledge about photography

To use knowledge about photography

To make good pictures

★ To develop photographic creativity

To express one's self

Figure 7.5
Purpose Hierarchy Example

Norton, M., Bozeman, W. C., & Nadler, G. *Student planned acquisition of required knowledge,*
1980. Englewood Cliffs: Educational Technology Publications, Inc., p. 41.

The second phase of PDA, possible solutions generation, involves creating a list of ways the selected purpose might be achieved. The basic "play" of this phase is brainstorming. An alternative recommendation is the Nominal Group Technique.[1]

Essentially, the Nominal Group Technique is a process in which group members work independently in each other's presence with information/feedback controlled by a group facilitator or coordinator. Though there are many variations on the general strategy, there are six basic, procedural stages or phases.

1. Silent generation of ideas in writing.
   A. Present the question to the group in writing.
   B. Read the question aloud.
   C. Avoid requests for clarification.

1. The Nominal Group Technique was developed in 1968 by Andre L. Delbecq and Andrew H. Van de Ven.

    D. Ask the group to write their ideas on a card or paper. The ideas should be stated in short phrases or sentences.

    E. Ask group members to work silently and independently.

    F. Discourage disruption of the silent, independent activity.

2. Round-robin recording of ideas on a flip pad. (Note: the flip pad is used rather than a chalkboard so that the information may be displayed and saved for future reference or transcription.)

    A. Emphasize that the goal of the process is to obtain each member's ideas while reflecting the total group's thinking.

    B. Stress the need to present ideas in brief phrases (no long discussions, deliberations, or lobbying for ideas).

    C. Accept ideas serially from members, one-at-a-time, as written on their paper.

    D. Allow group members to decide if ideas are duplicate.

    E. Members may "pass" when they have no more ideas.

    F. The moderator should record ideas exactly as presented, VERBATIM (no poetic license at this time).

3. Serial discussion of each recorded idea.

    A. Explain the purpose of this step is to clarify ideas and offer necessary explanations. The purpose is not to critique or evaluate.

    B. Encourage group discussion on each idea when appropriate.

    C. Sanction lobbying for ideas during this discussion.

4. Preliminary vote on ideas.

    A. Ask the group to select a specific number of ideas (5–10) from the list.

    B. Rank order the set of cards/ideas by assigning a value to each one. If there are 10 ideas, the most important idea or highest ranked idea will receive a "10." The least important idea in the set will receive a "1."

    C. The moderator will collect or tally the votes assigned to each idea. The ideas on the original list can then be placed in a priority order.

5. Discussion of the preliminary vote.

    A. Avoid pressure from group members toward consensus.

    B. Attempt to keep discussions and clarifications brief.

6. Final vote.

    A. Repeat Step 4.

    B. Bring process to closure.

Research has demonstrated that these group procedures produce a large number of innovative ideas while reducing the dominance of high-status, aggressive, highly articulate or "expert" persons. Because the technique is structured, maximum use is made of available time often eliminating rambling, unproductive discourse.

The Nominal Group Technique in Phase II will generate many solutions or ways to accomplish the selected purpose. Some will be unimaginative and re-

flect little creative thought. Others will be wild, theoretical, or totally impractical. The user of PDA should not be concerned at all about this phenomenon. In fact, occcasionally the more impractical sounding ideas are actually
the best.

Phase III of PDA is the selection of the target plan. This phase shapes the
ideas into possible major alternatives. The target plan should be a reasonably
practical plan which is not sufficiently detailed for actual implementation. It
is simply a target for which to aim. It does not include details or ways to handle the exceptions and problems that occur with any plan.

Once the specification of the target plan has been accomplished, Phase IV
of the PDA strategy, details specification, may be carried out. At this point,
the technique is to consider all the aspects and exceptions related to the plan.
This phase generally presents fewer problems since this is a stage of planning
that is quite familiar. All through the phase of detailing, the selected purpose
of Phase I should be remembered and considered in making decisions. Phase
IV activities can be most easily completed if a clear target plan has been out-
lined in Phase III. Without a target plan, planners often become confused and
frustrated when they try to consider all details of a plan. They become over-
whelmed with too much information and retreat to standard and less satisfactory solutions. A target plan offers a convenient way to deal with one part of
the plan at a time and avoid the frustration of considering too many factors at
once.

The last and obvious phase of PDA is the implementation of the plan, including evaluation and refinement. The planners should remember the desired purpose throughout the implementation. If this purpose is not being
achieved, it may be necessary to design a plan closer to the target or even review the planning process beginning with purpose selection.

Summary

Educational change and the implementation of new or different systems are
difficult at best. The situation is made even more difficult when a new or un-
familiar technology is involved. The change will be somewhat threatening to a
few individuals. Therefore, an understanding of the change process and
methods for planning and implementing change is most important. This insight, coupled with sufficient knowledge of computer-based education, can
bring about the "critical mass" necessary for success. The relationship between these systems can be depicted as in Figure 7.6.

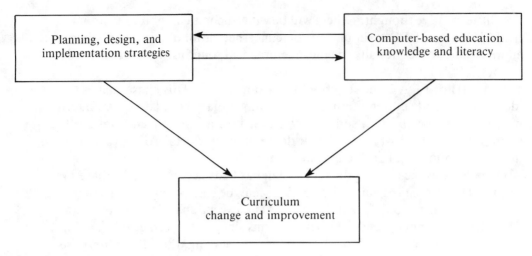

Figure 7.6
Systems in the Change Process

Experience has shown that this strategy and approach may reduce many of the traditional obstacles to change. At best, resistance will be minimal.

References

Berman, P., & McLaughlin, M. W. (1974). *Federal programs supporting educational change, Vol. I: A model of educational change* (R–1589/1). Santa Monica: The Rand Corporation.

Delbecq, A. L., Van de Ven, A. H., & Gustafson, D. (1975). Group decision making in modern organizations. Chapter 1 from *Group techniques for program planning*. Glenview, IL: Scott Foresman, and Company.

Hage, J., & Aiken, M. (1970). *Social change in complex organizations*. New York: Random House, Inc.

Havelock, R. G. (1973). *The change agent's guide to innovation in education*. Englewood Cliffs: Educational Technology Publications.

Lipham, J. M., & Rankin, R. E. (1982). *Change, leadership, and decision making in improving secondary schools*. Working Paper No. 331. Madison: Wisconsin Center for Educational Research.

Nadler, G. (1981). *The planning and design approach*. New York: John Wiley & Sons.

Norton, M., Bozeman, W. C., & Nadler, G. (1980). *Student planned acquisition of required knowledge*. Englewood Cliffs: Educational Technology Publications, Inc.

Speed, N. E. (1979). *Decision participation and staff satisfaction in middle and junior high schools that individualize instruction*. Technical Report No. 561. Madison: Wisconsin Research and Development Center for Individualized Schooling.

Suggested Readings

Bozeman, W. C., & Clements, M. S. (1981). Planning and design: A systems approach. *Planning and Changing, 12*(3), 131–144.

Bozeman, W. C. & Schmelzer, S. (1984). Strategic planning: Applications in business and education. *Planning and Changing, 15*(1), 35–49.

Dede, C., & Allen, D. (1981, January). Education in the 21st century: Scenarios as a tool for strategic planning. *Phi Delta Kappan*, 362–366.

Delbecq, A. L., & Van de Ven, A. H. (1971). A group process model for problem identification and program planning. *The Journal of Applied Behavioral Science, 7*(4), 466–492.

Nadler, G., & Bozeman, W. C. (1983). The relationship of planning and knowledge synthesis. In S. A. Ward and L. J. Reed (Eds.), *Knowledge structure and use: Implications for synthesis and interpretation*. Philadelphia: Temple University Press.

Glossary

Access Time   the elapsed time between a request for data from memory and the actual delivery of the data

Address   a group of characters which identify a given storage location

Algorithm   a set of well-defined rules or steps for the solution of a problem

Alphanumeric   a character set which contains letters of the alphabet, numerals, and special characters such as punctuation marks

ALU   arithmetic and logic unit; the part of the central processing unit which performs arithmetic functions and logical operations such as comparisons or decisions

Analog   pertaining to representation by a physical quantity; contrast with digital

Analog Computer   computer which uses analog data (e.g., slide rule)

ANSI   American National Standards Institute; an organization which establishes standards

APL   A Programming Language; a high-level programming language designed primarily for mathematical applications

Argument   one of the independent variables in a mathematical relation

Array   a matrix or rectangularly ordered set of elements

Artificial Intelligence   a computer application in which the system emulates human thought, reasoning, learning, and decision-making processes

ASCII   American National Standard Code for Information Interchange; a standard seven-bit coded character

Assembler   a computer program used to translate a program expressed in an assembly language into a machine language

Assembly Language   a specific computer-oriented language; instructions are in a one-to-one correspondence with the machine language

Asynchronous Transmission   method of data transmission in which the start of each character is arbitrary; contrast with synchronous transmission

Auxiliary Storage Device   a storage device (e.g., magnetic tape or disk) which supplements main memory

Backup Copy   a copy of an original data set or program (usually on tape or disk) that is kept in case the original is lost or destroyed

Bar Code   data representation consisting of lines that are machine readable

BASIC   Beginner's All-Purpose Symbolic Instructional Code; a high-level programming language which uses English-like statements

Batch Processing   processing of accumulated data or jobs in the same computer run

Baud   rate of transmission of digital data in bits per second

BCD   see binary coded decimal system

Binary Coded Decimal System (BCD)   a character set containing sixty-four six-bit characters

Binary   pertaining to two possible states or conditions (e.g., on/off, zero/one, clockwise/counterclockwise, etc.)

Bit   binary digit; the symbols 0 and 1 in the binary number system

Bits Per Inch (BPI)   a measure of magnetic tape storage density

BPI   see bits per inch

Bubble Memory   a memory or storage technology using the principle of magnetic fields

Buffer   a temporary storage device typically used for input/output operations

Bug   error or malfunction

Bus   conductor(s) used for transmission of data

Byte   a string of bits which represent one specific character

Central Processing Unit (CPU)   section of the computer which interprets and executes instruction; the CPU contains the control and arithmetic/logic units

Cathode-Ray Tube (CRT)   a vacuum tube employing a screen for the display of information; similar to a television picture tube

COBOL   Common Business Oriented Language: a high-level programming language used for business data-processing applications

Compile   to translate a computer program written in a high-level language into machine language

Compiler   a computer program used to compile

Computer   a device which can perform arithmetic computation and logical operations without human intervention

Computer Program   a set of instructions in a form acceptable to a computer

Computer Word   a character or bit string treated as a unit

Console   the part of a computer used for observation of and communication with the system

Core   see magnetic core

CPU   see central processing unit

CRT   see cathode-ray tube

Daisywheel Printer   a letter-quality printer using a flat wheel-shaped print element; the element has "petals," each of which contains one fully formed character

DASD   see direct-access storage device

Data   representation of facts, ideas, instructions, or concepts in a form suitable for manipulation or processing

Data Base   a set of organized data sufficient for user information needs

Data Base Management Systems (DBMS)   software used for the organization, storage, retrieval, and maintenance of data

Data Processing   the systematic sequence of operations on data

Decimal   pertaining to a base ten number system or a system with ten possible states, symbols, or values

Default   a value or choice assumed by a program when no other is specified

Digital   pertaining to representation of data in the form of digits or symbols of a numbering system

Digital Computer   a computer which processes data represented as numbers or digits

Direct Access Storage Device (DASD)   a storage device in which access time is not affected by the location of the data; example: magnetic disk

Disk Operating System (DOS)   a program which handles input and output functions related to disk storage; functions usually include storing and retrieving data, error recovery, and file management

Disk Pack   a removable set of magnetic disks

Documentation   a collection of instructions, information, and specifications about a system or program

DOS   see Disk Operating System

Double-Precision   the use of two computer words to represent a single number in order to gain more significant figures or precision

Duplex (Full Duplex)   simultaneous transmission of data in both directions

EBCDIC   Extended Binary Coded Decimal Interchange Code; an eight-bit code used to represent characters

EOF   End-of-File; a code signifying that the last record of a file has been read

EPROM   Erasable Programmable Read Only Memory; nonvolatile read only memory which can be erased using ultraviolet light and reprogrammed

Field   a specific area in a computer record used for a particular item of data

File   a set of related records

Firmware   a combination of hardware and software; software which resides in ROM

First-Generation Computer   a computer using vacuum tubes as the principal components

Floppy Disk   a secondary storage medium using a flexible magnetic platter; generally used with small computer systems

Flowchart   a schematic or pictorial representation of the sequence of operations leading to the solution of a problem

Format   the layout or location of data in a record

FORTRAN Formula Translation; a high-level computer-programming language especially suited for mathematical or scientific applications

Giga (G) ten to the ninth power (one billion); used as a prefix such as in gigahertz

Graphics Tablet an input device used to create computer graphics or pictures

Half Duplex alternate or one-way at a time data communication

Hard Copy a permanent copy (e.g., paper copy) of computer output

Hardware physical equipment in a computer system; contrast with software

Hertz a unit of frequency equal to one cycle per second

Hexadecimal base sixteen number system using the symbol 0, 1, 2, . . .9, A, B, C, D, E, F

Hollerith Card punched card used as a data input medium

Hollerith Code type of code used on a punched card to represent data

I/O Device input/output device used to enter and receive data from a computer system

IC see integrated circuit

Information meanings and interpretations which humans assign to data

Input data to be processed by the computer

Integrated Circuit (IC) miniature electronic circuit containing the equivalent of thousands of transistors and other components

Interface a connector device between two components of a computer system

Interpret to translate each source program statement to a machine language before translating the next statement

Interpreter a computer program used to interpret a high-level programming language (e.g., BASIC interpreter)

JCL Job Control Language used to direct an operating system

Joy Stick a lever used as an input device to control position on a display

K an abbreviation for kilo or 1000; 1 K equals 1024 when referring to storage capacity

Light Pen a photoelectric device used as an input/output device with a CRT

Line Printer output device which prints one line at a time rather than one character at a time

Load to enter data or programs into memory

Logical Record a collection of data or a record defined in terms of content rather than its physical location or attributes

Logoff the procedure used to terminate connection between a terminal and the computer

Logon the procedure used to begin a terminal session or connect a terminal to the computer

Loop a set of instructions which are executed repeatedly

LSI Large-Scale Integration; computer chips are considered LSI circuits

Machine Language language used directly by the computer; does not have to be compiled or interpreted

Magnetic Core Storage a type of main memory using an array of small iron cores, toroidal in shape

Magnetic Disk a flat circular platter surfaced with magnetic material used as a data storage medium

Magnetic Drum Storage a magnetic storage device in which data are stored on the surface of a rotating drum

Magnetic-Ink-Character Recognition mode of data input using machine-readable characters printed with magnetic ink

Main Memory principal storage of a computer for data and instruction; synonymous with main storage, core, real storage

Mb megabyte (roughly, one million bytes)

MICR see magnetic-ink character recognition

Microcomputer a complete computer, usually containing all circuitry on a single board; synonymous with personal computer or home computer

Microprocessor a complete central processing unit on a single chip

Microsecond one millionth of a second

Millisecond one thousandth of a second

Modem device used for transmission of data over communication facilities (e.g., telephone); acronym for modulator-demodulator

Motherboard printed circuit board into which circuit boards, chips, peripherals, etc. can be plugged

Mouse a tabletop, hand-held input device used to move a pointer on a CRT screen

Multiprocessing operation involving the parallel execution of two or more computer programs at the same time by two or more CPUs

Multiprogramming operation involving the execution of two or more computer programs at the same time by a single CPU

Nanosecond one billionth of a second

Object Code translated (e.g., compiled) form of a source language; executable machine code

OCR see optical character recognition

Octal pertaining to a base eight number system

Online System system in which input can be transmitted directly into the computer from point of origin and output returned

Operating System programs or software which control the overall operation of the computer

Optical Character Recognition (OCR) input device which can read characters directly from paper

Output data which has been processed; data delivered from an output device

Overlay Program computer program designed so that certain sections will use the same memory locations

Paper Tape input medium using a paper tape with punched holes

Parallel Input/Output the simultaneous transmission or reception of data signals or bits; contrasted with serial input/output

Password keyword or code which will permit user access to a system

Peripheral hardware (e.g., input, output, or storage device) attached to and used with a computer

PL/1 Programming Language 1; a high-level computer-programming language suitable for business or scientific applications

Program set of instructions to the computer which enable the system to perform some task

Punched Card see Hollerith card

Punched Tape see paper tape

Queue a waiting line, usually of jobs to be processed or printed

RAM see random access memory

Random Access Memory (RAM) temporary storage used by the computer; usually refers to semiconductor main memory

Read Only Memory (ROM) memory or storage which can be accessed (read) but cannot be changed

Real Time System generally refers to systems operating in a conversational mode; computer response time is sufficiently fast to support the application

Register a storage device intended for a special purpose; for example, the accumulator is a register that accumulates the result of an operation

Remote Job Entry (RJE) submission of a program or data through an input device not located at the immediate computer site

RJE see remote job entry

ROM see Read Only Memory

RPG (Report Program Generator) a programming language used to construct reports from data sets

Second-Generation Computer a computer using transistors as the principal components

Secondary Storage Device see auxiliary storage device

Security prevention of unauthorized access to a computer system, data, or programs

Semiconductor solid-state electronic component such as a transistor or diode

Serial Input/Output type of interface which transmits or receives data in a single stream of bits or signals; contrast with parallel input/output

Software computer programs, documentation, procedures, routines used in a data-processing system; contrast with hardware

Spooling simultaneous peripheral operations on line; use of auxiliary storage to enhance the efficiency input/output operations

Structured Programming an approach to computer program development which emphasizes use of modules

Synchronous Transmission method of data transmission in which a constant time frame is used during the sending and receiving of data elements; contrast with asynchronous transmission

Systems Analyst a data-processing specialist who works with users to facilitate their applications needs or requirements

Telecommunications transmission of data over communications facilities

Terminal an input/output device usually including a typewriter-like keyboard and some form of display (e.g., CRT) or printer

Thermal Printer dot-matrix printer which uses heat-sensitive paper

Third-Generation Computer a computer using integrated circuit devices as the principal components

Time-Sharing data-processing operation which permits two or more users to interact with the system concurrently

TTY teletypewriter equipment

Turnaround Time elapsed time between the submission of a job and the delivery of output

Verify to check entry of transcription of data

Virtual Storage technique using hardware and software to increase the amount of main memory available

Volatile Storage a storage device the contents of which are lost when power is removed

Wand Reader input device for entering data at point-of-sale (POS) terminals

Word see computer word

Word Processing manipulation of data, especially text; to store, manipulate, and generate text copy

APPENDIX B
SUGGESTED PUBLICATIONS

AEDS Journal
1201–16th Street, NW
Washington, DC 20036

AEDS Monitor
1201–16th Street, NW
Washington, DC 20036

A+
P.O. Box 2965
Boulder, CO 80321

BYTE
70 Main Street
Peterborough, NH 03458

Classroom Computer Learning
5616 West Cermak Road
Cicero, IL 60650

Computers and Electronics
P.O. Box 2744
Boulder, CO 80302

Computing Teacher
ICCE, 135 Education
University of Oregon
Eugene, OR 94701

Courseware Critique
The University of Iowa
224 Lindquist Center
Iowa City, IA 52242

Courseware Report Card
Educational Insights, Inc.
150 West Carob Street
Compton, CA 90220

Creative Computing
P.O. Box 5214
Boulder, CO 80321

Digest of Software Reviews: Education
1341 Bulldog Lane, Suite B
Fresno, CA 93710

Educational Technology
140 Sylvan Avenue
Englewood Cliffs, NJ 07632

Electronic Learning
Scholastic Inc.
730 Broadway
New York, NY 10003–9538

Home Computer Magazine
P.O. Box 5537
Eugene, OR 97405

LIST
3381 Ocean Drive
Vero Beach, FL 32963

MICRO
P.O. Box 6502
Chelmsford, MA 01824

Microcomputing
80 Pine Street
Peterborough, NH 03458

Peelings II
P.O. Box 188
Las Cruces, NM 88001

Personal Computing
P.O. Box 2942
Boulder, CO 80322

School Microware Reviews
Dresden Associates
P.O. Box 246
Dresden, ME 04342

Software Review
Meckler Publishing
520 Riverside Avenue
Westport, CT 06880

Index